Hire Your Kid

The Sole Proprietor's Guide to Creating a New Job

HireYourKid.com

Keith R. Hall, CPA

Ebook ISBN: 978-1-971478-50-0
Paperback ISBN: 978-1-971478-51-7
Hardback ISBN: 978-1-971478-52-4

Third Edition
Printed in U.S.A.
Paradigm Resources, Inc.
7110 Walnut Street
Frisco, Texas 75033

Table of Contents

Dedication 1

Note from the Author 2

Chapter One: Hire Your Kid 4
How much money do your give your child every year?

Chapter Two: Why Create a Job? 13
Convert the allowance to wages.

Chapter Three: Does This Work for Me? 21
Too good to be true?

Chapter Four: Creating the Job 35
Delegate and put your child to work.

Chapter Five: Hiring the New Employee 56
New Hire Paperwork!

Chapter Six: Paying the Employee 74
The kid's favorite part.

Chapter Seven: Filing and Reporting Requirements 84
Compliance Hoops.

Chapter Eight: A WARNING!!! It's All About The Paper 111
No short cuts!

Chapter Nine: A Call to Action! 121
The tax savings are waiting but you have to do it!

BONUS Chapter — Hire Your Kid – Retire Your Kid 134
No Way!!!

Appendix A: The Case Study – Meet Kelsey 138

Appendix B: Hire Your Kid Checklist 157

Appendix C: Completed Sample Forms: 161
Form SS-4 163
Job Description 164
Form I-9 165
New Hire Report 166
Time Cards 167
Form W-4 168
Form W-2 169
Form W-3 170
Form 944 171
Form 940 173
Form 1040 175

Appendix D: State Websites for New Hire Reporting 197

Appendix E: Resources 200

Dedication

For my kids….Stevie, Ryan and Kelsey! You guys will never know the positive impact you have had on my life and my very soul.

You have served as my inspiration in so many things, perhaps the least of which is the idea behind this book. I have hired each of you, deducted each of you, and saved thousands of tax dollars because of each of you. But mostly, I have just loved you.

Note from the Author

I have spent the better part of forty years working with small business owners just like you. I have spent thousands of hours with numerous small businesses; they have been of various types, with many different issues standing between them and their dreams of success. However, many of the problems small business owners face are the same. There are many differences, but also many similarities. All of us have to file a tax return and all of us usually end up thinking we are paying too much to Uncle Sam. I very rarely hear a small business owner, or any taxpayer for that matter, complaining that they were denied a chance to pay more in federal income tax. A vast majority of Americans are happy to pay their fair share of tax to support the country that we love....but dang it, every April 15th, it just doesn't seem fair.

In Texas, we say, "The fair comes in October!" But indeed this book is about fair. I would never recommend a tax deduction or a tax strategy that is anything other than fair. However, even more dramatically, I would never recommend that you forgo any tax deduction that supports your business. To me, fair means supporting our country with our appropriate portion of tax dollars paid. But it also means deducting all of those ordinary and necessary expenses that you incur in supporting the growth of your business and, therefore, the growth of our country.

That brings us to the very purpose of this book. This book is about hiring a new employee and the necessary paperwork required to do it correctly. This book is about documentation and reporting and compliance. But mostly, this book is about keeping more of the money you've worked so hard to earn. This book is about paying less in federal and state income taxes by creating a new job and hiring your child.

Creating a new job for your child will provide numerous benefits that are difficult to value. Your new employee will gain a new sense of responsibility, duty, and purpose. They will learn more about your business and about what makes a small business successful. This new job may even play a role in shaping their future and the choices they make for that future. But regardless of those higher-level goals, your goal of paying less in tax every year has already begun, simply by creating one more job. I love the idea of making a positive difference in a child's future, but this book is about saving tax dollars. Period!

You must answer two questions with a 'Yes' in order to benefit from this book:

Do you file a Schedule C for your business?

And

Do you have a kid at home?

That's it. If you can answer 'yes' to those two questions, then this book is for you. I will show you how to hire your child, complete all necessary employment documentation, and ensure compliance with all federal and state reporting requirements. There are literally thousands of dollars in tax savings waiting for you to claim by hiring your kid. But those dollars won't just jump on your tax return by themselves. You have to act. At the end of this book, I will challenge you with 'A Call to Action.' That call to action is a simple one…Do the things outlined in this book and save over $5,000 in taxes.

The Internal Revenue Code is on your side. The IRS is on your side. They will pay you for doing the things in this book. So read carefully and diligently. And then ACT. Hire Your Kid! On April 15th, you will be glad you did.

1

Hire Your Kid

Yes, it's the name of the book and yes, my editor told me you can't give the first Chapter the same name as the whole book. But I don't want to make you wait for the point or even make you read the entire book. If you own your own business and have a child at home between the ages of approximately 8 and 18, this book is for you. I will be writing about taxes and the IRS, as well as W-2s and W-3 forms, and various other compliance issues. However, there is only one key point to the pages of this book…

Create a job for your child - Hire Your Kid and
Save over $5,000 in taxes

That's it. That's the whole deal. Everything you need to know is included, as well as additional resources to call upon and even an offer to let someone else do the work for you. Sounds good? Let's do it.

The best tax planning ideas are those that can increase tax deductions without actually having to pay any more money. What if you went back to last year's tax return and simply added an additional tax deduction of $15,000? You didn't have to spend any extra money, but somehow realized that there was indeed $15,000 that you had already spent but just didn't know that it was deductible. The trick is to recognize that you will be spending this $15,000 anyway, regardless of any tax planning ideas. Converting that $15,000 from non-deductible personal expenses into fully deductible business expenses can save over $5,000 in federal income tax. And that is exactly what we are going to do.

Let me start by asking a personal question. How much money do you spend on your child every year? This is a difficult question to answer, but regardless of your situation, the amount is substantial. Consider the money you give them on Saturday afternoon at the mall, for a movie ticket, or their weekly allowance. If the kids are old enough to drive, do you pay for the gas for the car? The speeding tickets they get? What about food, clothing, and health care? If your daughters are anything like mine, there is always a new pair of designer jeans that somehow become a matter of life or death, with the potential to end their social advancement. Even more critical, how about money for a college savings account? But regardless of what the money is for, added all up, it's a big number.

From a tax standpoint, very few of these dollars translate into a tax deduction. The kids' allowance, their clothes, gas for the car, and the designer jeans will never be deductible and therefore will never provide any tax benefit. Regardless, you will continue to spend this money. You will spend this money whether or not you read this book, whether you hire your child, and whatever your ultimate tax liability might be. You will spend that money on your child, no matter what else happens.

The cost we incur to raise our children continues to grow at an alarming rate. In a nationwide survey completed in 2025, LendingTree reported an average annual cost of raising a child to be $29,419. (www.lendingtree.com/debt-consolidation/raising-a-child-study/). The total increase was a staggering 35.7% from their last survey completed in 2023. Those costs include housing, food, clothing, transportation, healthcare, etc., and vary from state to state. The highest monthly cost was in Hawaii at $36,472, and the lowest was in Mississippi at $16,490.

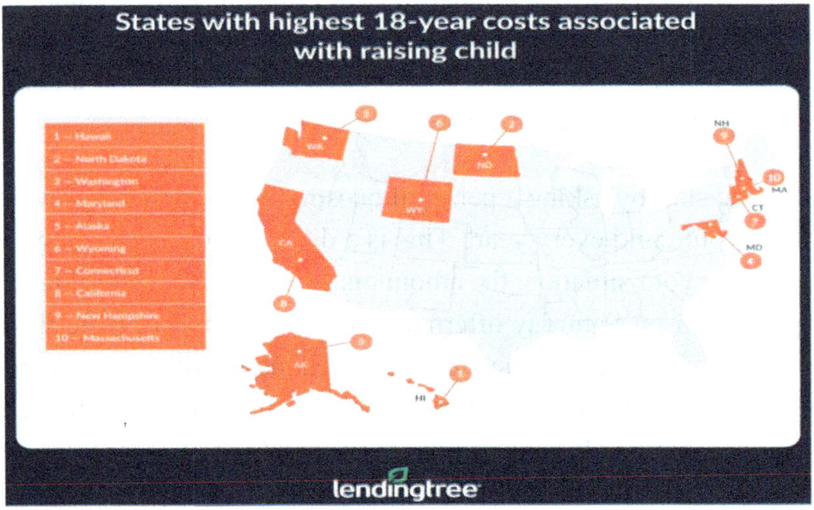

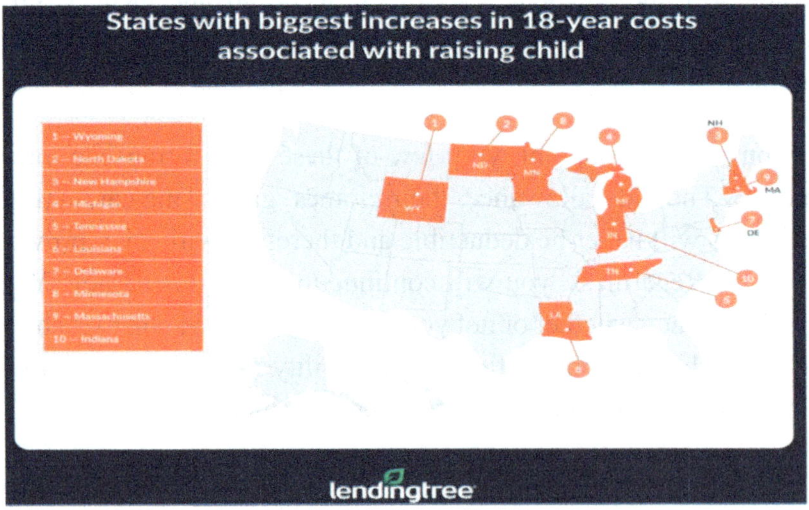

Unfortunately, I have more bad news. Those numbers do not include any amount set aside for college. According to the College Board's Advocacy and Policy Center, the average annual tuition and fees for a public four-year in-state university are currently $11,610 for the 2024-2025 enrollment year. Room and board will add another $13,310 for a total annual cost of your child's college education of $24,920. Those costs do not include transportation or any amount for designer jeans, which may or may not be even more important for the college social scene. Ugh!!!

Average Published Prices (Enrollment-Weighted) for Full-Time Undergraduates, 2023-24 and 2024-25

	Sector			
	Public Two-Year In-District	Public Four-Year In-State	Public Four-Year Out-of-State	Private Nonprofit Four-Year
Tuition and Fees				
2024-25	$4,050	$11,610	$30,780	$43,350
2023-24	$3,950	$11,310	$29,840	$41,740
$ Change	$100	$300	$940	$1,610
% Change	2.5%	2.7%	3.2%	3.9%
Housing and Food (Room and Board)				
2024-25	$10,390	$13,310	$13,310	$15,250
2023-24	$9,970	$12,770	$12,770	$14,650
Tuition and Fees and Housing and Food				
2024-25	$14,440	$24,920	$44,090	$58,600
2023-24	$13,920	$24,080	$42,610	$56,390

College Board, Trends in College Pricing and Student Aid, 2024
http://research.collegeboard.org/trends/college-pricing

The cost of attending a public two-year in-state university remains high, with an average annual tuition of $14,440. So now, just think about the cost of college for that 14-year-old child. In four short years, it will be time to leave high school behind and begin the next stage of education.

Even if you totally ignore the rising cost of college expenses, you will need to set aside over $6,000 during each of the next four years just to have enough for the first year of college expenses. Even if the plan is to start with a two-year Associate's degree, it will be expensive.

My goal for this chapter was not to present a comprehensive list of depressing facts about the cost of raising a child. My goal was to remind you that you will be spending this money anyway. Regardless of the goals of this book, regardless of decisions you make for future tax returns, and regardless of whether you ever create a new job, you WILL be spending this money on your child.

But what about taxes? Of the total amount that you spend on supporting and raising your child, how much will you get to deduct? You may be eligible for some tax benefits from the child tax credit and possibly a credit for part of your daycare expenses. Health insurance premiums that you pay for yourself and your kids may generate some level of tax deduction as a self-employed business owner. You most likely will qualify for some education credits once you start paying those college tuition bills. However, most of the money you give to your child or spend on their basic needs is not tax-deductible. You work every day and earn as much money as possible to provide those things for your kids. But before you can pay for anything, each dollar you bring home from your small business will be subject to federal income tax and to self-employment tax. Self-employment tax is roughly 15.3% on each dollar. And that is on top of federal income tax. If you are in the low to middle income tax bracket, meaning your combined household taxable income for both you and your spouse is about $97,000, then you will pay 22% in federal income tax on each additional dollar that you earn. Putting those two together, you can pay as much as 37.3% in total taxes on each new dollar of income. It is a bit oversimplified, but self-employment and federal income tax mean that you have only about 63 cents of every dollar you earn left over to pay for college, the movies, gas for the car, and all those designer jeans.

Let's say that you woke up last night from a nightmare about the cost of college for your eight-year-old son. You start today with a new, determined effort to earn extra money to start a college savings account. You find one more customer or work enough extra hours in your small business to earn an extra $6,000 with the intent of putting that money into a new college savings account. Guess what? You earned $6,000; nice job, but you only get to keep about $3,780 of that new money. What?? The new $6,000 will generate self-employment tax of approximately $900 and federal income tax of approximately $1,320, leaving you only $3,780 to put into your son's new college savings account. To get the extra $6,000 in college money that you need, you must actually generate an extra $9,524 in new earnings. That's right! $9,524 in new earnings would increase total taxes by about $3,524, leaving you with $6,000 for your son's future. Dang it, that just doesn't seem fair, but that is the math. (And I didn't even bring up that nasty thing called state income tax.)

Now that I have severely depressed you (I hope you are still reading), let's go back a step and talk about basic tax planning. Old textbook material that you may have encountered in college or around the water cooler and have likely done your best to forget. The first key point to tax planning is to always make sure you have included all income on your tax return. DO NOT intentionally exclude any money from the top line of your tax return, because a bunch of bad things can happen from there. Do not be creative or aggressive or any of those cool words when it comes to income....include everything. Always.

Key point number two for basic tax planning...Now that everything is on the tax return, be extremely creative, extremely aggressive, and extremely proactive in getting the money back off the tax return. That means deductions and exemptions and credits. Make sure that you take all of the possible deductions applicable to your business and the expenses that you have incurred. Don't wait until April 15th to think about potential deductions for your business. Most tax planning ideas end with the New Year's

Eve party. Once the calendar year is over, there are very few options for increasing the potential tax deductions related to managing your business. But most importantly, even before that New Year's Eve party, never spend money just to get a tax deduction. Let me say that again….

Never spend money just to get a tax deduction!!!

The math is the same for deductions as for the new income that you earned. For every dollar that you spend related to a tax deduction, you only reduce your tax liability by about thirty-seven cents. You have increased your deductions in order to save those thirty-seven cents but you are in the hole by the remaining sixty-three cents. Never, never, ever spend a dollar in order to save thirty-seven cents. If you need a new laptop or know you will be spending business funds on a new piece of furniture anyway, then spending those amounts prior to year-end can provide better cash flow by accelerating the deduction. But do not buy a laptop that you don't need so that you can take a thousand-dollar deduction. Do not purchase a new oven for your bakery business solely because it is tax-deductible. Do not take a friend out to lunch and pay the bill so that you can take a tax deduction.

As I mentioned before, the best tax savings ideas are those that can take money you are already spending and convert it from non-deductible expenses into fully deductible business expenses. So, how can we find a way to make that money, which you are already spending on your child, tax-deductible? I know that you have already guessed the answer…Hire Your Kid!!!

Instead of just giving your child the money you are currently giving them, have them work for it. Most likely, they already work for their money, but I am proposing that you make their work more formal. Rather than cleaning their room or helping with laundry, find something in your business for them to do. Create a job for your child and actually put them to work. As a small business owner, you have already learned that there are literally thousands of things that need to be done each and every day. There is inbound mail and outbound mail to sort, stamp, and file. There are shipping duties, filing duties, and returning phone calls. Someone has to clean the home office and someone has to shred sensitive documents. Someone has to stuff envelopes with marketing materials and someone has to lick stamps for all of those envelopes. There is a good chance that your child already performs some of those tasks for your business, but my guess is that they don't receive a specific payment for those tasks.

And what about new tasks? New ways to grow your business? Maybe ways that you haven't thought of yet. Things that your child can do that perhaps you don't know how to do. Let's talk about social media. Does your small business have a presence on Facebook or Twitter? If your children are in any way like mine, they are brilliant with Facebook. Your child may be able to build a Facebook page for your small business. They can post coupons or sale events or just post weekly updates on the services that you provide. How cool would it be to generate new customers from a place you never thought of, where your kid was the company marketing expert? And how cool will your kid be at school when they tell their friends that they get paid for playing on Facebook?

The point is that they are most likely already doing the work. If not, there are literally thousands of things that they can do to help you be more successful and productive in managing your small business. Make their working relationship with your company a formal employee/employer relationship. Create a formal job and Hire Your Kid. As always, the good things in life take a little effort, so you will need to do some paperwork. Your business will need its own Employer Identification Number (EIN) if this will be your first employee. You will need to develop a job description and decide on an hourly wage to pay your new employee. You will need to complete the IRS and US Citizenship paperwork. You will need to report the wages paid to your new employee to the IRS and to the Social

Security Administration. And you will actually need to pay your new employee; however, you are already doing that anyway.

This book will guide you through the step-by-step process of creating your new job and converting personal, non-deductible expenses into fully deductible business expenses. This IS the very best tax planning tool available. I will talk much more about the money in the coming chapters but here is a brief math example of what this means:

Assume that you create a job for your child to handle the mail, stuff envelopes, clean the home office, and possibly even manage your business's Facebook page. You schedule them to work a couple of hours on Tuesday night and a couple more on Thursday night. Perhaps a few more hours on Saturday or Sunday afternoon, so that they work about 12 hours a week or about 50 hours a month. You determine a reasonable hourly wage of $25.00 per hour. They do the work. You pay them for the hours that they actually work, meaning about $300 a week, or about $1,250 a month. At the end of the year, you will have paid your new employee $15,000 in wages and hopefully they will have created new benefits and new revenue for your small business, not to mention more time for you to do other things.

What have we actually accomplished? You've created a new job. Your child will be more mature, your business will be more successful, you will have more time to focus on growing your business, and much more. But let's not think about all of those inherent and idealistic benefits just yet; let's just trace the money. Remember the tax math: The $15,000 in new wages paid will be fully deductible on your business tax return. Self-employment tax will be reduced by approximately 15% of those new wages and federal income tax will be reduced by 22% (depending on your marginal income tax bracket). Combined, the $15,000 in wages will reduce your total tax by approximately $5,550. You have taken $15,000 in money that you were already spending, which was personal and non-deductible, and converted that money into a fully deductible business expense. That's it. That is what this book is all about.

2

Why Create a Job?

The easy and obvious answer to the question of why create a job is to save $5,000 in taxes on your very next tax return. Creating a new job for your child will significantly lower your overall tax liability and the only real cost of doing so is the required paperwork. There is over five thousand dollars in cash money just waiting for you to claim, but you must claim it. You must create that job in order to claim the savings. The concept that makes this idea so terrific and easy is that you are effectively moving taxable income off your personal tax return and onto your child's, where the tax rates are much lower, and in most cases, zero.

By creating the new job, your child has earned income and is subject to the same earned income tax rules as you and I. The good news is that your child can earn up to $15,000 in 2025 before they even have to file a tax return. This is the same rule for all taxpayers, not just children, which basically states that unless you earn at least a certain amount of money, you don't even have to file a tax return. That amount is different depending on your filing status, your age, and on many other factors, but for kids who are still claimed as a dependent on their parents' tax return, that number is $15,000 for 2025 and increases a little bit each year to account for rising inflation. In our example, your child will be working about 12 hours a week at $25.00 per hour and will therefore earn $15,000 in wages for the year which means no tax return needs to be filed. The reason that they don't have to file is that even though they will still be listed as a dependent on your tax return, they are still eligible for a standard deduction equaling $15,000, so that their taxable income will be zero. Since there will be no tax, there is no requirement to even file the tax return.

But what about payroll taxes? What about Social Security taxes, FICA and Medicare? What about the Federal unemployment tax or FUTA tax? The following is an excerpt from IRS Publication 15, Circular E, Employer's Tax Guide, Chapter 3, beginning on page 15:

3. Family Employees

Child employed by parents.

Payments for the services of a child under age 18 who works for their parent in a trade or business aren't subject to social security and Medicare taxes if the trade or business is a sole proprietorship or a partnership in which each partner is a parent of the child......(further)

....Payments for the services of a child under age 21 who works for their parent, whether or not in a trade or business, aren't subject to FUTA Tax.

IRS

Publication 15

(Circular E), Employer's Tax Guide

For use in **2025**

Contents

What's New 1
Reminders 2
Calendar 9
Introduction 11
1. Employer Identification Number (EIN) 12
2. Who Are Employees? 13
3. Family Employees 15
4. Employee's Social Security Number (SSN) 16
5. Wages and Other Compensation 17
6. Tips 21
7. Supplemental Wages 22
8. Payroll Period 24
9. Withholding From Employees' Wages 24
10. Required Notice to Employees About the Earned Income Credit (EIC) 29
11. Depositing Taxes 30
12. Filing Forms 941, Form 943, Form 944, or Form 945 35
13. Reporting Adjustments to Forms 941, Form 943, or Form 944 39
14. Federal Unemployment (FUTA) Tax 42
15. Special Rules for Various Types of Services and Payments 45
16. Third-Party Payer Arrangements 52
17. Federal Agency Certifying Requirements of Federal Income Taxes Withheld From U.S. Government Employees Working in, or Federal Pension Recipients Residing in, American Samoa, the CNMI, and Guam 53
How To Get Tax Help 55
Index 58

Future Developments

For the latest information about developments related to Pub. 15, such as legislation enacted after it was published, go to IRS.gov/Pub15.

What's New

Social security and Medicare taxes for 2025. The rate of social security tax on taxable wages is 6.2% each for

The bottom line is that the wages you pay to your child as an employee of your small business operated as a sole proprietorship are NOT subject to Social Security taxes. No FICA tax, or Medicare tax and no FUTA tax. No payroll taxes.

The wages are subject to federal income tax; however, as we noted above, the child earning about $15,000 in wages will have no tax liability and doesn't even have to file a tax return. Furthermore, if the child expects no tax liability, they may claim an exemption from withholding on the appropriate IRS Form W-4, which I will demonstrate how to complete in Chapter 5.

Therefore, your child working for your sole proprietorship will pay no tax and will be subject to no withholding requirement and will have no filing requirement related to the $15,000 in wages received. However, that same $15,000 is fully deductible on your business tax return.

Creating a job and paying a reasonable wage, rather than simply giving your child the money, converts personal, non-deductible allowances into fully deductible wages, which can be included directly on your Schedule C, Profit or Loss from Business.

Remember that the underlying logic for this tax planning strategy is that your child will be in a much lower income tax bracket than you are. This idea transfers taxable income from your tax return to their tax return. So, what if the child has a paper route or works at the local YMCA as a lifeguard in the summer and therefore already has some income? What if the child already has wages from other part-time jobs? The Hire Your Kid tax strategy still provides maximum tax savings, provided that you are indeed in a higher tax bracket. The only downside is that if the child has earned income in excess of $15,000, they will now be subject to the income tax filing requirement. They will file their own individual income tax return, including the wages received from the YMCA and the wages paid to them from your small business. If they have, say $20,000 in total wages, $5,000 from the YMCA and $15,000 from you, they will now have a tax liability. The $20,000 in gross wages will translate into $5,000 in taxable income after subtracting the standard deduction of $15,000 on their tax return. The child will still be listed as a dependent on your personal return and you will claim any related tax benefit.

The $5,000 in taxable income will be taxed at the lowest possible U.S. tax rate of 10% generating a total tax liability of $500. Notice in the table below from the IRS website at www.irs.gov that the child can have up to $11,600 in taxable income ($26,600 in gross wages before the standard deduction amount of $15,000) before they will get to the next tax bracket of 12%.

Schedule X—If your filing status is Single

If your taxable income is: Over—	But not over—	The tax is:	of the amount over—
$0	$11,600	------- 10%	$0
11,600	47,150	$1,160.00 + 12%	11,600
47,150	100,525	5,426.00 + 22%	47,150
100,525	191,950	17,168.50 + 24%	100,525
191,950	243,725	39,110.50 + 32%	191,950
243,725	609,350	55,678.50 + 35%	243,725
609,350	-------	183,647.25 + 37%	609,350

Excerpt from IRS 2024 Publication 17, Your Federal Income Tax, page 126

Even though the child will pay tax at the lowest tax rate of 10%, the wages that you have paid them for services provided to your small business will be deducted at your TOP marginal tax bracket. The table below, also from www.irs.gov, shows the tax table for married filing jointly. You will note that a combined household taxable income of just $201,050 will generate a marginal tax rate of 24%, which is the very middle income tax bracket. That means each additional dollar of wages that you pay to your child will reduce your federal income tax by 24 cents, while the child's tax will only increase by 10 cents.

Schedule Y-1—If your filing status is Married filing jointly or Qualifying surviving spouse

If your taxable income is: Over—	But not over—	The tax is:	of the amount over—
$0	$23,200	------- 10%	$0
23,200	94,300	$2,320.00 + 12%	23,200
94,300	201,050	10,852.00 + 22%	94,300
201,050	383,900	34,337.00 + 24%	201,050
383,900	487,450	78,221.00 + 32%	383,900
487,450	731,200	111,357.00 + 35%	487,450
731,200	-------	196,669.50 + 37%	731,200

Excerpt from IRS 2024 Publication 17, Your Federal Income Tax, page 126

In addition, since the child's wages are not subject to FICA or Medicare tax for the child, but are deductible for self-employment tax on your tax return, each additional dollar of wages saves another 15 cents.

The key point is that even if the child has other income, the transfer of taxable income from a higher tax bracket to a lower tax bracket will always satisfy the goal of reducing your overall tax liability. If you operate a sole proprietorship and have a child to whom you give money each year, there is no reason not to take advantage of this plan and put the child to work. But you may be tempted to skip the paperwork. You may be tempted just to include the $15,000 in wages right on line 26 of your Schedule C and call it good. AVOID this temptation. You must do the paperwork. It's not difficult but you must formally create the job and avoid just jumping to the end and taking a deduction. This book is here to help you step-by-step to saving thousands of dollars - but don't cut corners.

The first temptation to take a shortcut is to pay them in cash simply. This is a very common approach, and many small business owners ask why we can't just avoid all this tedious employee paperwork and treat them like independent contractors.

This is a very good question and it always comes from an experienced small business owner. I always know that when I get this question, it is coming from someone who knows about the paperwork, knows about hiring qualified workers, and most likely has a good instinct about the importance of compliance and its related headaches. It is tempting to compensate your child, the new worker, as an independent contractor simply because it is easier. The only reporting requirement for payments made to an independent contractor for services is the completion of an IRS Form 1099-NEC at the end of the year. And that is only for those independent contractors to whom you paid at least $600 per year. There is no job description, no employment verification, no time cards, no pay checks, no payroll tax returns, no W-2, no W-3. If the choice were based solely on the easiest road for paperwork, then utilizing the services of independent contractors instead of employees would almost always be easier. Much easier!

The problem lies in the use of the word 'choice,' and this is very important. The classification of a worker is NOT a matter of choice. The employer cannot just choose which classification applies to their new worker based on convenience or on an assumption of which option might generate the fewest headaches or paperwork. The worker is either an employee or an independent contractor based on the facts and circumstances of their particular working relationship. Those facts and circumstances will dictate which classification is appropriate and, therefore, which set of reporting requirements is required. It is up to the company to determine the classification and the appropriate compliance and paperwork requirements related to the new position, but it is not a matter of choice. When hiring your child, it won't be easy to support their classification as an independent contractor.

The key factor in evaluating which classification is correct for a new worker is control. Does the worker control the work product, or does the employer control it? If the employer tells the worker when to be at work, what to do at work, how to do the work, provides the necessary tools to do the work, and may even dictate what to wear, then the worker is most likely an employee. If the worker decides on many aspects, such as when, how, and where, and has their own tools, and in most cases, has other clients for whom they provide similar services, then the worker is most likely an independent contractor. Like many IRS rules and regulations, the classification of a new worker is a bit vague and depends on the specific facts and circumstances, but the evaluation related to your child will almost always indicate an employer/employee relationship instead of an independent contractor relationship.

Even if the facts of the situation could be interpreted as an independent contractor relationship, the idea just doesn't work. One of the most unbelievable benefits of this idea is the fact that the wages paid to your child are not subject to payroll taxes. If the child is an independent contractor, there are still no payroll taxes in the strict definition of such; however, the child will be subject to self-employment tax. Remember that extra 15.3% that we pay as self-employed business owners? If the child is indeed an independent contractor, they are also a self-employed business owner, just like you. This fact may provide some level of pride for a parent who is also a small business owner, but it means that if the child has at least $400 of net earnings from self-employment, then they will be required to file a federal income tax return. Remember that as an employee, the child could have earned income of as much as $15,000 before they would be required to file a tax return; however, as a self-employed business owner, that threshold is much lower.

The federal income tax will work out about the same since the child will still be under the individual standard deduction but the net earnings will be subject to self-employment tax at 15.3%. The $2,300 that you will save in self-employment tax by paying the child as an independent contractor will now show up on the child's income tax return. There is no rate shifting of tax from your return to their return, as the self-employment tax rate remains the same. The bottom line is that you are out $2,300, whether you have to pay the tax or the child has to pay it. Not only does the child most likely not qualify as an independent contractor based on the specific facts and circumstances, but it will also result in a $2,300 tax savings loss by choosing that classification.

In order for all of the goals we have set for hiring your child, you must create the job. Creating that one more job is exactly what the president and all of your congressional representatives are asking you to do and they are prepared to put their money where their mouth is. Creating this new job will contribute to economic growth in our country, and it will also put $5,000 back in your pocket in the form of lower taxes. The title of this chapter is "Why Create a Job?" and I would be more than happy for you to answer that question with any high-level political commitment to economic growth, community investment, or an altruistic belief in bettering humanity as a whole. But this book and this idea are about keeping $5,000 more of the money you work so hard to make. And the way to save that money is to create a job. Don't pretend, don't cut corners, and do not skip any of the paperwork!

3

Does This Work for Me?

I hope there are several questions floating in your head right now, including, "Why didn't I hear about this years ago?" As I mentioned at the very beginning, I have listened to literally thousands of small business owners over the last forty years and most of them have exactly the same questions as you. In this Chapter, I will answer the top 10 questions that I receive from small business owners like you when it comes to hiring their kids.

1. Is there a minimum age? How old does my kid have to be?

This is the first question that arises in almost every situation. Most of us have either heard or read about child labor laws or have the perception that a child must be at least 14 years old to have a job. The Fair Labor Standards Act (FLSA) does indeed provide minimum age requirements for various jobs, as do state employment agencies. However, minors working in a business solely owned or operated by the child's parent or parents are exempt from FLSA requirements. (See US Department of Labor, Child

Provisions for Nonagricultural Occupations Under the Fair Labor Standards Act, Child Labor Bulletin 101.) This is true provided that the job is not deemed to be hazardous, such as excavation, manufacturing of explosives, mining and operating power equipment. The only requirement is that the services provided by the child are 'reasonable' in connection with their age and skill set. The term 'reasonable' is one that we will encounter over and over, so keep that concept in mind. As parents, it is very unlikely that we would put our kids in danger or take advantage of their efforts on the job. This is the very reason that FLSA rules do not apply when we hire our own children.

For an example of 'reasonable,' consider that you own and operate an architectural design company and you have hired your child. The child is performing calculus operations to determine the second and third derivatives of a complex algebraic equation, which helps determine the level of vibration in a building during an earthquake. Further, your child is three years old. Most likely, that is not a reasonable job for the child's age and skill set. However, what if you were a photographer instead of an architect? What if that same three-year-old child was modeling the new fall line of children's clothing for your best client? The job is now clearly reasonable for the child's age and skill set. Not only would the job be totally reasonable for a three-year-old child, but only a three-year-old child could provide those specific services. Should that child be compensated for the services they provide? Of course, they should, just as you should take a valid deduction on your business tax return for the wages you pay the child.

A child working for their parents' sole proprietorship can be any age, provided the services they provide to the company are reasonable. Use your common sense and build a job that they can handle; however, there is no minimum age.

2. Is there a maximum age for my child?

Similar to the question regarding minimum age, there is NO maximum age limit for your child. The same standard applies for 'reasonable' both to skill set and to wages, but the child can be any age. Remember that the key to this tax-saving strategy is the concept of moving taxable income from a higher marginal tax bracket to a lower marginal tax bracket. If you are giving money to your child anyway, regardless of their age, AND they are in a lower marginal income tax bracket than you, then creating a job and having them work for the money will always save you some tax dollars. However, the math will be different depending on their age.

If the child is older than age 17, the wages paid to the child will be subject to Social Security taxes, FICA and Medicare. For children under the age of 18, the savings are expected to be 37% based on a federal income tax rate of 22% and a 15% self-employment tax rate. Since FICA and Medicare taxes are basically the same as self-employment tax, the savings for older children are limited to the reduced federal income tax. The wages paid will still reduce your self-employment tax by up to 15.3%, but the combined Social Security tax assessed on these new wages will also be 15.3%. You will still save taxes based on your marginal income tax bracket, but the tax savings will be less for the child who is at least 18 years of age.

3. Is this a red flag for the IRS? Will I get audited?

There are no guarantees regarding the IRS audit process, but I believe that your chances of being audited are actually lower if you follow the processes outlined in this guide. I certainly cannot prove that assertion but I do think I can convince you that it is true. The IRS will conduct approximately 1.5 million audits every year, which is about 1 percent of all returns filed. As a small business owner, your chances of being selected for one of those audits is about 2%, or twice as likely as the guy living next door to you. That may seem unfair, but as a small business owner who files a Schedule C, your tax return already has a few more complexities than the average employee's Form 1040 and therefore, you are more likely to make a mistake. The IRS is well aware of that possibility, so they tend to review our returns more frequently.

Also, keep in mind that not all audits are conducted with the goal of making most of us fearful of the IRS. Those audits are conducted for the sole purpose of generating more money for the U.S. Treasury. They are looking for returns that include mistakes or deductions without supporting documentation, so they can generate additional revenue for the Treasury. That is also why the more complicated your return is, the more likely you are to be selected for IRS scrutiny.

If you have several complexities, such as accelerated depreciation, net operating loss carryforwards, gain or loss on the sale of business assets, or the use of the Earned Income Credit, your chances of an IRS audit increase. The more likely there is a mistake included in your tax return, the more likely there will be an additional assessment of tax. That may sound a bit scary, but at the end of the day, it is all about the money.

So, let's talk about adding wages to your tax return and how that might affect those potential errors and, therefore, the potential audit. The wages that you pay to your child or any other employee will be supported by applicable payroll tax returns and W-2s. The payroll tax returns have been submitted to the IRS, and the W-2s for each employee, along with a W-3 transmittal, have been submitted to the Social Security Administration (see Chapter 7). The IRS computers and the Social Security Administration computers communicate the details that each has received and verify that the reports match. This may also be scary, but if the payroll tax returns submitted to the IRS don't match the W-2s submitted to the Social Security Administration, you will receive a notice. Guaranteed! The computers already know!

By the same token, the IRS also already knows when the reports match. Even if your tax return is selected for a random compliance audit, the IRS will know whether or not your wages are supported by appropriate documentation before they even contact you. By following the details in Chapter 7, your reports will always match. The wages reported on your Schedule C will match those filed with your annual IRS Form 944 and the total of all W-2s filed with the Social Security Administration. Before the IRS agent can even ask a question, the IRS computer has already verified that the supporting documentation has been filed, both internally and with the Social Security Administration. This is comparable to the IRS already having copies of all of your receipts before they even call you into their office. You have demonstrated that you filed all the reports, those reports are accurate and timely, therefore providing advanced evidence that you are doing things correctly. Remember that the IRS looks at our returns more often because their records indicate we make more mistakes. By adding this line item, you have advance proof that you don't make mistakes, which is why I believe including wages, with all the supporting documentation, can actually decrease your chances of an IRS audit.

4. Exactly HOW much will I save by hiring my kid?

This question is the most difficult to answer specifically, as there are numerous variables for each of our tax returns. I have included a detailed case study in Appendix A to provide an example of the effect of hiring your child with real numbers included on a real tax return. But as you probably already figured out, the total savings that you will realize will depend on your specific facts and circumstances. The key point is that hiring your child effectively moves taxable income from your tax return to the tax return of your child. The real savings is the difference between your marginal tax bracket and the child's marginal tax bracket; PLUS the savings you will realize by reducing your self-employment tax. If you are a married taxpayer filing a joint return and your taxable income is between $94,300 and $201,050, then your marginal tax bracket is 22%. If your taxable income is between $23,200 and $94,300, then your marginal tax bracket is 12%. In the chart below from the IRS website at www.IRS.gov, find the level of your projected taxable income and find the corresponding percentage rate in the middle-right-hand column. Multiplying the total wages paid to your new employee by the applicable tax rate will be the estimated amount that you will save by hiring your kid. Since the tax rates that apply to all of us are progressive, meaning the more taxable income you have, the higher the marginal tax rate will be, the more money you make, the more taxes you will pay.

Schedule Y-1—If your filing status is **Married filing jointly** or **Qualifying surviving spouse**

If your taxable income is: Over—	But not over—	The tax is:	of the amount over—
$0	$23,200	------- 10%	$0
23,200	94,300	$2,320.00 + 12%	23,200
94,300	201,050	10,852.00 + 22%	94,300
201,050	383,900	34,337.00 + 24%	201,050
383,900	487,450	78,221.00 + 32%	383,900
487,450	731,200	111,357.00 + 35%	487,450
731,200	-------	196,669.50 + 37%	731,200

Excerpt from IRS 2015 Publication 17, Your Federal Income Tax, page 262

The savings related to self-employment tax are even more cumbersome since there is a maximum amount of self-employment earnings that is subject to SE tax. Net earnings from self-employment that are under the maximum amount are taxed at 15.3% while self-employment earnings over the maximum are taxed at only 2.9%. Here is a quick guide on how much you can expect to save based on total taxable income for a married couple and a salary for your child of $15,000 per year:

Estimated Tax Savings Based on Total Wages of $15,000

Taxable Income	Marginal Tax Bracket	Federal Tax Savings	SE Tax Savings	Total Savings
$0 - $23,200	10%	$1,500	$2,295	$3,795
$23,200 - $94,300	12%	$1,800	$2,295	$4,095
$94,300 - $201,050	22%	$3,300	$2,295	$5,595
$201,050 - $383,900	24%	$3,600	$435*	$4,035
$383,900 - $487,450	32%	$4,800	$435*	$5,235
$487,450 - $731,200	35%	$5,250	$435*	$5,685
Over $731,200	37%	$5,550	$435*	$5,985

*Assumes net earnings from self-employment of at least $176,100 for 2025

The savings for a child who is at least 18 years of age will be less and will approximate the total Federal Tax Savings listed in the chart above. Remember that the self-employment tax will still be lower but will effectively be replaced with payroll taxes in the form of FICA and Medicare assessed on the wages paid to the child who is at least 18. However, as you can see by the numbers in the Federal Tax Savings column, the amounts are still significant.

Yes, there will always be more complications when we are discussing the IRS and tax compliance. The total savings will be affected by the deduction for self-employment taxes and other phase-out limits based on your specific situation, and potential additional tax on higher-earning taxpayers assessed under the Affordable Care Act. But regardless of your particular facts and circumstances, the tax savings for hiring your child are significant.

5. How much do I pay the kid? Is there a minimum wage?

The answer to this question is similar to the minimum age question discussed earlier and we will use the standard of 'reasonable' again. First, the Department of Labor and the FLSA do enforce a minimum wage. However, as you may have already guessed, the wages paid to a child working in a business owned solely by the child's parent or parents are exempt from minimum wage requirements. Therefore, there is NO minimum wage requirement relating to creating this new job for your child.

The only requirement is that the wages paid are 'reasonable' in connection with the services provided by the child to your small business. Keep in mind that our goal here is to maximize the tax deduction for wages paid to the child, so you may be tempted to pay an hourly wage that is too high. Consider how much you would pay an unrelated third party to do the same job. How much would you pay a neighborhood kid to mow your grass? How much would you pay that same neighborhood kid to help you clean out the garage? In my opinion, an unskilled youth could earn $15 to $25 an hour for manual labor around the house for their parents or a neighbor. Office work that may require a bit more education and skill, such as word processing, website review, or marketing assistance, might earn $20 to $30 an hour.

The key for the level of pay is based on the actual services provided and need only be 'reasonable.' Reasonable is in the eyes of the beholder, so when you create your specific job, it is up to you, as the owner, to decide on a reasonable wage. Don't be greedy, but do be fair and do your best to make the math come out to $15,000 in total wages for the year.

6. Can I just pay them in cash and not do all the paperwork?

I discussed this topic extensively in Chapter 2, but I wanted to include it again here because it is particularly important. The easy answer is "NO," you cannot just pay them in cash and forgo the required paperwork. This may be one of the biggest temptations for cutting corners, but fight that urge. I won't go back through all of the details, so refer to Chapter 2 if you need reminding, but the answer is "NO!"

7. Can I do this for last year, too?

All of my answers so far have been what I would call "good" answers, but unfortunately, this answer falls into the "not so good" category. Creating your new job and hiring your child is not something that can be accomplished retroactively. The key to this strategy and the accompanying tax savings is the formal creation of that new job. Formally having the child provide services, completing time cards, paying the child a reasonable wage, and then reporting those wages to the appropriate governmental agencies is the key to saving thousands of dollars in taxes. The only real cost related to the thousands that you will save is the paperwork. You must do the paperwork.

Unfortunately, you did not read this book last year and complete all of the steps that I will show you in the following chapters. Your child did not perform those duties, you did not pay them a reasonable wage, and you did not file the necessary paperwork. Since you did not complete those steps, the wages would not be a valid deduction and therefore should not be included on your tax return. So, as much as I would like to say otherwise, you cannot go back and create the job from last year. The quicker you create your new job and put your child to work, the quicker you will start saving money.

Now that I have typed that answer, let's look at this a different way. The most important factor is the validity of the job itself. Maybe your child did indeed work for your business last year. Maybe you did create a job for your child but simply did not type everything into a nice neat document.

Maybe you actually paid your child for the work that they completed during the year for your small business but simply failed to report those payments as wages. If this is true, then not only can you report those payments as wages, but you SHOULD report those payments as wages. Any reports that should have been filed should be filed as quickly as possible. There may be late filing fees and potential interest if any taxes are due with those returns; however, the returns should be filed as quickly as possible.

If you paid your child for services provided to your small business, those payments should have been reported as wages. Those wages should be included on the employee's W-2 and as deductible wages on your Schedule C. Even if the forms are late or if you will be required to file an amended tax return, you should still report the wages paid and take the corresponding deduction. It's never too late to file the correct forms and it's never too late to save a few thousand dollars.

8. What if I have two kids?

This is a great question and allows me to return to the "good" answers. If you have more than one child who is available and qualified to provide services to your small business, you should hire all of them. The jobs that you create for each child may be different and each could have different responsibilities. Make sure to use the standard of "reasonable" in evaluating the age and skill set for each child separately in designing a new job for each. You might even have a different hourly wage for each.

If you have two kids, you can save twice as much. If you have three kids, you can save three times as much. If you have....well, you get the idea. You should certainly avoid having additional kids just to create new jobs, but for each child who is able to provide services to the business, there is tax to be saved.

9. What about State income tax?

The case study included in Appendix A is based on the details for a small business owner living in Texas, which has no state income tax. If you reside in a state that does have a state income tax, the math is obviously a bit different. The good news is that the math difference will most likely be in your favor, meaning you will actually save MORE money in taxes by hiring your kid. Remember that the overriding tax concept that makes this such a great tax strategy is moving income off of your personal income tax return and onto your child's income tax return, where the tax rate will generally be lower. Many of the states that do assess state income tax have a flat tax rate, so that the tax will actually be the same whether it is included on your return or the child's return. Many of those same states also have an exemption and/or a standard deduction for your child's tax return that will save you some tax money, even if the rates are the same.

As a brief example, let's compare Texas, Georgia, and Illinois. Since there is no state income tax in Texas, and all wages paid to a child working for their parents' sole proprietorship are also exempt from state unemployment tax, Texas has no tax for the child and no tax for the sole proprietor either. Therefore, there is no tax impact or reporting requirement for state income tax in Texas related to the wages paid to your child. However, the State of Georgia does have a state income tax that requires a tax return if wages are at least $12,000. So, what does that mean? In our example, your child earning $15,000 in wages from your small business would not be required to file a federal income tax return; however, the child would be required to file a State of Georgia individual income tax return. The Georgia state return would include $15,000 in wages, a standard deduction of $12,000, resulting in state taxable income of $3,000.

In our case study example, Samantha, the new hire, would be required to file a tax return in the State of Georgia to report $15,000 in wages. Keep in mind that YOUR State of Georgia income tax return will also include that same $15,000 in wages paid to Samantha, but as a deduction. $3,000 in taxable income will generate approximately $90 in Georgia state income tax, but the same wages will reduce the state income tax on your state tax return by as much as $863, so you will save even more. Therefore, just like at the federal level, you have moved taxable income from your return over to your child's return, therefore paying less in state tax as well.

The State of Illinois provides no personal exemption for a child earning $15,000 and claimed as a dependent on their parents' return; therefore, the child will pay Illinois state income tax on the entire $15,000. YOU, the parent, will pay less in Illinois state income tax since you will also have a new $15,000 deduction. Since Illinois has a flat 4.95% tax rate, meaning the child will pay the same rate as you, the two actually just offset each other. No additional state tax savings amount is realized, but also no additional state tax net cost is incurred, even though your child will have to file a state income tax return. This is the worst-case scenario for state income tax, which is basically a break-even between the tax the child pays and the tax that you save but you still have the added hassle of filing a separate return for your child for the State of Illinois.

Some states are better than others, but you will never end up paying more in state taxes by hiring your child. The worst that can happen is that the state tax that you save will end up as the same amount to be paid on the child's tax return. Meanwhile, you still pocket the federal tax savings of $5,000 or more.

The bottom line is that you may need to file a tax return for your child for state income tax, but if you do, it will most likely save you even more money than if you had no state income tax at all. That may sound totally backward in that paying state tax will actually save you money but the key point is still that you are moving income from one tax return to another to be taxed at a lower rate.

10. This sounds too good to be true. Is it?

You most likely have heard the adage, "If it sounds too good to be true, then it probably is." However, by putting your kid to work and then doing a little bit of paperwork, you WILL save as much as $5,000 in taxes or more. Period! There is no doubt that the premise of this book sounds too good to be true. But it is totally true.

You have created a job. Your child is doing the work. That work is supported by time cards and actual payments. You have completed payroll tax returns and W-2s and complied with all reporting requirements. You have seen the specific exemption from payroll taxes for wages paid to your child in IRS Publication 15 (see page 15) and you have seen references to the Department of Labor exemptions for a child working solely for their parents. It should be clear from these references that Congress supports the hiring of your child, as evidenced by its favorable tax treatment. It should be clear that both the IRS and the Department of Labor are aware that small businesses are indeed hiring their children to work in their businesses, as these working relationships are specifically addressed in their publications and websites.

United States Department of Labor – Youth & Labor
Internal Revenue Service – Publication 15, Employer's Tax Guide
Texas Workforce Commission – Child Labor Exemptions

Each of the above entities specifically publishes rules, procedures, exemptions, and calculations related to small business owners hiring their kids. Take a few minutes to review the U.S. Department of Labor website at www.DOL.gov and search on "Hire Your Kid." Download a copy of IRS Publication 15, Employer's Tax Guide, and review Chapter 3, Family Employees, directly from the IRS website at www.IRS.gov. And finally, search your state's employment commission website for details related to child labor exemptions. As an example, search the Texas Workforce Commission website at www.TWC.state.tx.us for detailed requirements for hiring your child.

The point I am trying to make here is that I agree that this tax strategy does indeed sound too good to be true. Yet, each of these government organizations —the U.S. Department of Labor, the Internal Revenue Service, and the Texas Workforce Commission—provides specific rules and exemptions for hiring your child. This may sound too good to be true, but each of these organizations provides even more evidence of this tremendous benefit.

If this question is on your mind, take a few minutes and do your own research. Use your favorite search engine and search for "hire your kid." I actually have done some of this work for you in Chapter 9 of this guide, but do the search yourself. You will find sources such as CBS MarketWatch, Forbes Magazine, and The Wall Street Journal. All of them have posted articles about the benefits of hiring your kid. I agree with the old adage of, "If it sounds too good to be true, then it probably is," but this is the exception. Take some time and read a few articles for yourself, then Hire Your Kid.

11. How do I know for sure if this is right for me?

Okay, I know this is the 11th question but let's just call it a bonus question and I saved the easiest one for last. If you file a Schedule C for your business AND you have a kid who can help with your business, this plan is right for you. There is nothing else to consider. Create a job, pay them a reasonable wage, do the paperwork, and you will save thousands in taxes. That's it.

4

Creating the Job

Perhaps the most common complaint among self-employed business owners, aside from tax-related issues, is the lack of time to complete all necessary tasks. As a self-employed business owner, you are required to be the CEO, the CFO, the CIO, the one who answers the phone, the one who takes the trash out at night, and everything in between. The work is never complete, and it's just you there to get it all done. It would be helpful to have an employee's assistance. Someone to whom you could delegate some of those tasks, not only to get those tasks completed but also to free your time for getting one more customer and achieving one more step toward your business goals.

The fact is that all of us could use some help, but very few of us have the extra cash flow available to hire a new employee. But now that you have this book, you know that you have some extra cash. Cash that used to be called allowance money, gas money, or college savings is now available for creating a new job. Before you decide who to hire for your new position (although we already have a great candidate in mind), you should set parameters for the job. The following steps should be included in creating your new job:

1. Obtain an Employer Identification Number.
2. Obtain a State Identification Number (if required).
3. Determine specific duties of the new position.
4. Determine an hourly wage based on those duties.
5. Complete a detailed job description.

1. Obtain an Employer Identification Number

Regardless of your entity form (sole proprietorship, partnership, Limited Liability Company, or Corporation), you MUST have an Employer Identification Number (EIN) if you will be hiring an employee. Corporations and LLCs will most likely already have an EIN, as these entities are separate from their owners. However, if you are a sole proprietor, you may not yet have an EIN associated with your business.

Even if you choose not to hire your child and save thousands of dollars, I recommend obtaining an EIN for your business and using it instead of your Social Security number in all business correspondence. I am sure you have read and heard way too much about identity theft and stolen account numbers and credit card details, so I won't waste a lot of space rehashing those details. However, I will always choose to have my personal Social Security number in as few places as possible, so having a separate EIN for the business is a valuable effort.

The good news is that getting your new EIN may be much easier than you ever thought it could be. There are four options for obtaining the new tax ID number, all of which start with completing IRS Form SS-4, Application for Employer Identification Number.

Form **SS-4** (Rev. December 2023) Department of the Treasury Internal Revenue Service

Application for Employer Identification Number
(For use by employers, corporations, partnerships, trusts, estates, churches, government agencies, Indian tribal entities, certain individuals, and others.)
See separate instructions for each line. Keep a copy for your records.
Go to *www.irs.gov/FormSS4* for instructions and the latest information.

OMB No. 1545-0003
EIN

Type or print clearly.

1 Legal name of entity (or individual) for whom the EIN is being requested
2 Trade name of business (if different from name on line 1)
3 Executor, administrator, trustee, "care of" name
4a Mailing address (room, apt., suite no. and street, or P.O. box)
5a Street address (if different) (Don't enter a P.O. box.)
4b City, state, and ZIP code (if foreign, see instructions)
5b City, state, and ZIP code (if foreign, see instructions)
6 County and state where principal business is located
7a Name of responsible party
7b SSN, ITIN, or EIN
8a Is this application for a limited liability company (LLC) (or a foreign equivalent)? ☐ Yes ☐ No
8b If 8a is "Yes," enter the number of LLC members
8c If 8a is "Yes," was the LLC organized in the United States? ☐ Yes ☐ No
9a **Type of entity** (check only one box). **Caution:** If 8a is "Yes," see the instructions for the correct box to check.
☐ Sole proprietor (SSN)
☐ Partnership
☐ Corporation (enter form number to be filed)
☐ Personal service corporation
☐ Church or church-controlled organization
☐ Other nonprofit organization (specify)
☐ Other (specify)
☐ Estate (SSN of decedent)
☐ Plan administrator (TIN)
☐ Trust (TIN of grantor)
☐ Military/National Guard ☐ State/local government
☐ Farmers' cooperative ☐ Federal government
☐ REMIC ☐ Indian tribal governments/enterprises
Group Exemption Number (GEN) if any
9b If a corporation, name the state or foreign country (if applicable) where incorporated | State | Foreign country
10 **Reason for applying** (check only one box)
☐ Started new business (specify type)
☐ Hired employees (Check the box and see line 13.)
☐ Compliance with IRS withholding regulations
☐ Other (specify)
☐ Banking purpose (specify purpose)
☐ Changed type of organization (specify new type)
☐ Purchased going business
☐ Created a trust (specify type)
☐ Created a pension plan (specify type)
11 Date business started or acquired (month, day, year). See instructions.
12 Closing month of accounting year
13 Highest number of employees expected in the next 12 months (enter -0- if none). If no employees expected, skip line 14.
Agricultural | Household | Other
14 If you expect your employment tax liability to be $1,000 or less in a full calendar year **and** want to file Form 944 annually instead of Forms 941 quarterly, check here. (Your employment tax liability will generally be $1,000 or less if you expect to pay $5,000 or less, $6,536 or less if you're in a U.S. territory, in total wages.) If you don't check this box, you must file Form 941 for every quarter. ☐
15 First date wages or annuities were paid (month, day, year). **Note:** If applicant is a withholding agent, enter date income will first be paid to nonresident alien (month, day, year)
16 Check **one** box that best describes the principal activity of your business. ☐ Health care & social assistance ☐ Wholesale—agent/broker
☐ Construction ☐ Rental & leasing ☐ Transportation & warehousing ☐ Accommodation & food service ☐ Wholesale—other ☐ Retail
☐ Real estate ☐ Manufacturing ☐ Finance & insurance ☐ Other (specify)
17 Indicate principal line of merchandise sold, specific construction work done, products produced, or services provided.
18 Has the applicant entity shown on line 1 ever applied for and received an EIN? ☐ Yes ☐ No
If "Yes," write previous EIN here

Third Party Designee
Complete this section **only** if you want to authorize the named individual to receive the entity's EIN and answer questions about the completion of this form.
Designee's name
Designee's telephone number (include area code)
Address and ZIP code
Designee's fax number (include area code)

Under penalties of perjury, I declare that I have examined this application, and to the best of my knowledge and belief, it is true, correct, and complete.
Applicant's telephone number (include area code)
Name and title (type or print clearly)
Applicant's fax number (include area code)
Signature
Date

For Privacy Act and Paperwork Reduction Act Notice, see separate instructions. Cat. No. 16055N Form **SS-4** (Rev. 12-2023)

IRS Form SS-4, Application for Employer Identification Number

You can download a copy of Form SS-4 directly from the IRS website (www.irs.gov/pub/irs-pdf/fss4.pdf) along with detailed instructions, or you can simply fill in the blanks on page 38. The form is relatively easy to complete, so let's get started.

The first seven lines of the form request contact information about you and your business. As a sole proprietor, Line 1 will be YOU. Not the name of the business or the name that you use in your marketing efforts, but just you as an individual. If you operate your business using a DBA (Doing Business As) or under an assumed name certificate, then you can include the business name on Line 2; however, this detail is not required.

Lines 4a and 4b should include the mailing address of the business or the place that you wish to receive correspondence from the IRS. In most cases, for the sole proprietor hiring their first employee, Lines 3, 5a, and 5b will be left blank. These lines relate to estates or trusts requesting an EIN and do not apply to the sole proprietor.

On Line 6, you will include the county and state for your business location, and Line 7 provides additional details about you as the small business owner. Line 7a should be YOU, and Line 7b should be YOUR Social Security number. Including your personal Social Security number is essential, as it serves as the key link between your new EIN for the business and you, the individual owner of that business.

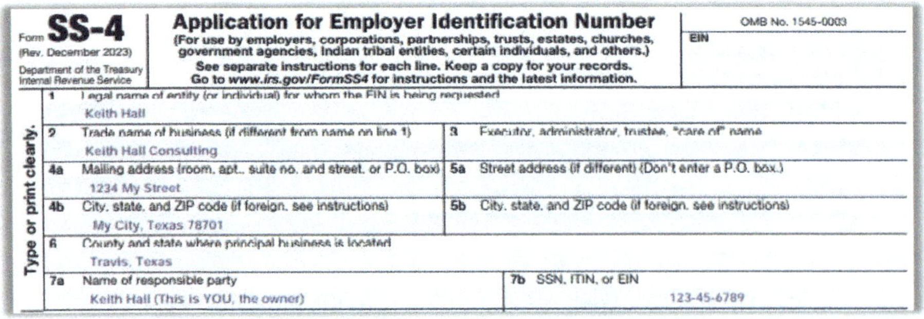
Form **SS-4** (Rev. December 2023) Department of the Treasury Internal Revenue Service

Application for Employer Identification Number
(For use by employers, corporations, partnerships, trusts, estates, churches, government agencies, Indian tribal entities, certain individuals, and others.)
See separate instructions for each line. Keep a copy for your records.
Go to *www.irs.gov/FormSS4* for instructions and the latest information.

OMB No. 1545-0003
EIN

Type or print clearly.

1 Legal name of entity (or individual) for whom the EIN is being requested Keith Hall	
2 Trade name of business (if different from name on line 1) Keith Hall Consulting	3 Executor, administrator, trustee, "care of" name
4a Mailing address (room, apt., suite no. and street, or P.O. box) 1234 My Street	5a Street address (if different) (Don't enter a P.O. box.)
4b City, state, and ZIP code (if foreign, see instructions) My City, Texas 78701	5b City, state, and ZIP code (if foreign, see instructions)
6 County and state where principal business is located Travis, Texas	
7a Name of responsible party Keith Hall (This is YOU, the owner)	7b SSN, ITIN, or EIN 123-45-6789

Lines 8 through 10 request information about your business entity type and why you are requesting the EIN. Lines 8a, 8b, and 8c ask for details if your entity is a Limited Liability Company: how many owners or members are in the LLC, and whether the LLC was organized in the United States. If your small business is operated as a sole proprietorship, then you will check the box for 'No' on Line 8a and then leave Lines 8b and 8c blank.

Lines 9a and 9b request details about the entity form, excluding LLCs. As a sole proprietor, you will check the first box and include your Social Security Number in the blanks provided. You may wonder why you need to include the Social Security Number again, since it is already listed above on Line 7b. In many situations, an individual other than the owner, such as a financial officer, CPA, or attorney, may request the EIN. In that case, the IRS still wants details about the owner. Line 9b will only be used for corporations and will be left blank for your business operating as a sole proprietorship.

Line 10 includes several options to indicate the reason for applying for the new EIN. Note that the IRS only requires us to select one box, even though more than one box may apply. In this case, you will be obtaining the new EIN for hiring new employees, so check the box for "Hired employees."

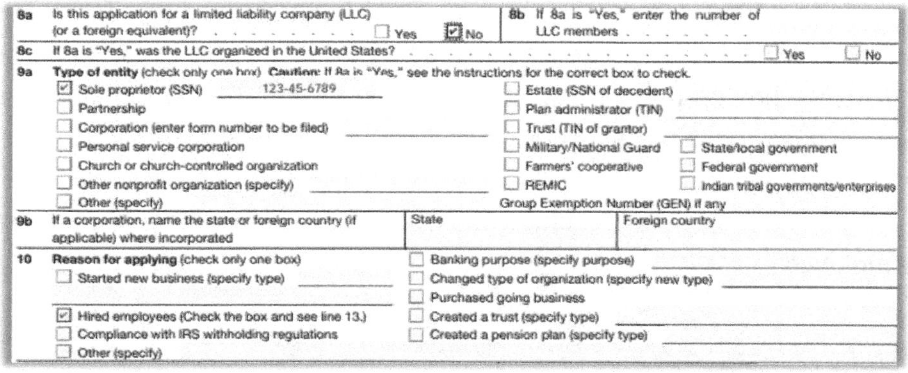
8a Is this application for a limited liability company (LLC) (or a foreign equivalent)? ☐ Yes ☑ No

8b If 8a is "Yes," enter the number of LLC members

8c If 8a is "Yes," was the LLC organized in the United States? ☐ Yes ☐ No

9a **Type of entity** (check only one box) **Caution:** If 8a is "Yes," see the instructions for the correct box to check.

- ☑ Sole proprietor (SSN) 123-45-6789
- ☐ Partnership
- ☐ Corporation (enter form number to be filed)
- ☐ Personal service corporation
- ☐ Church or church-controlled organization
- ☐ Other nonprofit organization (specify)
- ☐ Other (specify)
- ☐ Estate (SSN of decedent)
- ☐ Plan administrator (TIN)
- ☐ Trust (TIN of grantor)
- ☐ Military/National Guard
- ☐ State/local government
- ☐ Farmers' cooperative
- ☐ Federal government
- ☐ REMIC
- ☐ Indian tribal governments/enterprises

Group Exemption Number (GEN) if any

9b If a corporation, name the state or foreign country (if applicable) where incorporated | State | Foreign country

10 **Reason for applying** (check only one box)

- ☐ Started new business (specify type)
- ☑ Hired employees (Check the box and see line 13.)
- ☐ Compliance with IRS withholding regulations
- ☐ Other (specify)
- ☐ Banking purpose (specify purpose)
- ☐ Changed type of organization (specify new type)
- ☐ Purchased going business
- ☐ Created a trust (specify type)
- ☐ Created a pension plan (specify type)

Lines 11 through 15 request details about when the business was formed, when it files its tax return, and about its current or expected employees. The most important line in this section for our purposes is Line 14 - pay close attention to that little check box.

Line 11 requests the date the business was started or acquired, and Line 12 asks for the closing month of the accounting year. Most small business owners, particularly those operating as sole proprietors, operate on a calendar year basis, meaning the closing month will typically be December. If you file a Schedule C with your personal income tax return for your business each April 15th, then you are indeed a calendar-year taxpayer, and Line 12 should be "December."

Line 13 requests information about the type and number of employees you will have. If you will be hiring your child as your first and only employee, you will include the number "1" under "Other" on Line 13. The child will be a bona fide employee of your business and not classified as an agricultural or household employee.

Line 14 is very important and asks about the amount you expect to pay in related payroll taxes and federal withholding. This is important because it will inform the IRS of the tax forms you wish to file for the wages you pay to your new employees. Remember that your child under age 18 will be exempt from all payroll taxes. And since you will expect to pay the child $15,000 or less, there will be no withholding requirement. Therefore, your total payroll tax liability is expected to be ZERO. Make sure you check the box on line 14 indicating that you wish to file the annual Form 944. More on this in Chapter 7. Fax the form to the IRS

Lastly, Line 15 will include the first date you expect to pay your new employee.

11 Date business started or acquired (month, day, year). See instructions. January 1, 2024	**12** Closing month of accounting year December
13 Highest number of employees expected in the next 12 months (enter -0- if none). If no employees expected, skip line 14. Agricultural: — Household: — Other: 1	**14** If you expect your employment tax liability to be $1,000 or less in a full calendar year **and** want to file Form 944 annually instead of Forms 941 quarterly, check here. (Your employment tax liability will generally be $1,000 or less if you expect to pay $5,000 or less, $6,536 or less if you're in a U.S. territory, in total wages.) If you don't check this box, you must file Form 941 for every quarter. ☑

15 First date wages or annuities were paid (month, day, year). **Note:** If applicant is a withholding agent, enter date income will first be paid to nonresident alien (month, day, year) . . . . January 31, 2025

Lines 16 through 18 request details about the specific business conducted and then ask for your signature. Check the box on Line 16 that best matches your principal business activity. If the list does not include a close match for your business, select the "Other" option and provide a brief description of what you do. Examples include "Consulting," "Insurance Sales," and "Landscape Maintenance." Line 17 simply requests more details regarding the services or products you provide. Finally, Line 18 asks if the applicant entity has ever applied for an EIN before. This question pertains to your small business, not to you as an individual. You may have had another business in which you requested an EIN in the past, but if this particular business has not requested an EIN, then the answer for this question should be "No."

Complete the process by signing and dating the form, and include your phone numbers in case the IRS needs to contact you. Once the form is completed, signed, and dated, take a few minutes to review the details to ensure you have all the information included and correct. Check your Social Security Number in particular to make sure you haven't transposed or omitted a number. Ensure that you have completed Line 14 related to filing Form 944, and you are all set.

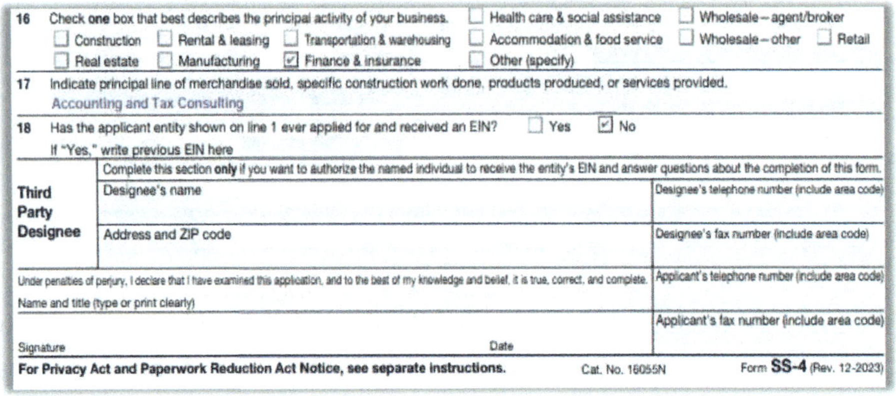

16 Check **one** box that best describes the principal activity of your business. ☐ Health care & social assistance ☐ Wholesale—agent/broker
☐ Construction ☐ Rental & leasing ☐ Transportation & warehousing ☐ Accommodation & food service ☐ Wholesale—other ☐ Retail
☐ Real estate ☐ Manufacturing ☑ Finance & insurance ☐ Other (specify)

17 Indicate principal line of merchandise sold, specific construction work done, products produced, or services provided.
Accounting and Tax Consulting

18 Has the applicant entity shown on line 1 ever applied for and received an EIN? ☐ Yes ☑ No
If "Yes," write previous EIN here

Third Party Designee	Complete this section **only** if you want to authorize the named individual to receive the entity's EIN and answer questions about the completion of this form.	
	Designee's name	Designee's telephone number (include area code)
	Address and ZIP code	Designee's fax number (include area code)

Under penalties of perjury, I declare that I have examined this application, and to the best of my knowledge and belief, it is true, correct, and complete. Applicant's telephone number (include area code)
Name and title (type or print clearly)
Applicant's fax number (include area code)
Signature Date

For Privacy Act and Paperwork Reduction Act Notice, see separate instructions. Cat. No. 16055N Form **SS-4** (Rev. 12-2023)

Now that you have a completed Form SS-4, you can choose the method that works best for you to obtain the EIN from the IRS. As I mentioned earlier, there are four different options for obtaining the new number.

A. Apply for the EIN online at www.IRS.gov.

Applying online is a relatively new option that effectively reviews names, addresses, social security numbers, and other information, and approves them in real-time. Correct numbers and spelling matter, and the related security issues can certainly cause the process to be longer and more cumbersome for some applicants. Based on my experience, this option is the easiest and quickest method for obtaining the EIN, typically taking about 10 to 15 minutes, start to finish. Perhaps the best part of this option is that once the process is complete, you will have your new EIN available for immediate use.

Go to www.IRS.gov and using the site's search function, search on "EIN" or "Apply for EIN." From there, click on the option for "Apply for an Employer Identification Number (EIN) Online." Under the section "Get an EIN," click on the link for "APPLY for an EIN," which will direct you to the IRS's EIN Assistant site:

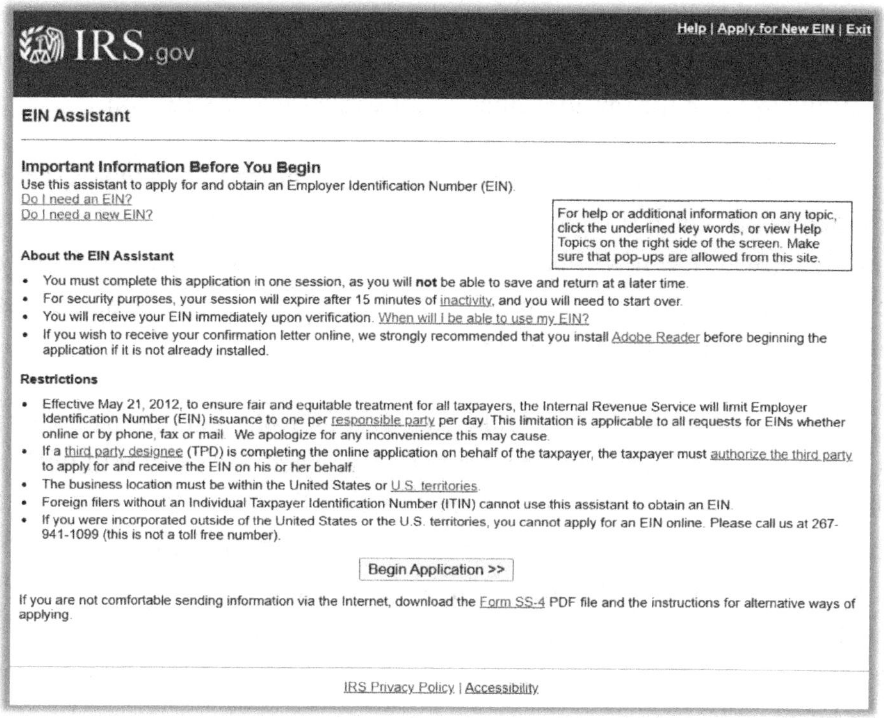

IRS.gov

Help | Apply for New EIN | Exit

EIN Assistant

Important Information Before You Begin
Use this assistant to apply for and obtain an Employer Identification Number (EIN).
Do I need an EIN?
Do I need a new EIN?

For help or additional information on any topic, click the underlined key words, or view Help Topics on the right side of the screen. Make sure that pop-ups are allowed from this site.

About the EIN Assistant

- You must complete this application in one session, as you will **not** be able to save and return at a later time.
- For security purposes, your session will expire after 15 minutes of inactivity, and you will need to start over.
- You will receive your EIN immediately upon verification. When will I be able to use my EIN?
- If you wish to receive your confirmation letter online, we strongly recommended that you install Adobe Reader before beginning the application if it is not already installed.

Restrictions

- Effective May 21, 2012, to ensure fair and equitable treatment for all taxpayers, the Internal Revenue Service will limit Employer Identification Number (EIN) issuance to one per responsible party per day. This limitation is applicable to all requests for EINs whether online or by phone, fax or mail. We apologize for any inconvenience this may cause.
- If a third party designee (TPD) is completing the online application on behalf of the taxpayer, the taxpayer must authorize the third party to apply for and receive the EIN on his or her behalf.
- The business location must be within the United States or U.S. territories.
- Foreign filers without an Individual Taxpayer Identification Number (ITIN) cannot use this assistant to obtain an EIN.
- If you were incorporated outside of the United States or the U.S. territories, you cannot apply for an EIN online. Please call us at 267-941-1099 (this is not a toll free number).

Begin Application >>

If you are not comfortable sending information via the Internet, download the Form SS-4 PDF file and the instructions for alternative ways of applying.

IRS Privacy Policy | Accessibility

Make sure you have completed the Form SS-4 and then click "Begin Application." The process does not follow the same format or order of information as included on the SS-4, but the details are basically the same. The website will prompt you with a number of questions that are included on the SS-4, but not necessarily using the exact words. Questions include details about you, the business, as well as your Social Security numbers and phone numbers. The site will also ask you some questions that are not included on the Form SS-4, such as:

Does your business own a highway motor vehicle with a taxable gross weight of 55,000 pounds or more?

and

Does your business involve gambling or wagering?

The purpose of these questions is to determine if your business may need to file other licenses or reports or pay other taxes. Simply answer each question based on the circumstances applicable to your situation.

Make sure to indicate that your business is indeed operated as a sole proprietorship. Once you select sole proprietorship, the site will also ask you to confirm if you will have household employees or regular employees. Ensure you choose the option to hire regular employees, rather than selecting the option for household employees.

This is very important!!! Make sure you indicate that you will expect to incur less than $1,000 in total tax liability. Therefore, you will wish to file IRS Form 944, Employer's Annual Federal Tax Return, instead of IRS Form 941, Employer's Quarterly Federal Tax Return. Of course, if you expect to hire other employees or incur those liabilities, then indeed indicate that via the application process. However, if you are hiring your child as your first employee, consider taking the easier option of filing the annual Form 944.

Once you complete the process, the website will confirm your new EIN. Make sure you print a copy of the confirmation and keep it with your business records. Your new EIN is ready to use.

B. Call the IRS directly.

Obtaining your new EIN by calling the IRS directly is my second favorite option and will take about the same amount of time as the online option, which is about 10 to 15 minutes. You can call the IRS from 7:00 a.m. to 10:00 p.m. Eastern Time to complete the application process. The toll-free number within the United States is:

800-829-4933

International callers may call 267-941-1099, where applicable; long-distance charges will apply. Make sure you have the completed Form SS-4 with you when you call. You will likely be on hold for a few minutes before being connected to an IRS employee, so it's a good idea to have this book with you so you can read the next chapter while you wait.

Once you have been connected with an IRS representative, you will indicate that you would like to get an EIN for your business, and the agent will ask if you have a completed Form SS-4. From there, the call will go something like this:

Agent:	What do you have on Line 1?
You:	Keith Hall
Agent:	Is there anything on Line 2?
You:	Yes, Keith Hall Consulting
Agent:	What do you have on Line 7a?
You:	Keith Hall
Agent:	How about Line 7b?
You:	123-45-6789

I won't make you read through the entire script here because you get the idea. The IRS agent will ask you questions throughout the form. It may sound strange, but they don't always ask you about every line on the form, and they don't always ask the questions in the same order as they appear on the form. Regardless of which items they ask about, you will have all the answers at your fingertips since you have already completed the form. Once the agent has asked their questions, they will put you on hold, and you will have a minute or two to read a bit more of the next chapter.

While you are reading, the agent will be checking for name availability, your Social Security Number, previously requested EINs, and most likely other details from a security standpoint. When they do come back to the phone, they will ask you to write your new EIN at the top of your Form SS-4 and then ask you to read it back to them. That number is active and available for immediate use to file a return, make a payment, or open a new business bank account. As I mentioned, the entire phone process should take approximately 10 to 15 minutes. You will receive a letter confirming the new number within a few days. This option is slightly more cumbersome than completing the process online due to the hold time on the phone, but it is a faster process for obtaining your new EIN than mailing or faxing the form to the IRS.

C. Mail the form directly to the IRS.

This method will take the longest to obtain the new EIN, but it is relatively straightforward. Simply sign the form, making sure you include your contact information and your phone number, and mail it directly to the IRS at:

Internal Revenue Service Center
Attn: EIN Operation
Cincinnati, OH 45999

If you are located outside the U.S. or do not have a legal residence, you will mail the Form SS-4 to the IRS at:
Internal Revenue Service Center
Attn: EIN International Operation
Cincinnati, OH 45999

The IRS recommends allowing four to five weeks for receipt of the new EIN via mail. Be sure to keep a copy of the form for your records.

D. Fax the form to the IRS.

Faxing the form is only slightly more difficult than mailing the form, and for many people it may even be easier. The IRS states that faxing the form can complete the process in as little as 4 days. If faxing the form is best for you, simply fax the form to:

Fax TIN – 855-641-6935 If you reside in the United States

Fax TIN – 855-215-1627 If you are outside the United States

As with mailing the form, be sure to keep a copy for your records.

2. Obtain a State Employer Identification Number (if necessary)

In addition to federal payroll reporting, you must also meet State payroll reporting requirements. The good news is that you most likely are not required to report wages paid to your child under age 18 from a sole proprietorship to your state's employment agency. Even if you do need to file a state report, there will most likely be no tax payment due. Many states will still require you to register as an employer with the state, and all states will require you to register your new employee (as we will discuss in Chapter 5). Again, even though you may need to register with your state and file a wage report, there will most likely be no tax liability for payroll taxes. I have included excerpts from California and Texas state employment agencies as examples of how most states address hiring minors.

State of California:

"Section 631 of the CUIC (California Unemployment Insurance Code) states, in part, that "Employment" does not include service performed by a child under the age of 18 years in the employee of his [or her] father or mother, or service performed by an individual in the employee of his [or her] son, daughter, or spouse (including, effective January 1, 2005, the employee's registered domestic partner). Section 631-1 of Title 22, California Code of Regulations, specifies that this exemption includes adopted children under the age of 18. Still, stepchildren, foster children, sons-in-law, or daughters-in-law are not included. Once a child reaches his or her eighteenth birthday, this exclusion no longer applies."

The above is quoted from the State of California, Employment Development Department, as per its Family Employment Information Sheet. To download a copy of the information sheet, go to:

http://www.edd.ca.gov/pdf_pub_ctr/de231fam.pdf

State of Texas:

The Texas Unemployment Compensation Act requires that any Employing Unit that becomes liable for reporting and paying unemployment tax in the State of Texas must register with the State within ten days of becoming liable for such tax. The State also provides a detailed list of services that are specifically exempt from the Act, and therefore, are not included in determining liability or reporting requirements under the Act.

Exempt Services: In order for the following services to be exempt and not included on the TWC Tax Reports, one or more of the following conditions must exist: Please get in touch with your nearest Texas Workforce Commission (TWC) Tax Office for specifics.

- Service of an Individual in the employ of the individual's spouse.

- Services of a Minor Child (under 21) in the employ of the parents.

- Services of Parents in the employ of their sons or daughters.

The above is quoted from the Texas Workforce Commission and the Texas Unemployment Compensation Act. To review this information, go to:

http://www.twc.state.tx.us/

I have included California and Texas just as examples, but most states follow the same general guidelines for the taxability of wages paid to your minor child. Many states have different minimum wage reporting standards compared to federal rules, so be sure to check your state's rules and regulations regarding hiring family members, particularly those under the age of 18. If your only employee is your child under age 18, you will most likely incur no tax and absolutely no additional costs for state unemployment insurance or any other employment-related cost. You may have to file another piece of paper or two with your state, but if you do, you will most likely save even more money by reducing your state income tax as well as your federal income tax. The bottom line here is that you should check with your state's reporting requirements to make sure you file correctly with the State. The good news is that most reports follow a general outline similar to federal reports, so the processes included in this guide will also be helpful in addressing state reports. (See Chapter 7 for reporting requirements.)

I have included a list of resources and state websites in Appendix D to help with researching your state's specific payroll requirements.

3. Determine the specific duties of the new position

Remember that the prevailing rule for compliance is almost always based on the vague concept of "reasonable." The specific duties required in the new position that you create must ultimately be reasonable in relation to the individual who will be completing those duties. From a technical standpoint, we are creating a new job that will help you manage your business and promote your own success by freeing your time for more important tasks. Ensure that the tasks assigned to your new position are reasonable, considering the skill set of your particular child.

There are literally thousands of tasks that must be addressed in your business. The goal is to set aside those tasks that your new employee can accomplish. We previously discussed the requirements for your child and the skill set they will bring to your company, helping you achieve your goals. Simply ensure that the tasks you are asking them to perform for your business are indeed things they can actually accomplish. Some of the more common duties assigned to minor children working in the parents' small businesses include:

- Answering the phone
- Greeting guests and customers
- Sorting incoming mail
- Processing outgoing mail
- Stuffing envelopes, affixing stamps, and sealing envelopes
- Making copies
- Faxing documents
- Filing and organizing files, both electronic and physical

This list is not exhaustive and covers only the basic duties that are most likely to be evident in all business environments. Be creative. If you can find tasks that will motivate and challenge your child as well as meet the needs of your company, you will have created even more benefits than just the thousands in tax dollars that you will save. Once you have completed the list of duties that are to be accomplished, include those in a formal job description and discuss those duties with your new employee. They may very well have some ideas of their own that can be included.

4. Determine an hourly wage based on those duties

Remember that minimum wage requirements do not apply to wages paid to a child under 18 employed in their parents' business, so there is no need to worry about setting an hourly wage that is too low. Also, remember that our goal here is to reimburse you for the money you are already giving your child. The hourly salary must meet the same "reasonable" requirement as the specific functions to be accomplished, so avoid paying your child $600 an hour for stuffing envelopes. It is easy to be tempted by a high hourly rate, as the more you pay them, the more you will save. However, be careful. Try to determine a reasonable wage that would be consistent with amounts that you might pay an unrelated worker for similar services.

I personally prefer an hourly wage of $25.00 for most administrative duties related to my small business, as outlined in the following scenario. I currently live in Dallas, Texas, and my neighbors have a 14-year-old son, Jason, who works in my yard every summer for extra money. He picks weeds, mows the grass, and occasionally plants new flowers whenever my wife decides that it is time for such things. On a typical Saturday, he mows the grass, trims a few bushes that need it, and then sweeps up the mess. He works for about two hours, and I always pay him $50. He is satisfied with that amount, and it appears to be the right total. I wouldn't feel good if I paid him less, and I wouldn't feel that good either if I paid him more. Fifty dollars for two hours' work is $25.00 per hour. This is the wage that I would be willing to pay an unrelated 14-year-old for services provided, so that is the basis for determining what is "reasonable" in terms of wages I should pay to my own child working in my business.

Your concept of a reasonable wage may be slightly less or slightly more. It would be appropriate to assume that a child working in your business at age eight might make a little less than a child who is 16 years old. Likewise, your 16-year-old may earn a bit more per hour for services related to your website and SEO optimization than your eight-year-old, who is stuffing envelopes and cleaning the home office. The key remains "reasonable." If you have two kids who will be providing services to your business, they don't necessarily have to be paid the same wage. By the same token, just because one is older, smarter, or providing more complicated services, it may still be reasonable to pay them a similar wage.

5. Complete a detailed job description

Once you have identified the specific duties to be accomplished, the skills required, and a reasonable wage, the formal job description can be completed. Have your new employee read the job description and allow them to make additions or deletions as needed. Get their 'buy-in." Once both of you are comfortable, have your new employee sign the job description and file a copy in the newly created personnel file folder. I have attached two sample job descriptions that hundreds of small businesses have used to create new jobs for their children. The first one is for an Administrative Assistant, and the second is for a Social Media Director.

Kelsey Busby Real Estate Sales

Job Description

SUMMARY

Provide administrative support to the company's Owner and Manager.

Job Title: Administrative Assistant   Reports to: Owner

Wages, Hourly: $25.00   Last Revision: January 1, 2025

Duties include general clerical, receptionist, and project-based work. Project a professional company image through in-person and phone interactions.

PRIMARY RESPONSIBILITIES

1. Answer the telephone and transfer the call to the appropriate staff member.
2. Meet and greet clients and visitors as needed.
3. Create and modify documents using Microsoft Office software.
4. Perform general clerical duties to include: photocopying, faxing, mailing, and filing.
5. Maintain a hard copy and electronic filing system.
6. Sign for and distribute UPS, FedEx, and Airborne packages.
7. Coordinate and maintain records for staff office space, phones, parking, and other related items.
8. Set up and coordinate meetings and conferences.
9. Support staff in assigned project-based work.
10 Other duties as assigned.

ADDITIONAL DUTIES

1. Maintain overall safety and cleanliness of the office.
2. Accomplish travel and delivery-related duties outside the office as necessary.

KNOWLEDGE AND SKILL REQUIREMENTS

1. Basic reading, writing, and arithmetic skills required.
2. Knowledge of Microsoft Office and telephone protocol.

WORKING CONDITIONS

1. Working conditions are normal for an office environment.
2. No hazardous duties will be assigned.

________________________   ________________

Employee Signature   Date

Kelsey Busby Real Estate Sales

Job Description

Job Title: Social Media Director Reports to: Owner

Wages, Hourly: $30.00 Last Revision: January 1, 2025

SUMMARY

Develop, implement, and maintain the company's social media presence. Develop a Facebook page, Twitter account, and any other application deemed appropriate. Provide monthly updates, broadcasts, and reports to maintain an overall social media presence.

PRIMARY RESPONSIBILITIES

1. Update the company website as needed.
2. Maximize search engine optimization with new content.
3. Post the current agenda, sales, and marketing details to the company's Facebook page.
4. Maintain a company presence on social media outlets, including Twitter, Facebook, and others.
5. Prepare a monthly report of social media presence.
6. Set up and coordinate meetings and conferences.
7. Support staff in assigned project-based work.
8. Other duties as assigned.

ADDITIONAL DUTIES

1. Maintain overall safety and cleanliness of the office.
2. Accomplish travel and delivery-related duties outside the office as necessary.

KNOWLEDGE AND SKILL REQUIREMENTS

1. Basic reading, writing, and arithmetic skills required.
2. Knowledge of Microsoft Office and telephone protocol.
3. Knowledge of SEO and social media outlets.
4. Experience with Facebook, Twitter, and other social media platforms

WORKING CONDITIONS

1. Working conditions are normal for an office environment.
2. No hazardous duties will be assigned.

_______________________ _______________

Employee Signature Date

Once you have completed your specific position's job description, make sure not to view it as permanently etched in stone. The detailed job requirements can certainly change with duties being added and deleted. It is always a good idea to review the details periodically and dust off the cobwebs. The key point of the job description is to document the services to be provided. If the question ever arises, the more paperwork you have, the better, which is true of almost all discussion points concerning the IRS. You have a couple of examples here that will fit many situations, but you can also use this format to build a specific job description for your new job.

Now that you have your job defined and your Employer Identification Number, you're ready to proceed. It's time to go out and hire that new employee. Let's do it.

5

Hiring the New Employee

If I were writing this book about hiring any random new employee, this section would need to include details about finding the best candidate for the position that you have created. However, the fact is that you already have a great candidate in mind for your new position. In fact, this position was truly designed with a specific new candidate in mind. Therefore, this chapter is about actually hiring your child for the new position that you have just created.

We will discuss the paperwork required to document the hiring process and the steps for getting the new employee started on their personal growth, as well as meeting the needs of your small business. I am not recommending that you forget that the new employee is indeed your child, but please keep in mind that you need to ensure you fulfill all the requirements for adequate documentation, just in case the IRS someday requests it. Avoid the temptation to take a shortcut here and take the time to build a little stack of paper that will always provide the answers to any question that could potentially be asked.

The first and most obvious task is to create a new personnel file for your new employee. This file will include the job description and salary details that you created in Chapter 4, as well as the details that you will complete in this Chapter. The new personnel file does not have to be anything fancy, but simply a place where you know all the details reside. So, find a nice hanging file folder or manila file folder and label it with your new employee's name. Insert a copy of the new job description, and we're ready to proceed.

There are three important steps and three important pieces of paper to complete for your new employee:

1. Verify Employment Eligibility

2. Complete Employee Withholding Allowance Certificate

3. Report the New Hire to Your State's New Hire Reporting System.

Each of these steps is extremely easy, with each requiring only a few minutes to complete. However, each is also an important document to maintain in your new employee's personnel file. It will take you more time to actually read each section of this chapter than it will to complete the actual forms, but don't allow that to let you think the forms are not important.

1. Verify Employment Eligibility

The Department of Labor and the United States Citizenship and Immigration Service have some level of jurisdiction over your new employee, the new job, the services that are provided, and even some benefits that must be provided. Your state's workforce commission will also want to dictate certain factors, such as hourly wage, overtime, reporting requirements, and the age of the workers, among others. As we have already discussed, your child working in your sole proprietorship is exempt from Department of Labor laws and regulations, as well as from your state's wage and hour laws. However, for some reason, you still need to formally verify the new worker's eligibility actually to hold the job within the United States.

The good news is that the form for verifying eligibility is very easy to complete and will take you less than 5 minutes. It may be tempting, but don't skip this step. I will walk you through the form line by line, give you a link to download a blank copy for your new employee, and you will have everything you need.

The form required for documenting a new employee's identity and employment authorization is called Form I-9, Employment Eligibility Verification, and is issued and maintained by the United States Citizenship and Immigration Services under the Department of Homeland Security. The bottom line is to verify that your new employee is indeed authorized to work within the United States. That authorization may be in the form of U.S. citizenship, a Social Security Card, a resident alien work permit, or a work visa, among others. Try not to get too bogged down in the logic or the necessity of the form; just spend a few minutes filling it out, stick it in the personnel file, and move on to more important things.

This particular part of the process will become more important once your small business grows and you need to hire unrelated employees. Making sure your new employees are actually authorized to work within the United States is a legal requirement and will be something to take seriously. Obviously, this is less important with your own child, and the need for this paperwork will most likely never come up.

The USCIS Form I-9 is four pages long and is very user-friendly. Page 1 is the only page you will actually have to complete for your child as your first new employee, and will be where we spend all of our time in this Chapter. Page 2 is actually just a menu of things to choose from in completing Page 1. Pages 3 and 4 are included for unique situations such as rehiring a former employee or when you have needed a translator or third party to help your new employee complete in answering your questions about their eligibility. These pages will not be required with your child's employment verification.

http://www.uscis.gov/files/form/i-9.pdf

Go to the above URL and print a blank copy to complete as you read the next few pages. I know this may seem unnecessary, but it will be very painless and only take a few minutes.

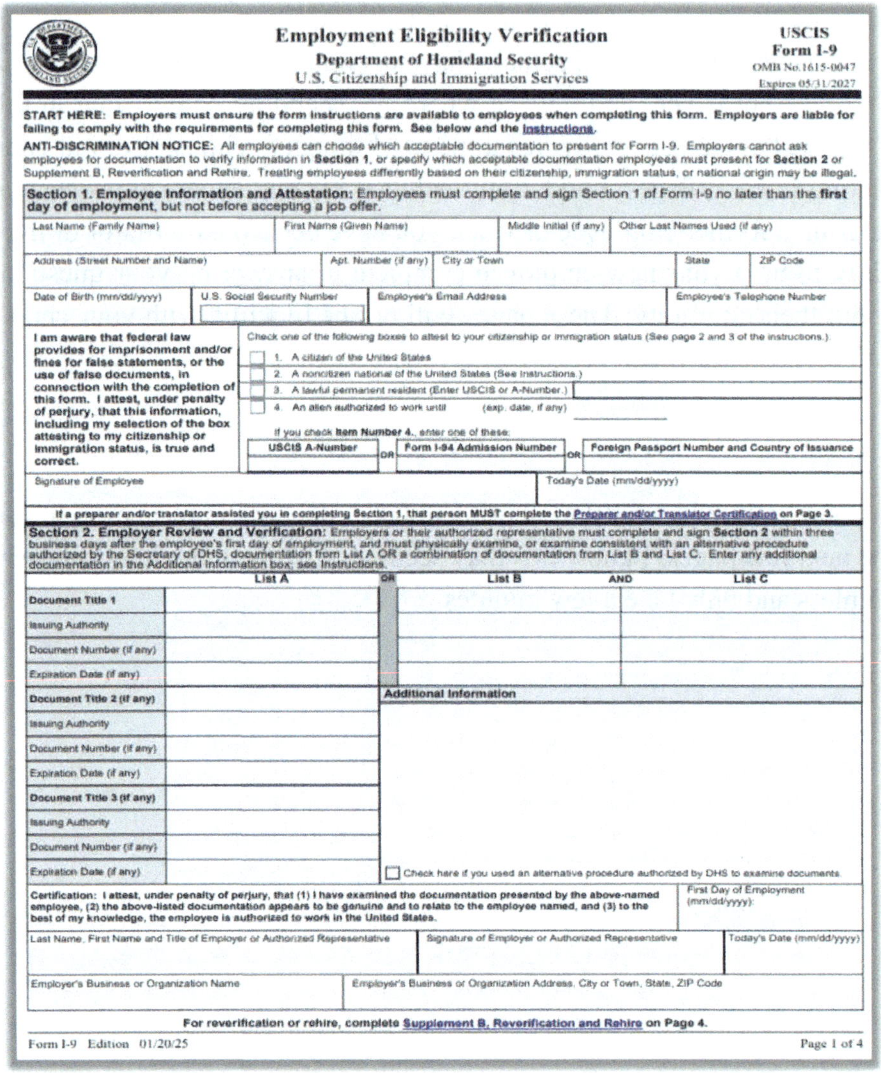

Employment Eligibility Verification
Department of Homeland Security
U.S. Citizenship and Immigration Services

USCIS Form I-9
OMB No.1615-0047
Expires 05/31/2027

START HERE: Employers must ensure the form instructions are available to employees when completing this form. Employers are liable for failing to comply with the requirements for completing this form. See below and the Instructions.

ANTI-DISCRIMINATION NOTICE: All employees can choose which acceptable documentation to present for Form I-9. Employers cannot ask employees for documentation to verify information in **Section 1**, or specify which acceptable documentation employees must present for **Section 2** or Supplement B, Reverification and Rehire. Treating employees differently based on their citizenship, immigration status, or national origin may be illegal.

Section 1. Employee Information and Attestation: Employees must complete and sign Section 1 of Form I-9 no later than the **first day of employment**, but not before accepting a job offer.

Last Name (Family Name)	First Name (Given Name)	Middle Initial (if any)	Other Last Names Used (if any)

Address (Street Number and Name)	Apt. Number (if any)	City or Town	State	ZIP Code

Date of Birth (mm/dd/yyyy)	U.S. Social Security Number	Employee's Email Address	Employee's Telephone Number

I am aware that federal law provides for imprisonment and/or fines for false statements, or the use of false documents, in connection with the completion of this form. I attest, under penalty of perjury, that this information, including my selection of the box attesting to my citizenship or immigration status, is true and correct.

Check one of the following boxes to attest to your citizenship or immigration status (See page 2 and 3 of the instructions.):

- [ ] 1. A citizen of the United States
- [ ] 2. A noncitizen national of the United States (See Instructions.)
- [ ] 3. A lawful permanent resident (Enter USCIS or A-Number.)
- [ ] 4. An alien authorized to work until (exp. date, if any)

If you check **Item Number 4.**, enter one of these:

USCIS A-Number	OR	Form I-94 Admission Number	OR	Foreign Passport Number and Country of Issuance

Signature of Employee	Today's Date (mm/dd/yyyy)

If a preparer and/or translator assisted you in completing Section 1, that person MUST complete the Preparer and/or Translator Certification on Page 3.

Section 2. Employer Review and Verification: Employers or their authorized representative must complete and sign **Section 2** within three business days after the employee's first day of employment, and must physically examine, or examine consistent with an alternative procedure authorized by the Secretary of DHS, documentation from List A OR a combination of documentation from List B and List C. Enter any additional documentation in the Additional Information box; see Instructions.

	List A	OR	List B	AND	List C
Document Title 1					
Issuing Authority					
Document Number (if any)					
Expiration Date (if any)					
Document Title 2 (if any)		**Additional Information**			
Issuing Authority					
Document Number (if any)					
Expiration Date (if any)					
Document Title 3 (if any)					
Issuing Authority					
Document Number (if any)					
Expiration Date (if any)		☐ Check here if you used an alternative procedure authorized by DHS to examine documents.			

Certification: I attest, under penalty of perjury, that (1) I have examined the documentation presented by the above-named employee, (2) the above-listed documentation appears to be genuine and to relate to the employee named, and (3) to the best of my knowledge, the employee is authorized to work in the United States.

First Day of Employment (mm/dd/yyyy):

Last Name, First Name and Title of Employer or Authorized Representative	Signature of Employer or Authorized Representative	Today's Date (mm/dd/yyyy)

Employer's Business or Organization Name	Employer's Business or Organization Address, City or Town, State, ZIP Code

For reverification or rehire, complete Supplement B, Reverification and Rehire on Page 4.

Form I-9 Edition 01/20/25 Page 1 of 4

The first page, as I mentioned above, is the only page that you will most likely have to complete and should take you less than about one minute. Okay, maybe two minutes because you will want to print neatly on the form. Section 1 of the form is technically to be completed by the employee; however, an employee under the age of 18 can certainly solicit the help of their parent with the form. (That is also YOU by the way!) Section one requests general information about the new employee, including name, address, Social Security number, date of birth, email address, and phone number. It will also ask you to check a box to identify citizenship in the United States or residency status. For most of us, simply checking U.S. Citizen will be applicable. If so, check that first box indicating "A citizen of the United States" and then have the new employee, your child, sign the form. That's it! Page one of the form is done.

If your child is not a United States citizen, then fill out the applicable parts of this page to ensure they are indeed eligible to work in the United States.

Section 2 of the form, the bottom half, is intended for completion by the employer. The purpose of this section is to record the documentation that you, as the employer, reviewed to verify that the new employee is who they say they are, and to verify their working status and eligibility. The point is that as an employer, you are responsible for examining documentation that verifies the employee's identity and also verifying a specific document that confirms their authorization to hold a job. Some documents can verify both, such as a United States passport.

Page 2 of the form provides a list of possible documents that the employer can potentially review in order to verify both identity and authorization. This page may look confusing at first, but try to view it like a restaurant menu. You can review one item from List A, or if that is not applicable, then you must review one item from List B AND one item from List C. The most common items for employers to review are either a US Passport, from List A, or a valid driver's license from List B and a Social Security Card from List C. If your child has a US Passport, then simply enter "US Passport" on the first line of List A, sign it, and you are all done.

LISTS OF ACCEPTABLE DOCUMENTS

All documents containing an expiration date must be unexpired.

* Documents extended by the issuing authority are considered unexpired.

Employees may present one selection from List A or a combination of one selection from List B and one selection from List C.

Examples of many of these documents appear in the Handbook for Employers (M-274).

LIST A Documents that Establish Both Identity and Employment Authorization	OR	LIST B Documents that Establish Identity	AND	LIST C Documents that Establish Employment Authorization
1. U.S. Passport or U.S. Passport Card		1. Driver's license or ID card issued by a State or outlying possession of the United States provided it contains a photograph or information such as name, date of birth, sex, height, eye color, and address		1. A Social Security Account Number card, unless the card includes one of the following restrictions: (1) NOT VALID FOR EMPLOYMENT (2) VALID FOR WORK ONLY WITH INS AUTHORIZATION (3) VALID FOR WORK ONLY WITH DHS AUTHORIZATION
2. Permanent Resident Card or Alien Registration Receipt Card (Form I-551)		2. ID card issued by federal, state or local government agencies or entities, provided it contains a photograph or information such as name, date of birth, sex, height, eye color, and address		2. Certification of report of birth issued by the Department of State (Forms DS-1350, FS-545, FS-240)
3. Foreign passport that contains a temporary I-551 stamp or temporary I-551 printed notation on a machine-readable immigrant visa		3. School ID card with a photograph		3. Original or certified copy of birth certificate issued by a State, county, municipal authority, or territory of the United States bearing an official seal
4. Employment Authorization Document that contains a photograph (Form I-766)		4. Voter's registration card		4. Native American tribal document
5. For an individual temporarily authorized to work for a specific employer because of his or her status or parole: a. Foreign passport; and b. Form I-94 or Form I-94A that has the following: (1) The same name as the passport; and (2) An endorsement of the individual's status or parole as long as that period of endorsement has not yet expired and the proposed employment is not in conflict with any restrictions or limitations identified on the form.		5. U.S. Military card or draft record		5. U.S. Citizen ID Card (Form I-197)
6. Passport from the Federated States of Micronesia (FSM) or the Republic of the Marshall Islands (RMI) with Form I-94 or Form I-94A indicating nonimmigrant admission under the Compact of Free Association Between the United States and the FSM or RMI		6. Military dependent's ID card		6. Identification Card for Use of Resident Citizen in the United States (Form I-179)
		7. U.S. Coast Guard Merchant Mariner Card		7. Employment authorization document issued by the Department of Homeland Security For examples, see **Section 7** and **Section 13** of the M-274 on **uscis.gov/i-9-central**. The Form I-766, Employment Authorization Document, is a List A, **Item Number 4.** document, not a List C document.
		8. Native American tribal document		
		9. Driver's license issued by a Canadian government authority		
		For persons under age 18 who are unable to present a document listed above:		
		10. School record or report card		
		11. Clinic, doctor, or hospital record		
		12. Day-care or nursery school record		

Acceptable Receipts

May be presented in lieu of a document listed above for a temporary period.

For receipt validity dates, see the M-274.

• Receipt for a replacement of a lost, stolen, or damaged List A document. • Form I-94 issued to a lawful permanent resident that contains an I-551 stamp and a photograph of the individual. • Form I-94 with "RE" notation or refugee stamp issued to a refugee.	OR	Receipt for a replacement of a lost, stolen, or damaged List B document.	Receipt for a replacement of a lost, stolen, or damaged List C document.

*Refer to the Employment Authorization Extensions page on **I-9 Central** for more information.

Form I-9 Edition 01/20/25 Page 2 of 4

If your child doesn't have a passport, the process is almost as simple. You will need to include one item from List B AND one item from List C. There are many items included as optional documentation noted under List B, most of which will most likely be irrelevant. If your child has a driver's license, that will most likely be the easiest choice for this section, in which case you will include the words, "State Driver's License."

Note that exceptions are listed for minors under the age of 18, as numbers 10, 11, and 12. Therefore, if your child does not have a driver's license for List B, simply include on the first line the words, "Minor Under Age 18." Then on line 2 for List B, enter the description for any school report or school report card, doctor or hospital record, or day care record. (The completed Form I-9 on page 64 includes this option as an example.)

The very first item included for List C is "A Social Security Account Number Card" and the second item is a valid state-issued birth certificate. You most likely have your child's Social Security card and their original birth certificate. Keep in mind that you will need the Social Security number for the child even if you don't have the card, so if there is no Social Security number or card, you will need to request the new number for your child. In the last column, under List C, include "Social Security Card" or "Birth Certificate," whichever is easiest for you to find while filling out the form.

Sign the bottom of the form and indicate the employee's first day of work, and you are all done. Your new employee has now been declared eligible to work for your small business in the United States. There is no applicable fee or tax with the Form I-9, and the completed form isn't even mailed to anyone. Place the completed and signed form in the new personnel file, and you are ready for the next form. I am guessing it took you more time to read this second than it did actually to complete the form. I have included a link to detailed instructions for the Form I-9 if you are interested in reading more.

https://www.uscis.gov/sites/default/files/document/forms/i-9instr.pdf

Employment Eligibility Verification
Department of Homeland Security
U.S. Citizenship and Immigration Services

USCIS
Form I-9
OMB No.1615-0047
Expires 05/31/2027

START HERE: Employers must ensure the form instructions are available to employees when completing this form. Employers are liable for failing to comply with the requirements for completing this form. See below and the Instructions.

ANTI-DISCRIMINATION NOTICE: All employees can choose which acceptable documentation to present for Form I-9. Employers cannot ask employees for documentation to verify information in **Section 1**, or specify which acceptable documentation employees must present for **Section 2** or Supplement B, Reverification and Rehire. Treating employees differently based on their citizenship, immigration status, or national origin may be illegal.

Section 1. Employee Information and Attestation: Employees must complete and sign Section 1 of Form I-9 no later than the **first day of employment**, but not before accepting a job offer.

Last Name (Family Name)	First Name (Given Name)	Middle Initial (if any)	Other Last Names Used (if any)
Busby	Samantha	R	

Address (Street Number and Name)	Apt. Number (if any)	City or Town	State	ZIP Code
30603 Lotus Ave		Plano	TX	75075

Date of Birth (mm/dd/yyyy)	U.S. Social Security Number	Employee's Email Address	Employee's Telephone Number
07/26/2008	4 5 7 2 7 3 9 0 1	Sammy.Busby@gmail.com	(214) 620-2437

I am aware that federal law provides for imprisonment and/or fines for false statements, or the use of false documents, in connection with the completion of this form. I attest, under penalty of perjury, that this information, including my selection of the box attesting to my citizenship or immigration status, is true and correct.

Check one of the following boxes to attest to your citizenship or immigration status (See page 2 and 3 of the instructions.):

- [x] 1. A citizen of the United States
- [ ] 2. A noncitizen national of the United States (See Instructions.)
- [ ] 3. A lawful permanent resident (Enter USCIS or A-Number.)
- [ ] 4. An alien authorized to work until (exp. date, if any)

If you check **Item Number 4.**, enter one of these:

USCIS A-Number	OR	Form I-94 Admission Number	OR	Foreign Passport Number and Country of Issuance

Signature of Employee	Today's Date (mm/dd/yyyy)
Samantha Busby	01/01/2025

If a preparer and/or translator assisted you in completing Section 1, that person MUST complete the Preparer and/or Translator Certification on Page 3.

Section 2. Employer Review and Verification: Employers or their authorized representative must complete and sign **Section 2** within three business days after the employee's first day of employment, and must physically examine, or examine consistent with an alternative procedure authorized by the Secretary of DHS, documentation from List A OR a combination of documentation from List B and List C. Enter any additional documentation in the Additional Information box; see Instructions.

	List A	OR	List B	AND	List C
Document Title 1			Minor Under Age 18		Social Security Card
Issuing Authority			Hospital Records		
Document Number (if any)					
Expiration Date (if any)					
Document Title 2 (if any)			**Additional Information**		
Issuing Authority					
Document Number (if any)					
Expiration Date (if any)					
Document Title 3 (if any)					
Issuing Authority					
Document Number (if any)					
Expiration Date (if any)			☐ Check here if you used an alternative procedure authorized by DHS to examine documents.		

Certification: I attest, under penalty of perjury, that (1) I have examined the documentation presented by the above-named employee, (2) the above-listed documentation appears to be genuine and to relate to the employee named, and (3) to the best of my knowledge, the employee is authorized to work in the United States.

First Day of Employment (mm/dd/yyyy):

Last Name, First Name and Title of Employer or Authorized Representative	Signature of Employer or Authorized Representative	Today's Date (mm/dd/yyyy)
Busby, Kelsey - Owner	*Kelsey Busby*	01/01/2025

Employer's Business or Organization Name	Employer's Business or Organization Address, City or Town, State, ZIP Code
Kelsey Busby Real Estate	30603 Lotus Ave, Plano, Texas 75075

For reverification or rehire, complete Supplement B, Reverification and Rehire on Page 4.

Form I-9 Edition 01/20/25

Page 1 of 4

2. Complete Employee Withholding Allowance Certificate

Each employee must complete IRS Form W-4, Employee Withholding Allowance Certificate. The purpose of this form is for the employee to communicate to the employer the amount of tax to withhold from their paycheck. The factors necessary for an employer to determine how much to withhold include the employee's filing status (married, single, head of household, etc.), the number and amount of any dependents and credits that may be claimed, and estimates of other income and deductions that might be expected. The employer also needs the employee's name, address, and Social Security number. As you can see from the copy below, the W-4 is designed to provide the employer with all the necessary information to pay their employee and withhold the correct amount of tax.

It is the employee's responsibility to complete the form, but it is the employer's responsibility to make sure the form is indeed completed. In this case, since your new employee is your child, it is a great idea to complete the form with your child. They will have fun helping with the form, learn a little bit about the job and the IRS, and you will need their signature on the form at the end.

At first glance, the form may look complicated, but in our case, we get a shortcut. If your child paid no tax last year and will not expect to pay any tax this year, then they will be eligible to claim an exemption from withholding. I don't like to use the words "logic" and "IRS" in the same sentence, but the logic here is that if the new worker will have no tax liability, then there should be no tax. Paying no tax is the plan for this Hire Your Kid Guide, so complete the W-4 for your new worker based on this exemption.

As you can see on the completed Form W-4 on Page 67, complete the top portion with name, address, and social security number, and then include the word "EXEMPT" in the space below item 4(c). Have your child sign the form, and the second step is also done.

Like the Form I-9, there is no applicable fee and no filing requirement. The form is not mailed to the IRS or any other government agency, but the employer is required to keep a copy of the form. Include the form in the new personnel file.

Form **W-4**

Department of the Treasury
Internal Revenue Service

Employee's Withholding Certificate

Complete Form W-4 so that your employer can withhold the correct federal income tax from your pay.
Give Form W-4 to your employer.
Your withholding is subject to review by the IRS.

OMB No. 1545-0074

2025

Step 1: Enter Personal Information

(a) First name and middle initial: Samantha R
Last name: Busby
(b) Social security number: 457-27-3901

Address: 30603 Lotus Ave

City or town, state, and ZIP code: Plano, Texas 75075

Does your name match the name on your social security card? If not, to ensure you get credit for your earnings, contact SSA at 800-772-1213 or go to www.ssa.gov.

(c) ☑ **Single** or **Married filing separately**
☐ **Married filing jointly** or **Qualifying surviving spouse**
☐ **Head of household** (Check only if you're unmarried and pay more than half the costs of keeping up a home for yourself and a qualifying individual.)

TIP: Consider using the estimator at *www.irs.gov/W4App* to determine the most accurate withholding for the rest of the year if: you are completing this form after the beginning of the year; expect to work only part of the year; or have changes during the year in your marital status, number of jobs for you (and/or your spouse if married filing jointly), dependents, other income (not from jobs), deductions, or credits. Have your most recent pay stub(s) from this year available when using the estimator. At the beginning of next year, use the estimator again to recheck your withholding.

Complete Steps 2–4 ONLY if they apply to you; otherwise, skip to Step 5. See page 2 for more information on each step, who can claim exemption from withholding, and when to use the estimator at *www.irs.gov/W4App*.

Step 2: Multiple Jobs or Spouse Works

Complete this step if you (1) hold more than one job at a time, or (2) are married filing jointly and your spouse also works. The correct amount of withholding depends on income earned from all of these jobs.

Do **only one** of the following.

(a) Use the estimator at *www.irs.gov/W4App* for the most accurate withholding for this step (and Steps 3–4). If you or your spouse have self-employment income, use this option; **or**

(b) Use the Multiple Jobs Worksheet on page 3 and enter the result in Step 4(c) below; **or**

(c) If there are only two jobs total, you may check this box. Do the same on Form W-4 for the other job. This option is generally more accurate than (b) if pay at the lower paying job is more than half of the pay at the higher paying job. Otherwise, (b) is more accurate . . . . ☐

Complete Steps 3–4(b) on Form W-4 for only ONE of these jobs. Leave those steps blank for the other jobs. (Your withholding will be most accurate if you complete Steps 3–4(b) on the Form W-4 for the highest paying job.)

Step 3: Claim Dependent and Other Credits

If your total income will be $200,000 or less ($400,000 or less if married filing jointly):

Multiply the number of qualifying children under age 17 by $2,000 $ ______

Multiply the number of other dependents by $500 . . . . . . $ ______

Add the amounts above for qualifying children and other dependents. You may add to this the amount of any other credits. Enter the total here . . . . **3** $

Step 4 (optional): Other Adjustments

(a) Other income (not from jobs). If you want tax withheld for other income you expect this year that won't have withholding, enter the amount of other income here. This may include interest, dividends, and retirement income . . . . **4(a)** $

(b) Deductions. If you expect to claim deductions other than the standard deduction and want to reduce your withholding, use the Deductions Worksheet on page 3 and enter the result here . . . . **4(b)** $

(c) Extra withholding. Enter any additional tax you want withheld each **pay period** . . **4(c)** $

Exempt

Step 5: Sign Here

Under penalties of perjury, I declare that this certificate, to the best of my knowledge and belief, is true, correct, and complete.

Samantha Busby — 01-01-25

Employee's signature (This form is not valid unless you sign it.) — **Date**

Employers Only

Employer's name and address: Kelsey Busby Real Estate, 30603 Lotus Ave, Plano, Texas 75075
First date of employment: 01-01-2025
Employer identification number (EIN): 27-1234567

For Privacy Act and Paperwork Reduction Act Notice, see page 3. Cat. No. 10220Q Form **W-4** (2025)

As I mentioned earlier, most states follow the federal lead in determining the information that must be obtained from new employees. If your business operates in a state that has an income tax provision for individuals, you should also have your new employee complete a state withholding form as well. Even the form itself will be very similar to the federal requirement. For example, George uses the following form:

Form G-4 (Rev. 08/15/24)

2511004015

STATE OF GEORGIA EMPLOYEE'S WITHHOLDING ALLOWANCE CERTIFICATE

1a. YOUR FULL NAME	1b. YOUR SOCIAL SECURITY NUMBER
2a. HOME ADDRESS (Number, Street, or Rural Route)	2b. CITY, STATE AND ZIP CODE

PLEASE READ INSTRUCTIONS ON REVERSE SIDE BEFORE COMPLETING LINES 3 – 8

3. MARITAL STATUS
Enter letter below on Line 7.

A. Single
B. Married Filing Separate or Married Filing Joint, both spouses working
C. Married Filing Joint, one spouse working
D. Head of Household

4. DEPENDENT ALLOWANCES [ ]

5. GEORGIA ADJUSTMENTS ALLOWANCE [ ]
(See instructions for details. Worksheet below must be completed)

6. ADDITIONAL WITHHOLDING $________

WORKSHEET FOR CALCULATING ADDITIONAL ALLOWANCES
(Must be completed for step 5)

A. Federal Estimated Itemized Deductions (If Itemizing Deductions)........ $________
B. Georgia Standard Deduction (enter one): $________
  Single/Head of Household $12,000
  Married Filing Joint $24,000
  Married Filing Separate $12,000
C. Subtract Line B from Line A (If zero or less, enter zero) .... $________
D. Allowable Georgia Adjustments to Federal Adjusted Gross Income .... $________
E. Add the Amounts on Lines C and D .... $________
F. Estimate of Taxable Income not Subject to Withholding .... $________
G. Subtract Line F from Line E (if zero or less, stop here)........ $________
H. Divide the Amount on Line G by $4,000. Enter total here and on Line 5 above .... ________
(This is the number of Georgia Adjustments Allowances you can claim. If the remainder is over $1,500 round up)

7. LETTER USED (Marital Status A, B, C or D) ________ **TOTAL ALLOWANCES** (Total of Lines 4 - 5) ________
(Employer: The letter indicates the tax tables in Employer's Tax Guide)

8. EXEMPT: (Do not complete Lines 4 - 7 if claiming exempt) **Read the Line 8 instructions on page 2 before completing this section.**
a) I claim exemption from withholding because I incurred no Georgia income tax liability last year **and** I do not expect to have a Georgia income tax liability this year. **Check here** ☐
b) I certify that I am not subject to Georgia withholding because I meet the conditions set forth under the Servicemembers Civil Relief Act as provided on page 2. My state of residence is ________. My spouse's (servicemember) state of residence is ________. The states of residence must be the same to be exempt. **Check here** ☐

I certify under penalty of perjury that I am entitled to the number of withholding allowances or the exemption from withholding status claimed on this Form G-4. Also, I authorize my employer to deduct per pay period the additional amount listed above.

Employee's Signature ________________ Date ________

Employer: Complete Line 9 and mail entire form only if the employee claims over 14 allowances or exempt from withholding. If necessary, mail form to: Georgia Department of Revenue, Taxpayer Services Division, P.O. Box 105685, Atlanta, GA 30348-5685

9. EMPLOYER'S NAME AND ADDRESS: **EMPLOYER'S FEIN:**________

EMPLOYER'S WH#:________

Do not accept forms claiming additional allowances unless the worksheet has been completed. Do not accept forms claiming exempt if numbers are written on Lines 4 - 7.

Notice that the form requests the same information as the IRS federal form, including name, address, Social Security number, filing status, and number of exemptions claimed. The state will also provide the new employee with the option to claim an exemption from tax withholding, just as with the IRS form. The following is Line 8 of the State of Georgia's Form G-4 above:

8. EXEMPT: (Do not complete Lines 4 - 7 if claiming exempt) **Read the Line 8 instructions on page 2 before completing this section.**
a) I claim exemption from withholding because I incurred no Georgia income tax liability last year **and** I do not expect to have a Georgia income tax liability this year. **Check here** ☐
b) I certify that I am not subject to Georgia withholding because I meet the conditions set forth under the Servicemembers Civil Relief Act as provided on page 2. My state of residence is _______________. My spouse's (servicemember) state of residence is _______________. The states of residence must be the same to be exempt. **Check here** ☐

Without including a copy of each state's form, the point here is that you should comply with your state's tax reporting and payment rules. A vast majority of these rules are identical to the federal rules. Some states have a lower "exempt" level of income than the federal level, so it is essential to check your state's Department of Revenue and ensure you pay your new employee less than the required amount.

If your child earns more than your state's maximum excludable income, it could actually work out even better for you. Keep in mind that if your child does file a state tax return for their new wages, which means they earned more than the maximum excludable amount, you will save even more money than we have discussed thus far. This is because they will be paying tax at a much lower rate than you would have paid if the wages had not been moved from your state tax return onto their state tax return. This just gets better and better.

The key point I am trying to make here is that you still need to comply with your state's rules and regulations, even though most will correspond to similar federal requirements that we are discussing in this Guide.

3. Report the New Hire to Your State's New Hire Reporting System

Federal and state laws require that all new hires be reported to the state new hire reporting agencies. The Personal Responsibility and Work Opportunity Reconciliation Act (PRWORA) of 1996, 42 U.S.C. 653A, initiated the existing reporting requirement and provides no exceptions. All employers must comply, and all new and rehired employees must be included. As a general rule, the new hire must be reported within ten days of their first day of work.

Once again, the good news is that the form is very easy to complete, and there is no fee associated with either the form or the filing process. This form, unlike the I-9 and the W-4, must be mailed to the appropriate state agency. Most states offer an online option that makes the reporting process very easy; however, it is also straightforward to simply fill out the form and mail it in. The required data is as follows:

- Company Name
- Company Mailing Address
- Company EIN
- Employee Name
- Employee Address
- Employee Social Security Number
- Employee Work Start Date

The state reports generally request additional data, such as the employee's birth date, salary amount, and employer and employee email addresses, but most are optional fields and do not need to be completed. I recommend completing the form in full to avoid confusion about which fields are optional and which are required. Most states will not accept the form if the required information is missing. The forms are brief and straightforward, so please fill them out completely. I have included two examples of New Hire Reporting forms. One from the Texas New Hire Reporting System and the second from the Georgia New Hire Reporting System:

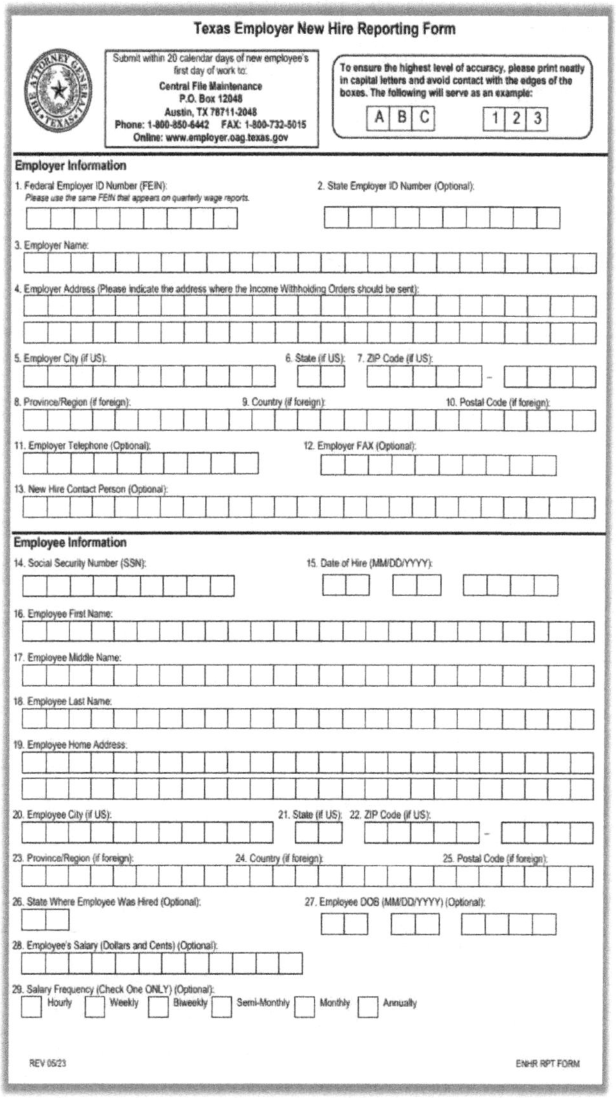

Texas Employer New Hire Reporting Form

THE ATTORNEY GENERAL • TEXAS •

Submit within 20 calendar days of new employee's first day of work to:
Central File Maintenance
P.O. Box 12048
Austin, TX 78711-2048
Phone: 1-800-850-6442 FAX: 1-800-732-5015
Online: www.employer.oag.texas.gov

To ensure the highest level of accuracy, please print neatly in capital letters and avoid contact with the edges of the boxes. The following will serve as an example:

A B C 1 2 3

Employer Information

1. Federal Employer ID Number (FEIN):
Please use the same FEIN that appears on quarterly wage reports.

2. State Employer ID Number (Optional):

3. Employer Name:

4. Employer Address (Please indicate the address where the Income Withholding Orders should be sent):

5. Employer City (if US):

6. State (if US):

7. ZIP Code (if US):

8. Province/Region (if foreign):

9. Country (if foreign):

10. Postal Code (if foreign):

11. Employer Telephone (Optional):

12. Employer FAX (Optional):

13. New Hire Contact Person (Optional):

Employee Information

14. Social Security Number (SSN):

15. Date of Hire (MM/DD/YYYY):

16. Employee First Name:

17. Employee Middle Name:

18. Employee Last Name:

19. Employee Home Address:

20. Employee City (if US):

21. State (if US):

22. ZIP Code (if US):

23. Province/Region (if foreign):

24. Country (if foreign):

25. Postal Code (if foreign):

26. State Where Employee Was Hired (Optional):

27. Employee DOB (MM/DD/YYYY) (Optional):

28. Employee's Salary (Dollars and Cents) (Optional):

29. Salary Frequency (Check One ONLY) (Optional):
Hourly Weekly Biweekly Semi-Monthly Monthly Annually

REV 05/23

ENHR RPT FORM

Georgia New Hire Reporting Form

Federal and state legislation (Georgia statute 19-11-9.2), requires all Georgia employers, both public and private, to report to the New Hire Reporting Program all newly hired, rehired, or returning to work employees. Information about new hire reporting and online reporting is available on our website: **www.GA-newhire.com**

Send completed forms to:
Georgia New Hire Reporting Program
PO Box 90728 East Point, GA 30364-0728
Fax: (404) 525-2983 or toll-free: (888) 541-0521

To ensure the highest level of accuracy, please print neatly in capital letters and avoid contact with the edges of the boxes. The following will serve as an example:

A	B	C		1	2	3

EMPLOYER INFORMATION

Federal Employer ID Number (FEIN): *(Please enter the same FEIN used to report the employee's quarterly wages)*

__ - _______

Primary Insurance Company Name (if available to the employee):

Employer Name:

Employer Address: *(Please indicate the address where the Wage Withholding Orders should be sent)*

Employer City: State: Zip Code:

Employer Phone (optional): Extension: Employer Fax (optional):

Email Address:

EMPLOYEE INFORMATION

Employee Social Security Number (SSN): ___ - __ - ____

Employee Starting Salary (Monthly):* .00

Employee First Name: Middle Initial

Employee Last Name:

Employee Address:

Employee City: State: Zip Code:

Start Date (MMDDYY): Date of Birth: *Optional

Medical Insurance Company Name:*

Reports must be submitted within 10 days of hire or rehire date.

REPORTS WILL NOT BE PROCESSED IF REQUIRED INFORMATION IS MISSING

Questions? Call us at (404) 525-2985 or toll-free at (888) 541-0469

As you can see, the two states, Texas and Georgia, have very similar forms, and most other states also follow the same general outline. This is not a coincidence since the Federal law that gave rise to the reporting requirement was specific as to the minimum information that was to be included. I have included a list of URLs for new hire reporting home pages for all fifty states, plus the District of Columbia, in Appendix D.

Find your state on the list to access your specific reporting form. Remember that each state will have several options for compliance, including an online filing option and a manual form that can be mailed. Regardless of which method is the easiest for you, make sure you complete the form and make a copy for your files. Once you have the copy, date the form and include that copy in your new personnel file.

You have now completed all of the initial paperwork for your new employee. Ensure you create a positive work environment and a safe place to work. This will most likely be their first job, and it's up to you to make that first experience a positive one. You have the chance to be the boss that you have always wanted to work for. So, make this one a good one.

6

Paying the Employee

Of all the chapters included in Hire Your Kid, this may well be your favorite one. However, it is guaranteed to be the favorite among your new employees. Whether it is your favorite or your child's favorite, I will tell you that this is the most important chapter.

Keeping up with the paperwork is very important, and you should follow all the steps that we have discussed. However, at the end of the day, the deduction that we are creating is based on wages paid. Wages PAID! It is crucial that you pay your employees a reasonable amount and in a timely manner. Employees like to get paid, and your company should recognize that and pay them accordingly.

Don't forget that you are also the child's parent. You are their employer AND their parent. Just because you pay them a reasonable wage for their efforts and contributions to the success of your business does not mean they have free access to the money, nor free will in how to spend it.

You still must guide them and instruct them on how to manage that money. So, make sure to pay your new employee, but also help them manage the money they have earned. This is money that you are already giving them anyway, but now it is more formal and structured, and it's a great time to add a similar level of structure to their spending and saving habits.

This chapter is about paying the employee, which, intuitively, is the easiest of all the things we are asking you to do in this guide for hiring your kid. But don't take this part for granted. Everything here ties together, and all of it points toward the tax savings that you will realize when you file your tax return at the end of the year. But it all starts with your new employee actually doing the work. This is a genuine job with real responsibilities and duties. On a day-by-day basis, the documentation for that work is evidenced by their time card for that particular pay period. This is kind of like a math test to which we already have the answers, but the teacher is demanding that we show our work.

Each pay period should have a time card that supports twenty-five hours worked. I recommend a set work schedule so that everyone is on the same page. Which specific days work best in your situation will be fine as long as the total hours still end up at twenty-five hours per pay period. The pay rate that we have discussed is set at $25.00 per hour. With twenty-five hours worked each pay period for a total of 24 pay periods during the year, the total annual wages will be exactly $15,000. Ensure that you initiate the pay process with the new employee actually working the agreed-upon number of hours. You have already set the pay rate, so as long as they work the required hours and you complete the necessary paperwork, you will save as much as $5,000 in taxes, just as we planned.

From a documentation standpoint, the tax savings start with the time card. Having your new employee submit a time card showing the hours they actually worked each pay period is a great idea and will always provide the correct answer if the question ever comes up.

There is neither a formal requirement for what a time card should look like nor any required minimum information to be included. The real purpose of the time card is to document the hours worked. It is a great idea to have the time cards prepared in advance so that your child already knows the actual times that they are expected to work. Once they actually work those hours, then simply signing the pre-prepared time card will document the hours worked. Your time cards could look something like this:

Kelsey Busby Real Estate **Pay Period # 15 August 1 - August 15, 2025**

Time Card

Position: **Administrative Assistant** Employee: **Samantha Busby**

	Fri 1-Aug	Sat 2-Aug	Sun 3-Aug	Mon 4-Aug	Tue 5-Aug	Wed 6-Aug	Thu 7-Aug	Fri 8-Aug	Sat 9-Aug	Sun 10-Aug	Mon 11-Aug	Tue 12-Aug	Wed 13-Aug	Thu 14-Aug	Fri 15-Aug
Hours Worked	1	4	2		3		3		5	2		2		3	
Overtime Hours															
Total Hours	1	4	2	0	3	0	3	0	5	2	0	2	0	3	0

Total Hours - Pay Period #15 25.00

Samantha Busby — Employee Signature

8/15/25 — Date

Notice that the time card requests just a couple of hours on Tuesday night, a couple more on Thursday night, and then a few hours on Saturday and possibly Sunday after church. That schedule results in twenty-five hours during the pay period, which translates into $625 in gross pay per pay period, or $15,000 for the year, assuming the child works for the entire year. The point is that it doesn't take a great commitment of hours for your new employee to generate $15,000 in wages, which will translate into over $5,000 in tax savings for you, the small business owner.

From a practical standpoint, I love the idea of completing the time cards for the entire year. Sit down with a calendar and a pencil (not a pen, since you will most likely have to erase and adjust) and build the work schedule for the entire year. Recognizing that your child will have homework and other activities as well, pencil in a couple of hours several days a week, and before long, you will have a complete plan for the entire year. Concentrate on building a plan based on twenty-five hours per pay period so that at the end of the day, your new employee will reach $15,000 in annual wages. The first page of your time card plan could look something like this:

Kelsey Busby Real Estate **Pay Period # 1 January 1 - January 15, 2025**
Time Card
Position: **Administrative Assistant** Employee: **Samantha Busby**

	Wed 1-Jan	Thu 2-Jan	Fri 3-Jan	Sat 4-Jan	Sun 5-Jan	Mon 6-Jan	Tue 7-Jan	Wed 8-Jan	Thu 9-Jan	Fri 10-Jan	Sat 11-Jan	Sun 12-Jan	Mon 13-Jan	Tue 14-Jan	Wed 15-Jan
Hours Worked		3	1	3	3		3		4		3	2		3	
Overtime Hours															
Total Hours	0	3	1	3	3	0	3	0	4	0	3	2	0	3	0

Total Hours - Pay Period #15 25.00
Samantha Busby — Employee Signature 1/15/25 — Date

Kelsey Busby Real Estate **Pay Period # 2 January 16 - January 31, 2025**
Time Card
Position: **Administrative Assistant** Employee: **Samantha Busby**

	Thu 16-Jan	Fri 17-Jan	Sat 18-Jan	Sun 19-Jan	Mon 20-Jan	Tue 21-Jan	Wed 22-Jan	Thu 23-Jan	Fri 24-Jan	Sat 25-Jan	Sun 26-Jan	Mon 27-Jan	Tue 28-Jan	Wed 29-Jan	Thu 30-Jan	Fri 31-Jan
Hours Worked	2	1	3	2		2		3	2	3	2	0	2		2	1
Overtime Hours																
Total Hours	2	1	3	2	0	2	0	3	2	3	2	0	2	0	2	1

Total Hours - Pay Period #15 25.00
Samantha Busby — Employee Signature 1/31/25 — Date

Kelsey Busby Real Estate **Pay Period # 3 February - February 15, 2025**
Time Card
Position: **Administrative Assistant** Employee: **Samantha Busby**

	Sat 1-Feb	Sun 2-Feb	Mon 3-Feb	Tue 4-Feb	Wed 5-Feb	Thu 6-Feb	Fri 7-Feb	Sat 8-Feb	Sun 9-Feb	Mon 10-Feb	Tue 11-Feb	Wed 12-Feb	Thu 13-Feb	Fri 14-Feb	Sat 15-Feb
Hours Worked	1	4		2		3		3	4		2		2		4
Overtime Hours															
Total Hours	1	4	0	2	0	3	0	3	4	0	2	0	2	0	4

Total Hours - Pay Period #15 25.00
Samantha Busby — Employee Signature 2/15/25 — Date

Kelsey Busby Real Estate **Pay Period # 4 February 16 - February 28, 2025**
Time Card
Position: **Administrative Assistant** Employee: **Samantha Busby**

	Sun 16-Feb	Mon 17-Feb	Tue 18-Feb	Wed 19-Feb	Thu 20-Feb	Fri 21-Feb	Sat 22-Feb	Sun 23-Feb	Mon 24-Feb	Tue 25-Feb	Wed 26-Feb	Thu 27-Feb	Fri 28-Feb
Hours Worked	4		3		3	1	4	3		2		3	2
Overtime Hours													
Total Hours	4	0	3	0	3	1	4	3	0	2	0	3	2

Total Hours - Pay Period #15 25.00
Samantha Busby — Employee Signature 2/28/25 — Date

Once you have completed the expected timecards for each pay period, you will now have a work schedule to share with your new employee. At the end of each pay period, the employee will document the completion of the hours by signing and dating the time card. If adjustments need to be made, simply indicate the changes right on the card. However, ensure that the employee works the planned twenty-five hours per week and accomplishes each of the work tasks that you have set for them.

The time cards will document the work actually done by the new employee and provide the basis for your payroll calculation. Now it's time to actually pay your kid.

If you have been successful in building the work plan based on 25 hours per pay period, the amount of pay will always be the same. Twenty-five hours actually worked times $25.00 per hour results in $625 per pay period. The same amount, paid twice a month for 12 months, generates annual wages of $15,000.

If you have other employees or have ever had an employee, you know that the most common method of payment is a payroll check. You most likely remember that calculating the amount of that payroll check may be the most difficult part of managing employees. The key issue is that the gross pay the employee has earned for any particular pay period is not necessarily the same amount as their actual paycheck. As the employer, you are required to withhold any relevant federal income tax, as well as FICA and Medicare tax, in determining the employee's net payroll check.

This IRS provides withholding tables based on filing status and exemptions, including amounts to be withheld for FICA and Medicare tax, as well as state withholding requirements. In addition, the IRS provides detailed instructions in Publication 15, Circular E, Employer's Tax Guide, as we discussed in Chapter 2, on page 15. Here is a link to the IRS publication, in case you ever need it for reference or a quick cure for insomnia.

https://www.irs.gov/pub/irs-pdf/p15.pdf

Based on an unrelated new employee with applicable tax withholding for FICA, Medicare, and federal income tax, here is what a typical check might look like…

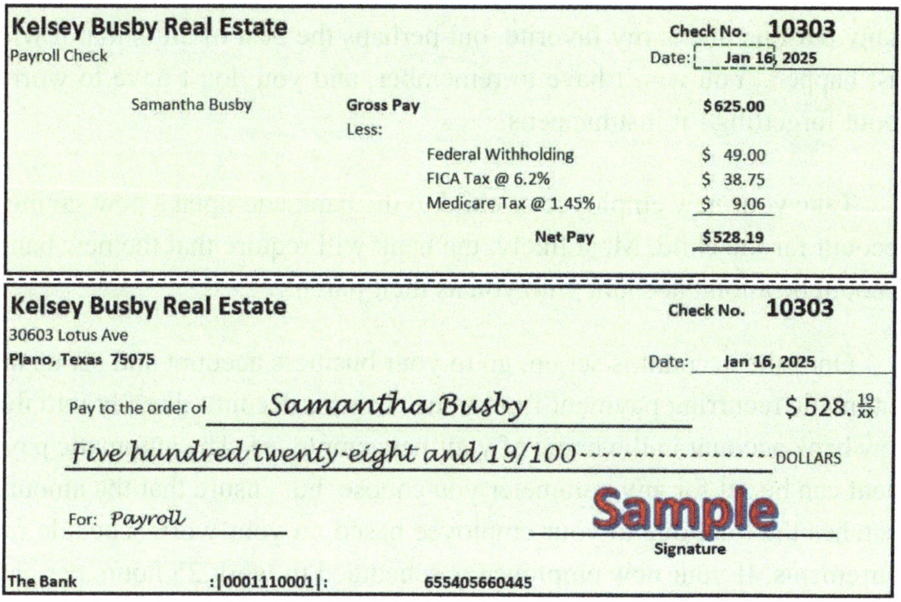

Kelsey Busby Real Estate — Check No. **10303**
Payroll Check — Date: Jan 16, 2025

Samantha Busby	**Gross Pay**		**$625.00**
	Less:		
		Federal Withholding	$ 49.00
		FICA Tax @ 6.2%	$ 38.75
		Medicare Tax @ 1.45%	$ 9.06
		Net Pay	**$528.19**

Kelsey Busby Real Estate — Check No. **10303**
30603 Lotus Ave
Plano, Texas 75075
Date: **Jan 16, 2025**

Pay to the order of *Samantha Busby* $ 528. 19/xx

Five hundred twenty-eight and 19/100 ------------------ DOLLARS

For: *Payroll*

Sample

Signature

The Bank **:|0001110001|:** **655405660445**

Maybe the best news for Hire Your Kid is that most of this simply does not apply. Since your new employee is a child working in the parent's business and earns no more than $15,000, the wages paid are exempt from FICA and Medicare tax, federal income tax, as well as state-related income and payroll tax. The net check is exactly the same as the gross wages. There is no need to provide any other documentation for payroll other than the actual payment of $625 to your new employee each pay period.

I started this chapter by saying that it is actually critical to pay your new employee. There are three basic methods for accomplishing that payment, and each is totally acceptable. Regardless of which option is best for you, choose one and then pay the employee every pay period.

1. Direct Deposit to Your Employee's Savings Account.

Let me tell you now, before you read any further, that this is my favorite option and the one I recommend above the other two. There are many reasons this is my favorite, but perhaps the best of all is that it will just happen. You won't have to remember, and you don't have to worry about forgetting - it just happens.

Take your new employee or child to the bank and open a new savings account for the child. Most likely, the bank will require that the new bank account be a joint account with you as their parent.

Once the account is set up, go to your business account and set up an automatic recurring payment from your business account directly into the new bank account in the name of your new employee. The automatic payment can be set for any parameter you choose, but ensure that the amount matches the total due to your employee based on your work schedule requirements. If your new employee is scheduled to work 25 hours per pay period and you will be paying them $25.00 per hour, then each of their semi-monthly net pay deposits will be $625. No withholding for federal tax or payroll tax, ensuring that all payment amounts remain the same throughout the year. Setting up automatic payments or transfers for the 1st and 16th of each month, each for $625, will ensure your payroll obligations are met each pay period, even if you never think about the process again.

At the end of the year, you will have paid your new employee $625 twice a month for a total annual pay of $15,000. You will have set up the automatic payment one time and then it just happens. No tax withholding, no checks to cut, no deposits to make, and most important, nothing to remember.

2. Issue a Payroll Check Twice a Month

I like the process of issuing actual checks for the wages paid to your new employee, as the documentation is perfect. Paying wages with an actual check demonstrates typical payroll and provides 24 cancelled checks in support of the wages actually paid. Those 24 cancelled checks are the best support that you can provide if the IRS ever asks.

The checks are also very easy to calculate since there is no applicable withholding amount or any other complication. Remember the sample check we discussed earlier, which included federal withholding, as well as FICA and Medicare, resulting in a net payroll check that was less than the gross wages. With your new employee, the payroll check will be much easier and will look something like this:

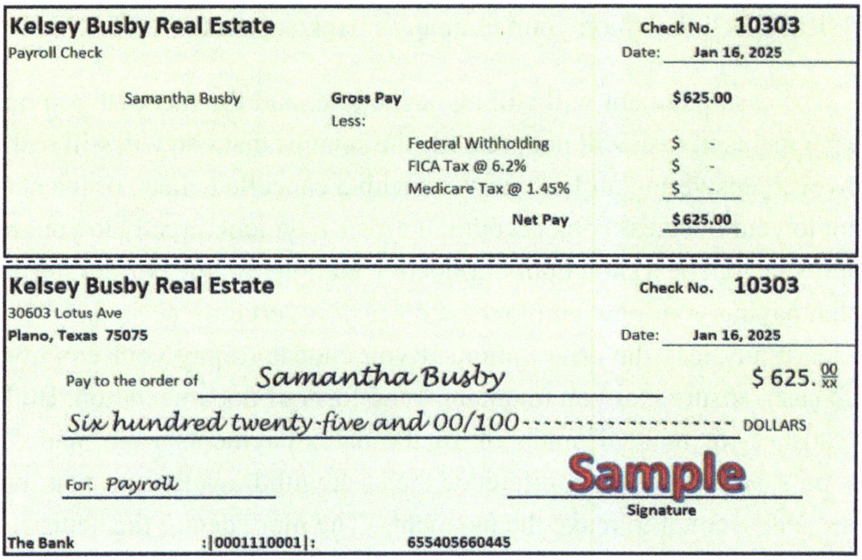
Kelsey Busby Real Estate Check No. **10303**
Payroll Check Date: Jan 16, 2025

Samantha Busby **Gross Pay** $625.00
Less:
Federal Withholding $ -
FICA Tax @ 6.2% $ -
Medicare Tax @ 1.45% $ -
Net Pay $625.00

Kelsey Busby Real Estate Check No. **10303**
30603 Lotus Ave
Plano, Texas 75075 Date: Jan 16, 2025

Pay to the order of *Samantha Busby* $ 625.00/xx
Six hundred twenty-five and 00/100 DOLLARS

For: *Payroll* Sample
Signature

The Bank :|0001110001|: 655405660445

Preparing and issuing actual paychecks for your new employee is only slightly more difficult than setting up a direct deposit system, and it will provide all the support you need. The details in your business bank account will be the same as those for the direct transfers. You can even prepare all the checks in advance, since you have already built your work plan for the year and know exactly how much each check will be. The only real downside is remembering actually to issue the checks.

3. Pay Your New Employee in Cash

I include this option here, as it is entirely acceptable, but I don't recommend it as a method. Many small business owners hiring their first employee are tempted by this method because it is so easy—no checks, no direct deposits, no issues with the bank. Just pay them with cash and move on. This is an acceptable method because there is no requirement for how wages are to be paid or in what form the actual payment must be made. I hope, however, that this is one fact that you choose to forget. You can certainly pay them in cash, but I strongly recommend paying them on a more formal basis, such as a direct deposit to a bank account or with a physical check drawn on your company's bank account.

The cash payment will still be deductible, and the fact that you made the payments in cash will not preclude the savings that you will still realize. However, answering an IRS question with a cancelled check or the actual debit to your business bank account, noting a payment directly to your new employee, will be a slam dunk for documentation. So, the bottom line here is that paying your new employee with cash is certainly acceptable, but it is clearly my least favorite option. If you choose to pay your employees with cash, ensure that you maintain some form of documentation. Build a spreadsheet or manual notebook of the dates payments were made, the amounts, and, if possible, reference the cash withdrawals from your business bank account to make the payments. The more detail, the better.

Remember that you are an employer and have created a new job to help your business grow. If the IRS ever asks you a question about this new job or any job that you create in the life of your small business, the question will most likely be Did you really pay this employee? The documentation for actual payment will always be easier to produce if the payment is in a form that leaves a trail. One of our goals here will always be to provide the evidence necessary to support the deduction. That paper trail will begin with the actual payment made to your new employee.

Regardless of how you choose to pay your new employee, just make sure that you pay them. And make sure you pay them for the work that they actually performed.

7

Filing and Reporting Requirements

This chapter may appear to be the most complicated and confusing. This chapter will contain the most IRS forms and publications, and perhaps the most numbers to deal with, so it may be the most complicated. However, it is my belief that once you get to the end of the chapter, you will confidently say, "Is that it? Is that all I have to do?"

Yes, it is my belief that the IRS makes things way more complicated than they absolutely have to. Yes, it is my belief that you still need to complete all the necessary paperwork to save the thousands of dollars in taxes that you are about to save. And most assuredly, YES, I am certain that you will find this very easy to accomplish once you have been through the process.

In Chapter 8, I will emphasize the importance of paperwork in accomplishing our goals. In this chapter, I will tell you that the paperwork is no big deal to complete. Just like eating an elephant, one bite at a time is the way to go. Follow the details on the next few pages, and I am confident that not only will you save thousands of dollars in taxes on your personal income tax return, but you will also be knowledgeable enough to write your own book on saving taxes.

As we go through the year-end paperwork, remember that these forms and calculations are the main level of support for the $15,000 tax deduction that is going to save you over $5,000 in federal income tax. This is where the rubber meets the road as far as the IRS is concerned. I truly believe that you will find each of these IRS forms to be incredibly easy to understand and complete for your small business. The forms that represent the core of the annual reporting requirement include the following:

1. From W-2, Wage and Tax Statement
2. Form W-3, Transmittal of Wage and Tax Statements
3. Form 944, Employer's ANNUAL Federal Tax Return
4. Form 940, Employer's Annual Federal Unemployment (FUTA) Tax Return

In this chapter, we will provide step-by-step instructions for each of these forms, including calculations and filing instructions. But before we get to that, let's skip to the end for a reconciliation discussion. Don't forget that the IRS will end up with a copy of each of these forms, and each of these forms will be subject to the big, secret underground IRS computer. Each of these forms will be automatically reviewed and recalculated, and each will be compared to the others. If the details on all of these forms do not match, you will wake up on some random Friday morning with a nice letter from the IRS asking for more details. Not the most fun way to start any new weekend.

All four of these forms will have several things in common, such as your business name, business tax ID number or EIN, business address, etc. However, more importantly, each of these forms will include the total wages paid to your new employee. Therefore, the total wages included on each of these forms should match. Line 1 of Form W-2, Line 1 of Form W-3, Line 1 of Form 944, and Line 3 of Form 940 should all match! That same total should also exactly equal the total amount that you actually paid your new employee in wages AND the amount that you included on Line 26 of your Schedule C for wages.

Without trying to be too scary, the IRS computer will be checking, so before you mail any form or send any piece of paper to anyone, ensure that you reconcile all the paperwork to verify that all the numbers match.

There is no required format or process to complete your payroll reconciliation. The key is to find a system that makes sense to you and guarantees that all the numbers match. I strongly recommend that the reconciliation be in writing and not just in your head. Take out a piece of paper and actually record the amounts included on each form. Don't cheat. Check the numbers from each form and include them on your reconciliation worksheet. I know that there is only one number and only one employee, so the process should be easy, but that is usually when mistakes occur. Take your time and reconcile!!! The following is a simple example that could work for you:

Wage and Payroll Tax Reconciliation

Form and Line	Total Wages	Form Delivered
Form W-2 Line 1	$15,000.00	Done, Jan 25th
Form W-3 Line 1	$15,000.00	Done, Jan 25th
Form 944 Line 1	$15,000.00	Done Jan 31st
Form 940 Line 3	$15,000.00	Done Jan 31st
Sch C Line 26	$15,000.00	Done, Apr 15th
Total Employee Checks	$15,000.00	Done

This may seem a bit obvious, and perhaps you're shaking your head, saying, "Is that really all that necessary?" I guess I agree that this may be a bit of overkill, but I recommend that you complete this process anyway. Yes, I am a CPA, and, yes, I would love for you to think I have never made such a silly mistake, but I have. Take a few extra minutes to fill out your reconciliation form, whatever it may look like. The key point is that all the numbers should match. Make sure to pay particular attention to the number you included on your Schedule C, as you will likely be completing that form several months after completing the other forms.

Remember my comment from Chapter 3: it is my opinion that if all of your payroll numbers match, you are actually less likely to be audited by the IRS than if you had no wages on your Schedule C. So, hiring your child can actually reduce your chances of being audited, provided that all of your numbers match. Perform the reconciliation before mailing any forms.

1. Form W-2, Wage and Tax Statement

You can start with any of the forms you wish, especially since you will be completing your payroll reconciliation at the end, but I recommend starting with the W-2. Although the IRS will ultimately have access to the data that is included on each W-2, the forms are actually mailed to the Social Security Administration. I say that the forms are mailed to the Social Security Administration, but you also have the option to complete and file the forms online at www.SSA.gov. The method that works best for you will always be the easiest option, so let's discuss both and then you can choose the one that makes the most sense for your specific situation.

The completed copy of the W-2 that is sent to the employee is generally due to the employee no later than January 31. This is true regardless of whether you file the government copies online or mail the completed forms physically. If mailing the forms, they must be postmarked by the last day of February, but if you file online, you will generally have until the end of March. Don't let the extra time be the reason to choose the online approach. Remember that this is all about the paperwork, so don't put this off. Fill out the forms and complete the task, and you will be happy that you did.

The reason the W-2 is due to the employee a full month before they are due to the Social Security Administration is for the practical reason of correcting errors. By sending the W-2 to each employee by January 31st, there is a full month for the employee to review the totals or correct a Social Security number or address before the form is actually filed with the government entity. As you might guess, it is much easier to adjust the W-2 or correct the error before the government has the information.

Since you will be completing the forms for your new employee who is also your child, the process of allowing the employee time to review and or correct any errors or mistakes may be somewhat unnecessary. You have some extra time to file the forms, but I recommend completing all the necessary forms at approximately the same time. File the reports and check them off your list. Don't wait until the last minute, and you will end up spending way less time in total than if you had waited for each due date.

Unlike other tax forms, such as your personal tax return (Form 1040) and even the payroll tax returns (Forms 944 and 940), the W-2 must be completed on a specific machine-readable form. You can't just print a copy from the internet or the IRS website, but you must use the preprinted forms like you see below:

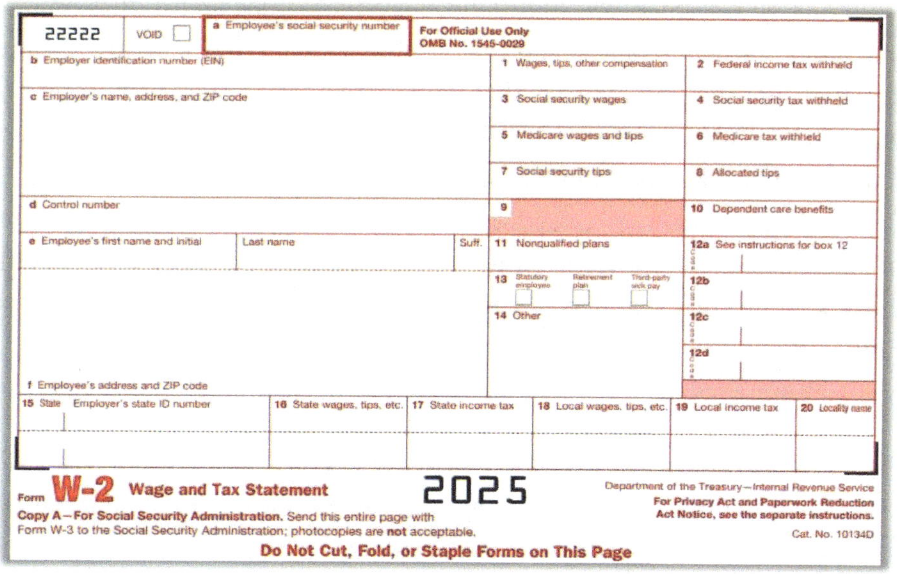
22222 VOID
a Employee's social security number
For Official Use Only
OMB No. 1545-0029
b Employer identification number (EIN)
1 Wages, tips, other compensation
2 Federal income tax withheld
c Employer's name, address, and ZIP code
3 Social security wages
4 Social security tax withheld
5 Medicare wages and tips
6 Medicare tax withheld
7 Social security tips
8 Allocated tips
d Control number
9
10 Dependent care benefits
e Employee's first name and initial
Last name
Suff.
11 Nonqualified plans
12a See instructions for box 12
13 Statutory employee Retirement plan Third-party sick pay
12b
14 Other
12c
12d
f Employee's address and ZIP code
15 State Employer's state ID number
16 State wages, tips, etc.
17 State income tax
18 Local wages, tips, etc.
19 Local income tax
20 Locality name
Form W-2 Wage and Tax Statement 2025
Department of the Treasury—Internal Revenue Service
Copy A—For Social Security Administration. Send this entire page with Form W-3 to the Social Security Administration; photocopies are not acceptable.
For Privacy Act and Paperwork Reduction Act Notice, see the separate instructions.
Cat. No. 10134D
Do Not Cut, Fold, or Staple Forms on This Page

Most office supply stores, such as Office Depot and Staples, will have a package of several W-2s along with several W-3s for approximately $25. You can also get a limited quantity directly from the IRS for free. You can call them directly at 800-TAX-FORM (800-829-3676) or you can order forms online at www.IRS.gov. You can order up to 1,000 of any particular form for free. The order process will take about four to six weeks, so make sure you plan accordingly.

Once you get the forms, you will notice there are multiple copies for each W-2. There are actually six different copies named as follows (and in this order):

Copy A
Copy 1
Copy B
Copy C
Copy 2
Copy D

And, NO, I am not kidding, those are the names and in that order. I have told you that I hate using the words "logic" and "IRS" in the same sentence, but the logic here is that the lettered series represents copies to meet federal requirements, and the numbered series represents the state requirements. The good news is that when hiring your child under age 18 (and provided you are indeed exempt from your state's filing requirements), the only copy we need to worry about is Copy A. Copy A is the red-inked top copy that needs to be sent to the Social Security Administration.

The form itself also features a series of lines with letters, such as "a," "b," "c," …, and a series of lines with numbers, "1," "2," "3," … The letter series, a-f, details for the company and the employee, including names, addresses, and tax identification numbers.

Enter the employer's name and address as well as the employee's name and address. Line d provides an option for a "control number" that could be helpful for large employers, but for us, this line is unnecessary and can be left blank. The key point for the letter series of lines on the W-2 is to make sure you correctly enter the Social Security number for your employee (Line a) and the company's Employer Identification Number

(EIN) (Line b). Once you enter these numbers, check them for accuracy. And once you have checked the numbers, then check them one more time.

There are numerous lines and requests for information on the W-2, but only a few of them will pertain to your new employee. The most important lines, as you might expect, are Lines 1 through 6, which are wages and applicable withholding amounts. Remember that your child, under the age of 18, working for their parent or parents in a sole proprietorship is exempt from Social Security and Medicare taxes. Therefore, no matter how much you have paid the child during the year, Lines 3 and 5 will be "0." Likewise, the applicable tax calculation included on Lines 4 and 6 will also be "0." The total to include on Line 1, "Wages, tips, and other compensation," should be the total that you actually paid the child during the year. If you have completed the recommended time cards and work schedule contained in this guide, the child worked the recorded hours, and you paid the child the suggested amounts, the total to be included on Line 1 would be $15,000. Since you also have a W-4, signed by your new employee indicating that they are "EXEMPT" from Federal withholding, you will also include "0" on Line 2. If you have done all the things included in this guide, Lines 1 through 6 of your new employee's W-2 should look like this:

1 Wages, tips, other compensation $15,000	2 Federal income tax withheld $0
3 Social security wages $0	4 Social security tax withheld $0
5 Medicare wages and tips $0	6 Medicare tax withheld $0

Again, there are many more lines on the W-2, but none will apply to our situation. Lines 7 and 8 provide tips for industries such as restaurants. Lines 10 through 14 contain information related to retirement plans and other benefit plans, including health insurance, life insurance, and other deferrals. Lines 15 through 20 represent state and local detail, all of which will be irrelevant to your new employee, under age eighteen and earning less than $15,000 per year, unless your state requires those wages to be reported. If so, simply include the total wages for your state on line 16. However, remember that these wages are not subject to state unemployment tax and are also exempt from withholding.

As I noted above, the actual W-2 consists of six different copies. However, the good news is that the layout of each copy is exactly the same. Once you have completed Copy A, each of the other copies, if applicable, will include exactly the same numbers. If you have paid your new employee based on the details recommended, then your W-2, Copy A, will look like this:

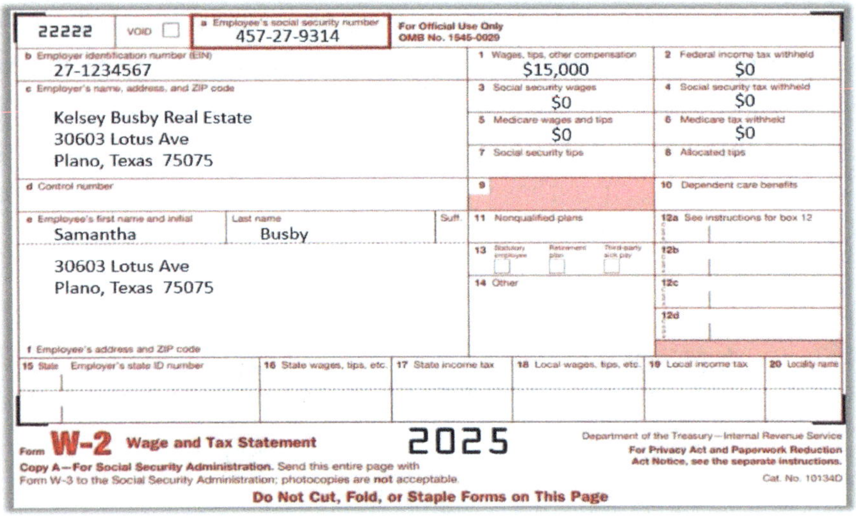
22222 VOID ☐
a Employee's social security number 457-27-9314
For Official Use Only
OMB No. 1545-0029
b Employer identification number (EIN) 27-1234567
1 Wages, tips, other compensation $15,000
2 Federal income tax withheld $0
c Employer's name, address, and ZIP code
Kelsey Busby Real Estate
30603 Lotus Ave
Plano, Texas 75075
3 Social security wages $0
4 Social security tax withheld $0
5 Medicare wages and tips $0
6 Medicare tax withheld $0
7 Social security tips
8 Allocated tips
d Control number
9
10 Dependent care benefits
e Employee's first name and initial Samantha
Last name Busby
Suff.
11 Nonqualified plans
12a See instructions for box 12
13 Statutory employee ☐ Retirement plan ☐ Third-party sick pay ☐
12b
30603 Lotus Ave
Plano, Texas 75075
14 Other
12c
12d
f Employee's address and ZIP code
15 State Employer's state ID number
16 State wages, tips, etc.
17 State income tax
18 Local wages, tips, etc.
19 Local income tax
20 Locality name
Form W-2 Wage and Tax Statement 2025
Department of the Treasury—Internal Revenue Service
For Privacy Act and Paperwork Reduction Act Notice, see the separate instructions.
Copy A—For Social Security Administration. Send this entire page with Form W-3 to the Social Security Administration; photocopies are not acceptable.
Cat. No. 10134D
Do Not Cut, Fold, or Staple Forms on This Page

The W-2 does not need to be generated from a computer software program, does not need to be typed, nor does it require any other specific process, as long as it is legible. You can handwrite the information directly on the red, machine-readable form and meet all IRS and Social Security Administration guidelines. In my opinion, this is one of the easiest IRS forms that you will ever be asked to complete.

The Form W-2 is not sent to the IRS as you might expect, but instead is sent to the Social Security Administration.

2. Form W-3, Transmittal of Wage and Tax Statements

As we previously discussed, a copy of the Form W-2 must be provided to your employee by January 31st. The copy that must be sent to the Social Security Administration is not due until the last day of February. The Form W-2 should be mailed to the Social Security Administration with a W-3, Transmittal of Wage and Tax Statements, which is also a red, machine-readable form. When you order the W-2s from the IRS or when you buy copies of the form at your local office supply store, you will also get a Form W-3. The packages offered by suppliers such as Office Depot and Staples will include copies of both forms in the same package. The key point is that you must have one of the preprinted red W-3s completed before mailing the W-2 to the Social Security Administration.

The W-3 is even easier to complete than the W-2. The W-3 is essentially a simple cover sheet for all the W-2s that your business needs to complete and file. It includes your company's name, address, and your Employer Identification Number. There is a space to indicate the total number of W-2s included with the W-3, as well as the total amount included on all of those W-2s combined. If you have only one employee, your child, and therefore only one W-2, the W-3 itself is extremely easy.

As you can see, the W-3 is very easy to complete, especially if you have only one employee, which is your child. Notice that we have included an "x" in the 'Kind of Payer' box in the upper left-hand corner in the box for '944.' As we will discuss in the next section of this chapter, Form 944 is the annual payroll tax return, and Form 941 is the quarterly payroll tax return. Our plan, based on hiring your child, is to qualify for the annual filing option. Therefore, ensure that you check the box for Form 944 if that is indeed the form you will be filing. There are several specialty options for "Kind of Employer," which will not apply to our situation for Hire Your Kid. Include an "x" in the box notating "None apply." The related boxes with numbers and letters are identical to those on the Form W-2. With only one employee, all the blanks will contain exactly the same numbers as the W-2. Make sure to sign and date the form, and you're all set. The completed W-3 for Kelsey Busby Realty is included below.

DO NOT STAPLE

33333	a Control number	For Official Use Only: OMB No. 1545-0029	
b Kind of Payer (Check one)	941 [ ] Military [ ] 943 [ ] 944 [X] CT-1 [ ] Hshld. emp. [ ] Medicare govt. emp. [ ]	**Kind of Employer** (Check one) None apply [X] 501c non-govt. [ ] State/local non-501c [ ] State/local 501c [ ] Federal govt. [ ]	Third-party sick pay (Check if applicable) [ ]
c Total number of Forms W-2: 1	d Establishment number	1 Wages, tips, other compensation: $15,000	2 Federal income tax withheld: $0
e Employer identification number (EIN): 27-1234567		3 Social security wages: $0	4 Social security tax withheld: $0
f Employer's name: Kelsey Busby Real Estate		5 Medicare wages and tips: $0	6 Medicare tax withheld: $0
30603 Lotus Ave Plano, Texas 75075		7 Social security tips	8 Allocated tips
		9	10 Dependent care benefits
g Employer's address and ZIP code		11 Nonqualified plans	12a Deferred compensation
h Other EIN used this year		13 For third-party sick pay use only	12b
15 State	Employer's state ID number	14 Income tax withheld by payer of third-party sick pay	
16 State wages, tips, etc.	17 State income tax	18 Local wages, tips, etc.	19 Local income tax
Employer's contact person: Kelsey Busby		Employer's telephone number: 214-620-2437	For Official Use Only
Employer's fax number		Employer's email address: K.Busby@BusbyRE.com	

Under penalties of perjury, I declare that I have examined this return and accompanying documents, and, to the best of my knowledge and belief, they are true, correct, and complete.

Signature: *Kelsey Busby* Title: Owner Date: Jan 31, 2025

Form **W-3** **Transmittal of Wage and Tax Statements** 2025

Department of the Treasury Internal Revenue Service

Send this entire page with the entire Copy A page of Form(s) W-2 to the Social Security Administration (SSA). Photocopies are not acceptable. Do not send Form W-3 if you filed electronically with the SSA.
Do not send any payment (cash, checks, money orders, etc.) with Forms W-2 and W-3.

Reminder

Separate instructions. See the 2025 General Instructions for Forms W-2 and W-3 for information on completing this form. Do not file Form W-3 for Form(s) W-2 that were submitted electronically to the SSA.

Purpose of Form

Complete a Form W-3 transmittal only when filing paper Copy A of Form(s) W-2, Wage and Tax Statement. Don't file Form W-3 alone. All paper forms **must** comply with IRS standards and be machine readable. Photocopies are **not** acceptable. Use a Form W-3 even if only one paper Form W-2 is being filed. Make sure both the Form W-3 and Form(s) W-2 show the correct tax year and employer identification number (EIN). Make a copy of this form and keep it with Copy D (For Employer) of Form(s) W-2 for your records. The IRS recommends retaining copies of these forms for at least 4 years.

E-Filing

The SSA strongly suggests employers report Form W-3 and Forms W-2 Copy A electronically instead of on paper. The SSA provides two free e-filing options on its Business Services Online (BSO) website.

- **W-2 Online.** Use fill-in forms to create, save, print, and submit up to 50 Forms W-2 at a time to the SSA.
- **File Upload.** Upload wage files to the SSA you have created using payroll or tax software that formats the files according to the SSA's *Specifications for Filing Forms W-2 Electronically (EFW2).*

W-2 Online fill-in forms or file uploads will be on time if submitted by **February 02, 2026.** For more information, go to *www.SSA.gov/bso.*

When To File Paper Forms

Mail Form W-3 with Copy A of Form(s) W-2 by **February 02, 2026.**

Where To File Paper Forms

Send this entire page with the entire Copy A page of Form(s) W-2 to:

Social Security Administration
Direct Operations Center
Wilkes-Barre, PA 18769-0001

Note: If you use "Certified Mail" to file, change the ZIP code to "18769-0002." If you use an IRS-approved private delivery service, add "ATTN: W-2 Process, 1150 E. Mountain Dr." to the address and change the ZIP code to "18702-7997." Go to *www.irs.gov/PDS* for a list of IRS-approved private delivery services.

For Privacy Act and Paperwork Reduction Act Notice, see the separate instructions.

Cat. No. 10159Y

You will also notice at the bottom of the W-3 that the mailing address for the Social Security Administration has been included. Once you complete the W-2, complete the W-3, and make sure the totals match (remember the reconciliation), make a copy for your files, and then mail the two forms to:

Social Security Administration
Direct Operations Center
Wilkes-Barre, PA 18769-0001

You can also file the W-2 and W-3 online at the Social Security Administration's Business Services Online (BSO) website at http://www.ssa.gov/bso. From start to finish, the registration process and the filing process ultimately take about the same amount of time as completing the forms manually. The biggest benefit of the online option is that you don't have to drive to Office Depot to obtain those silly little red inked forms.

From the main webpage at BSO, search for a link titled "Create Account." If you already have an account, simply sign in to begin. Otherwise, choose "Create an Account with Login.gov and then Create an account." Using your email to begin, then select the language you would prefer.

The site will send you an email for verification, and then you will be prompted to select a password. Always a joy trying to decide on passwords. They required at least 12 characters, so choose something you will remember and consider writing it down somewhere. You will also need to authenticate your login using several options. The easiest is to select "Text Message." The system will send you a text with a six-digit code to authenticate your contact information. I know this sounds cumbersome, but the process works very smoothly and will only take a few minutes.

Now they will need to verify that it is actually you requesting access. This basically involves taking a picture of your ID and yourself with your phone, and then sending it to them. Sounds intrusive, so you may want to revert to the paper forms at this point. My advice is to keep going, because after completing this process, filing the forms online will become much easier each year.

If you haven't punched your computer monitor yet, the next step will be to request specific services offered by the Social Security Administration's Business Services Online. The only process we are interested in is filing W-2s for our employees, which will be the top item on the services we offer. Click the box for SSA Services Suite for Employers, which will enable the electronic filing of all wage reports.

Business Services Online

Main Menu | Contact Us | BSO Information | Keyboard Navigation

Request Access to BSO Services

Select Service Suites

You must request access to do specific functions within a service suite. Let us help you choose which functions to add.

☐ **SSA Services Suite for Employers:**

Electronic Wage Reporting Service and/or Social Security Number Verification Service (SSNVS)

Electronic Wage Reporting allows employers to Report Wages to Social Security and to view the status of their submission.

Social Security Number Verification Service (SSNVS)

Allows the completion of an online form or submission of a file to request verification of names and Social Security Numbers of employees free of charge to employers and their agents for wage reporting purposes only. To verify SSNs for other than wage reporting purposes, please select the Special Services Suite for Consent Based Social Security Number Verification Service (CBSV) below.

Social Security Administration, Business Services Online
www.SSA.gov/bso

The site will confirm the services for which you are authorized to perform, and you will be ready to file the W-2 and W-3. Take your time and ensure that you enter your Social Security numbers correctly. Then, double-check them before clicking "submit." Don't forget your reconciliation process. If you have paid your new employee $15,000 for the year, ensure that the W-2 reflects this amount and that the same amount is also listed on the W-3 Transmittal.

The online process will most likely take about the same amount of time as completing the forms manually, so it is up to you to decide which option is best for your situation. Regardless of which one works for you, ensure that you keep copies of all the forms and verify that all the information is accurate. Verify the Social Security numbers one more time and refer to your payroll reconciliation to ensure the amounts are accurate as well.

It has likely taken you longer to read this section of the guide than it will take you to complete the Forms W-2 and W-3. Don't get frustrated or let the forms be more complicated than they actually are. And don't forget that you are saving over $5,000 for doing this little bit of paperwork.

3 . Form 944, Employer's ANNUAL Federal Tax Return

I'm sure you're getting tired of me saying this, but the next form we'll tackle is also very easy to complete. There are two basic forms available for payroll tax reporting, IRS Form 941 and Form 944. Form 941 is a quarterly report, so it is completed four times per year. The Form 944 is an annual report and, therefore, only needs to be filed once at the end of the year. The key is that you expect to pay less than $1,000 is total payroll tax. Since we will have no tax with our new employee, we will qualify for the annual filing requirement.

The annual payroll tax return for your business may sound and look complicated, but give me a few seconds to prove how easy it can be. The form is two pages long, but as you will see, page 2 of the form is almost completely blank, with a couple of boxes to check and a place for your signature. On page 1, we will be asked to complete 10 different lines with amounts related to your payroll activity for the year…but nine of those numbers will be "0."

You are likely aware that wages paid to a child working in their parents' business are exempt from FICA and Medicare tax. Since you have paid them $15,000, which is under the gross income for filing purposes, there is no federal withholding requirement either. That is why almost all of the blanks will include a zero. Once again, don't forget to reconcile the total wages paid for the year, which is $15,000, to your new employee.

So, let's take a look at the Kelsey Busby Real Estate annual payroll tax return below.

Form **944 for 2024: Employer's ANNUAL Federal Tax Return**

Department of the Treasury – Internal Revenue Service

OMB No. 1545-0029

Employer identification number (EIN)	2 7 – 1 2 3 4 5 6 7
Name *(not your trade name)*	Kelsey Busby
Trade name *(if any)*	Kesley Busby Real Estate
Address	30603 Lotus Ave
	Number / Street / Suite or room number
	Plano / TX / 75075
	City / State / ZIP code
	Foreign country name / Foreign province/county / Foreign postal code

Who Must File Form 944

You must file annual Form 944 instead of filing quarterly Forms 941 **only if the IRS notified you in writing**.

Go to *www.irs.gov/Form944* for instructions and the latest information.

Read the separate instructions before you complete Form 944. Type or print within the boxes.

Part 1: Answer these questions for this year. Employers in American Samoa, Guam, the Commonwealth of the Northern Mariana Islands, the U.S. Virgin Islands, and Puerto Rico can skip lines 1 and 2, unless you have employees who are subject to U.S. income tax withholding.

1	**Wages, tips, and other compensation**	1	15,000 . 00
2	**Federal income tax withheld from wages, tips, and other compensation**	2	0 . 00
3	**If no wages, tips, and other compensation are subject to social security or Medicare tax**	3	[X] **Check here and go to line 5.**
4	**Taxable social security and Medicare wages and tips:**		

	Column 1		Column 2
4a Taxable social security wages	.	× 0.124 =	.
4b Taxable social security tips	.	× 0.124 =	.
4c Taxable Medicare wages & tips	.	× 0.029 =	.
4d Taxable wages & tips subject to Additional Medicare Tax withholding	.	× 0.009 =	.

4e	**Total social security and Medicare taxes.** Add Column 2 from lines 4a, 4b, 4c, and 4d	4e	.
5	**Total taxes before adjustments.** Add lines 2 and 4e	5	0 . 00
6	**Current year's adjustments** (see instructions)	6	.
7	**Total taxes after adjustments.** Combine lines 5 and 6	7	0 . 00
8	**Qualified small business payroll tax credit for increasing research activities.** Attach Form 8974	8	.
9	**Total taxes after adjustments and nonrefundable credits.** Subtract line 8 from line 7	9	0 . 00
10	**Total deposits for this year, including overpayment applied from a prior year and overpayments applied from Form 944-X, 941-X, or 941-X (PR)**	10	0 . 00
11	**Balance due.** If line 9 is more than line 10, enter the difference and see instructions	11	. 00
12	**Overpayment.** If line 10 is more than line 9, enter the difference: 0 . 00		Check one: [ ] Apply to next return. [ ] Send a refund.

You MUST complete both pages of Form 944 and SIGN it.

For Privacy Act and Paperwork Reduction Act Notice, see separate instructions. Cat. No. 39316N Form **944** (2024)

Kelsey Busby Real Estate, Form 944, Page 1

Name (not your trade name)	Employer identification number (EIN)
Kelsey Busby	27 – 1234567

Part 2: Tell us about your deposit schedule and tax liability for this year.

13 Check one: [X] **Line 9 is less than $2,500. Go to Part 3.**

[ ] **Line 9 is $2,500 or more. Enter your tax liability for each month. If you're a semiweekly schedule depositor or you became one because you accumulated $100,000 or more of liability on any day during a deposit period, you must complete Form 945-A instead of the boxes below.**

13a	Jan. .	13d	Apr. .	13g	July .	13j	Oct. .
13b	Feb. .	13e	May .	13h	Aug. .	13k	Nov. .
13c	Mar. .	13f	June .	13i	Sept. .	13l	Dec. .

Total liability for year. Add lines 13a through 13l. Total must equal line 9. **13m** .

Part 3: Tell us about your business. If question 14 does NOT apply to your business, leave it blank.

14 If your business has closed or you stopped paying wages . . . . [ ] Check here, and

enter the final date you paid wages / / ; also attach a statement to your return. See instructions.

Part 4: May we speak with your third-party designee?

Do you want to allow an employee, a paid tax preparer, or another person to discuss this return with the IRS? See the instructions for details.

[ ] Yes. Designee's name and phone number

Select a 5-digit personal identification number (PIN) to use when talking to the IRS.

[X] No.

Part 5: Sign here. You MUST complete both pages of Form 944 and SIGN it.

Under penalties of perjury, I declare that I have examined this return, including accompanying schedules and statements, and to the best of my knowledge and belief, it is true, correct, and complete. Declaration of preparer (other than taxpayer) is based on all information of which preparer has any knowledge.

Sign your name here *Kelsey Busby*

Print your name here: Kelsey Busby

Print your title here: Owner

Date: 1-31-25

Best daytime phone: 214-620-2437

Paid Preparer Use Only

Check if you're self-employed [ ]

Preparer's name		PTIN	
Preparer's signature		Date	
Firm's name (or yours if self-employed)		EIN	
Address		Phone	
City	State	ZIP code	

Page **2** Form **944** (2024)

Kelsey Busby Real Estate, Form 944, Page 2

The top part of page one of the form is for the expected business information, including Employer Identification Number, business name, and business address. As always, ensure you enter the EIN correctly. Once you have checked the numbers, it is a good idea to double-check them again. The most common reason for receiving a letter from the IRS is the transposition of a number, so double-check it.

As I mentioned earlier, there are 15 separate line items on page one of the Form 944 that we must complete. However, as you can see on the Kelsey Busby Form 944, 14 of those amounts are either blank or include a "0." Line 1 of the form, titled "Wages, tips, and other compensation," is really the only line that we have to complete. Again, referring to our reconciliation concept, ensure that the amount you include on Line 1 matches the amount listed on the employee's W-2 and the W-3 Transmittal.

Pay particular attention to Line 3, where you verify that all wages paid during the year are exempt from Social Security and Medicare tax. This is the whole point! The wages that are paid to a child under age 18 working for their parents' sole proprietorship are exempt from all of these taxes. We still need to report to the IRS that the wages were paid, but they are exempt. Therefore, the payroll tax return itself is very easy since, as you can see, all of the numbers are just "0."

Page 2 of the Form 944 is even easier. There is no tax liability, so the top portion of the form is left completely blank. Since you completed the form yourself, you can click "No" to allow the IRS to discuss the form with another individual in Part 4. Make sure to date and sign the form, and you're all done.

Finally, check the numbers one more time against your payroll reconciliation. Verify the EIN and ensure that you have signed the form and confirmed the mailing address for your specific state. Make copies for your file, and be sure to mail the form by the due date, which is January 31st, after the end of the year. I am confident that you are getting very annoyed with me, but check the numbers one more time before you put the forms in the envelope.

Perhaps the most challenging aspect of Form 944 is determining where to actually mail the form. Included within the instructions for Form 944, the IRS provides different addresses depending on the state you call home and whether a payment is due with the form. Since our employee is exempt, there will be no payment with our Form 944. If you live in one of the following states:

Connecticut	Delaware	Wash, DC
Georgia	Illinois	Indiana
Kentucky	Maine	Maryland
Massachusetts	Michigan	New Hampshire
New Jersey	New York	North Carolina
Ohio	Pennsylvania	Rhode Island
South Carolina	Tennessee	Vermont
Virginia	West Virgina	Wisconsin

You will mail your completed and signed Form 944 to:

Department of the Treasury
Internal Revenue Service Center Kansas City, MO 64999-0044

If you live in one of the following states:

Alabama	Alaska	Arizona
Arkansas	California	Colorado
Florida	Hawaii	Idaho
Iowa	Kansas	Louisiana
Minnesota	Mississippi	Missouri
Montana	Nebraska	Nevada

New Mexico	North Dakota	Oklahoma
Oregon	South Dakota	Texas
Utah	Washinton	Wyoming

You will mail your completed and signed Form 944 to:

Department of the Treasury
Internal Revenue Service Center
Ogden, UT 84201-0044

4. Form 940, Employer's Annual Federal Unemployment (FUTA) Tax Return

The second annual payroll tax return, the Form 940, applies to Federal Unemployment Tax. As we have already discussed, your child working for your sole proprietorship is exempt from this tax as well. Even though no tax is due, the IRS still requires us to file the tax return. The good news is that this return is equally as straightforward and as easy as the Form 944, with the most confusing part being where to mail the completed form. As you can see from the Kelsey Busby Form 940 included on pages 106 and 107, the Form 944 and Form 940 are very similar.

The top part of the form requests the business name and address, as well as the Employer Identification Number, which is a crucial piece of information. Once again, if your only employee is the child you hired following this guide, most of the blanks on this form will be completed with "0." Form 940 can be completed very easily by simply reading the description for each line.

Part 1 of Form 940 requests information about state unemployment taxes. Your child is also exempt from any state unemployment tax; however, you still enter your state's two-digit abbreviation on line 1. The remainder of Part 1 should be left blank. Part 2 requests the total wages paid and then inquires whether any of those wages were exempt from FUTA tax. Since all of the wages paid to your child are indeed exempt, Lines 3 and 4 will be the same amount.

The wages that you pay are exempt since they are paid to a "Family Employee." Therefore, you will check the box for "Other" on Line 4e. Line 5 will also be left blank, again, since all wages are exempt. Line 6 is a calculation of Lines 4 and 5, ensuring the total on Line 6 is $15,000, the same as on Line 1.

Lines 7 and 8 are also calculations yielding zero taxable wages and zero tax. The remaining lines on the Form 940 will also be zero. After you have completed each line, your Form 940 will resemble Kelsey's, shown below.

Form **940 for 2024: Employer's Annual Federal Unemployment (FUTA) Tax Return** 850113

Department of the Treasury — Internal Revenue Service

OMB No. 1545-0029

Employer identification number (EIN) 2 7 – 1 2 3 4 5 6 7

Name *(not your trade name)* Kelsey Busby

Trade name *(if any)* Kelsey Busby Real Estate

Address 30603 Lotus Ave

Number Street Suite or room number

Plano TX 75075

City State ZIP code

Foreign country name Foreign province/county Foreign postal code

Type of Return
(Check all that apply.)

- [ ] **a.** Amended
- [ ] **b.** Successor employer
- [ ] **c.** No payments to employees in 2024
- [ ] **d.** Final: Business closed or stopped paying wages

Go to *www.irs.gov/Form940* for instructions and the latest information.

Read the separate instructions before you complete this form. Please type or print within the boxes.

Part 1: Tell us about your return. If any line does NOT apply, leave it blank. See instructions before completing Part 1.

1a **If you had to pay state unemployment tax in one state only, enter the state abbreviation** . **1a** T X

1b **If you had to pay state unemployment tax in more than one state, you are a multi-state employer** . . . **1b** ☐ Check here. Complete Schedule A (Form 940).

2 **If you paid wages in a state that is subject to CREDIT REDUCTION** . . . **2** ☐ Check here. Complete Schedule A (Form 940).

Part 2: Determine your FUTA tax before adjustments. If any line does NOT apply, leave it blank.

3 **Total payments to all employees** . . . **3** 15,000 . 00

4 **Payments exempt from FUTA tax** . . . **4** 15,000 . 00

Check all that apply: **4a** ☐ Fringe benefits **4c** ☐ Retirement/Pension **4e** ☒ Other
4b ☐ Group-term life insurance **4d** ☐ Dependent care

5 **Total of payments made to each employee in excess of $7,000** . . . **5** .

6 **Subtotal** (line 4 + line 5 = line 6) . . . **6** 15,000 . 00

7 **Total taxable FUTA wages** (line 3 – line 6 = line 7). See instructions . . . **7** 0 . 00

8 **FUTA tax before adjustments** (line 7 x 0.006 = line 8) . . . **8** 0 . 00

Part 3: Determine your adjustments. If any line does NOT apply, leave it blank.

9 **If ALL of the taxable FUTA wages you paid were excluded from state unemployment tax, multiply line 7 by 0.054** (line 7 × 0.054 = line 9). Go to line 12 . . . **9** .

10 **If SOME of the taxable FUTA wages you paid were excluded from state unemployment tax, OR you paid ANY state unemployment tax late** (after the due date for filing Form 940), complete the worksheet in the instructions. Enter the amount from line 7 of the worksheet . . **10** .

11 **If credit reduction applies,** enter the total from Schedule A (Form 940) . . . **11** .

Part 4: Determine your FUTA tax and balance due or overpayment. If any line does NOT apply, leave it blank.

12 **Total FUTA tax after adjustments** (lines 8 + 9 + 10 + 11 = line 12) . . . **12** .

13 **FUTA tax deposited for the year, including any overpayment applied from a prior year** . **13** .

14 **Balance due.** If line 12 is more than line 13, enter the excess on line 14.

- If line 14 is more than $500, you must deposit your tax.
- If line 14 is $500 or less, you may pay with this return. See instructions . . . **14** 0 . 00

15 **Overpayment.** If line 13 is more than line 12, enter the excess on line 15 and check a box below **15** 0 . 00

You **MUST** complete both pages of this form and **SIGN** it. Check one: ☐ Apply to next return. ☐ Send a refund.

For Privacy Act and Paperwork Reduction Act Notice, see separate instructions. Cat. No. 112340 Form **940** (2024)

Kelsey Busby Real Estate, Form 940, Page 1

850212

Name *(not your trade name)*	Employer identification number (EIN)
Kelsey Busby	27 – 1234567

Part 5: Report your FUTA tax liability by quarter only if line 12 is more than $500. If not, go to Part 6.

16 **Report the amount of your FUTA tax liability for each quarter; do NOT enter the amount you deposited. If you had no liability for a quarter, leave the line blank.**

16a **1st quarter** (January 1 – March 31)	**16a**	.
16b **2nd quarter** (April 1 – June 30)	**16b**	.
16c **3rd quarter** (July 1 – September 30)	**16c**	.
16d **4th quarter** (October 1 – December 31)	**16d**	.

17 **Total tax liability for the year** (lines 16a + 16b + 16c + 16d = line 17) **17** 0 . 00 **Total must equal line 12.**

Part 6: May we speak with your third-party designee?

Do you want to allow an employee, a paid tax preparer, or another person to discuss this return with the IRS? See the instructions for details.

☐ **Yes.** Designee's name and phone number

Select a 5-digit personal identification number (PIN) to use when talking to the IRS.

☒ **No.**

Part 7: Sign here. You MUST complete both pages of this form and SIGN it.

Under penalties of perjury, I declare that I have examined this return, including accompanying schedules and statements, and to the best of my knowledge and belief, it is true, correct, and complete, and that no part of any payment made to a state unemployment fund claimed as a credit was, or is to be, deducted from the payments made to employees. Declaration of preparer (other than taxpayer) is based on all information of which preparer has any knowledge.

Sign your name here *Kelsey Busby*

Print your name here: Kelsey Busby

Print your title here: Owner

Date: 1/31/25

Best daytime phone: 214-620-2437

Paid Preparer Use Only

Check if you are self-employed ☐

Preparer's name		PTIN	
Preparer's signature		Date	/ /
Firm's name (or yours if self-employed)		EIN	
Address		Phone	
City	State	ZIP code	

Page **2** Form **940** (2024)

Kelsey Busby Real Estate, Form 940, Page 2

The key points here, as we have discussed, are to ensure that the total wages included on this form match all the other forms and the total amount you actually paid in wages to your new employee. Ensure that you complete your payroll reconciliation by comparing the total wages as per the W-2, the W-3, the Form 944, and the Form 940. They should all match. Make sure to include your name and the EIN on page two, and sign and date the form. Make copies for your files and now you are ready to try and figure out where to mail the form.

You might think that we could just mail the form to the same place as we mailed the Form 944, but not so fast. That would be way too easy. The addresses are generally the same, depending on your state of residence and whether you are sending a payment with the form. The only difference is the extended zip code for each mailing address.

If you live in one of the following states:

Connecticut	Delaware	Wash, DC
Georgia	Illinois	Indiana
Kentucky	Maine	Maryland
Massachusetts	Michigan	New Hampshire
New Jersey	New York	North Carolina
Ohio	Pennsylvania	Rhode Island
South Carolina	Tennessee	Vermont
Virginia	West Virgina	Wisconsin

You will mail your completed and signed Form 940 to:

Department of the Treasury
Internal Revenue Service
Kansas City, MO 64999-0046

If you live in one of these following states:

Alabama	Alaska	Arizona	Arkansas
California	Colorado	Hawaii	Idaho
Iowa	Kansas	Louisiana	Minnesota
Mississippi	Missouri	Montana	Nebraska
Nevada	New Mexico	North Dakota	Oklahoma
Oregon	South Dakota	Texas	Utah
Washington	Wyoming		

You will mail your completed and signed Form 944 to:

Department of the Treasury
Internal Revenue Service
Ogden, UT 84201-0046

I hope that, at this point, you are in agreement regarding the total ease of completing all the necessary compliance reports for both the IRS and the Social Security Administration. If you have never seen any of these forms before, they may look a bit complicated, but I hope I have shown you how easy they can be.

One more time, be sure you review the reconciliation. Verify each form to ensure that all numbers match. Sign and date the form and mail by the due date of January 31st.

Wage and Payroll Tax Reconciliation

Form and Line	Total Wages	Form Delivered
Form W-2 Line 1	$15,000.00	Done, Jan 25th
Form W-3 Line 1	$15,000.00	Done, Jan 25th
Form 944 Line 1	$15,000.00	Done Jan 31st
Form 940 Line 3	$15,000.00	Done Jan 31st
Sch C Line 26	$15,000.00	Done, Apr 15th
Total Employee Checks	$15,000.00	Done

Don't get overconfident in the ease of the forms and skip this step. Take a few minutes to write down the numbers from each form and verify that they all match. Verify the Employer Identification Number on each form, paying close attention to the correct transposition of numbers. If you fail to catch one of those silly errors, it won't be the end of the world or even the end of the deduction, but it will mean that you will receive a big fat envelope from the IRS, which will most likely ruin a perfectly good Saturday morning. So, check the numbers one more time before you put all of that paper into the mailbox.

8

A WARNING!!!
It's All About The Paper

I will admit up front that I am not a fortune teller and have no working model for a crystal ball. However, I predict, just based on experience, that once you see and understand the tax benefits of hiring your child, you will want to put them to work today, and probably even yesterday. You will want to take advantage of those tax benefits right now! You may be tempted to take a shortcut and simply include the deductions on your tax return without following all the steps outlined in Chapters 1 through 7. Some readers will immediately start thinking about last year, amended returns, and getting a significant refund from Uncle Sam.

Don't give in to the temptation!!! Avoid the desire for a shortcut. Do the paperwork. The process of hiring your child incurs minimal financial cost and minimal exposure to an IRS audit adjustment. You don't have to pay anyone to accomplish the goal we have set for lowering your total tax bill by creating a new job. But there is a cost. And that cost is the paper-work!!! You must do the paperwork. Don't take any shortcuts.

The foundation for the savings you are about to realize is the stack of paper you will prepare. Some of those pieces of paper are simply stored in your own file cabinet, while some will be sent to the Internal Revenue Service. Some will be sent to the Social Security Administration, and some will be sent to your state employment regulators. We have shown you, step by step, how to complete each piece of paper and what to do with it. Some of the forms can be scary, and most of us have an unhealthy and, for the most part, an unreasonable fear of the IRS. However, don't forget that the IRS is primarily a computer-based system. Just big computers that are designed to read forms, do calculations, and (unfortunately) send us letters when they want more of our money. The forms communicate to the IRS the things that we need them to know. Without the forms, they won't know what we are trying to convey, which will only lead to more questions.

And when the IRS asks us questions, that is when we generally tend to get a bit nervous. By completing the paper trail that we have shown you how to build, that nervous feeling should be minimized. Your confidence will be expanded because you will already have the answers to any questions that could be asked. And those answers are almost always a simple piece of paper.

Consider the ultimate fear...well, at least the ultimate fear as it relates to the IRS. You wake up on some random Saturday morning, and all is good with the world. The morning is clear, and your coffee is rich and hot. You stroll to the mailbox whistling a tune. In the mailbox, right next to the birthday card from your Mom, is a big white envelope. The upper left-hand corner of the big envelope reads 'Internal Revenue Service.' The Saturday morning air is no longer clear and fresh, and your coffee is no longer rich or hot. Very few Saturdays start out more ominously than getting that big white envelope from the IRS.

Let's talk about what questions the IRS might be asking inside that big envelope. The questions they may want to ask you about your new employee and the deduction that you have included on Line 26 of your Schedule C can always be answered with a single piece of paper.

1. There is $15,000 included on line 26 of your Schedule C may I see your support for that deduction?

Although the probability of ever getting a question from the IRS is very low, if you get a question related to the wages you paid, this will be it. May I see your support? The answer, of course, is a resounding, "Yes, you may!" You will produce a Form W-3, Transmittal of Wages and Tax Statements, that shows a total of $15,000 in wages paid. You will produce a Form W-2, Wage and Tax Statement for your new employee that includes name, address, Social Security Number, Employer Identification Number, and total wages paid equaling $15,000. You will produce IRS Form 944, Employer's Annual Federal Tax Return, showing total wages paid of $15,000 as well as an IRS Form 940, Employer's Annual Federal Unemployment Tax Return, also showing total wages paid of $15,000.

All of the documents match. The total deduction on Line 26 of your Schedule C exactly matches the wage reports sent to the Social Security Administration. The wage reports sent to the Social Security Administration exactly match the payroll tax reports sent to the Internal Revenue Service. Remember that the IRS already has this information anyway, and they already know that the numbers match. This is why it is very unlikely that the IRS will ever ask a question about your new employee.

2. How did you determine the total wages of $15,000?

I have never been present during an IRS inquiry when this question was raised, but it could happen. The good news is that you already have a home run answer to this question as well. The hours worked by the employee determined the wages. You have paid them only for the hours that they worked at $25.00 per hour. You will produce semi-monthly time cards, signed by your employee, indicating total hours worked. You will produce bank statements showing transfers from your business account that match the total wages paid, or summary payment schedules detailing the total amounts paid for work completed. The total annual wage of $15,000 was determined by simply multiplying the number of hours the employee worked, as supported by the signed time cards, by the hourly wage of $25.00 per hour. That's it.

3. What does your employee do for the company?

Likewise, I have never been present during an IRS inquiry when this question was raised, but it could happen as well. More good news, you already have a homerun answer to this question as well. You will produce a signed job description detailing the exact duties and responsibilities of your employee. The job description provides details of the required skills, working conditions, and even documents the hourly wage agreed upon between the employee and employer.

Only a very small percentage of us will actually experience an IRS audit this year. The IRS will process approximately 150 million tax returns for the previous year. That is not a typo: 150,000,000, as in million, tax returns. Of those tax returns, the IRS will audit about 1.5 million returns, or just about 1%. Before any other discussions, your chances of getting that dreaded IRS envelope are about one out of one hundred. One out of one hundred is not a very good chance, but it is big enough to make most of us worry about it.

The odds get a little bit better or worse, based on your perspective, if you are a sole proprietor owning your own business. If you file a Schedule C, Profit or Loss from Business with your personal income tax return, then your chances of being audited go up to about 2%, or about one out of every fifty small businesses. But it gets worse. If you have over $25,000 in gross receipts from your business activity, then your chances increase to approximately 3%. About one out of every 33 small businesses with over $25,000 in gross revenue will receive a letter in the mail requesting some level of additional information. This is still a very small number in the overall scheme of things, but it is also THREE times as likely as someone who does not own a small business.

Why is that? Why are those of us who have chosen to create our own jobs and contribute to the U. S. economy by creating more jobs singled out to be audited three times as much as everyone else? This seems unfair, but the statistics are not concerned with fairness.

We are audited more frequently than anyone else because we tend to make more mistakes than others. Period! The IRS computers contain years of data indicating where mistakes are made, where adjustments should be applied, where taxpayers cut corners, where documentation is likely to be missing, and, yes, where they are most likely to generate new tax dollars for the U.S. Treasury.

Unfortunately, there isn't much we can do today about those statistics. But we can avoid the temptation to take a shortcut. We can avoid the temptation to skip the paperwork. If you do the paperwork, a vast majority of any issues will be resolved by the computer itself. That same big IRS computer will already know that your deductions are valid and that no further questions need be asked. The computer will already know that the wages you claimed on Schedule C match the totals submitted on IRS Form 944. The computer will even know that the Social Security Administration received your W-3, Transmittal of Wage and Tax Statements, showing exactly the same amount that was included on your Schedule C and on the Form 944. This is the very reason I believe your chances of having to answer any question from the IRS are actually reduced by hiring your kid and doing all the things we have suggested in these chapters.

This book has given you every answer to every question the IRS could ask about your new employee and your new $15,000 deduction. All the answers are in the paperwork, so please review it. Don't be tempted by that shortcut. Try to remember that the typical IRS employee with whom you might be speaking about your tax return is no different from you or me. He or she is neither a rocket scientist nor a bottom-of-the-class flunky. Instead, they are simply average workers just like us, doing their job every day. They get to work at 8:30 a.m. and want very badly to leave by 4:30 p.m. today because they have a kid's soccer game that they just can't miss.

The IRS agent has approximately 400 cases, all of which require their highest priority and must be resolved by the end of the quarter. And, guess what? They have a budget! Not a cost budget, but a collection budget. A budget for additional tax that should be found by examining those 400 cases! It would be ideal to assume that the IRS dedicates the entirety of its enforcement efforts to ensuring that we have the necessary support to complete error-free tax returns. It would even be somewhat comforting to assume that their main goal in examining our tax returns is to help us "get it right" the first time. But my opinion is that the primary goal addressed by each examining agent, each day, is to determine which of their 400 cases will generate additional tax and which ones won't. Which may have an error and which do not.

I will only ask you to do this once, but put yourself in their shoes. Which of those tax files would you expect to find additional taxes? Which of those files would you spend your time reviewing in hopes of covering some of your budget before the end of the day? Don't forget that the agent is overworked, underpaid, and underappreciated, and will do anything to ensure they arrive at that soccer game on time.

Would you spend most of your time looking at those case files with incomplete forms, missing forms, handwritten forms, or forms with obvious errors and omissions? Or would you spend more time on those case files that are complete, neat, and orderly? Even if the IRS computer has already selected the case files to be reviewed, and meetings have been scheduled, would you spend more time with those taxpayers who have a shoebox full of receipts or those with neat and orderly files containing all the paperwork completed and available for review?

It is my opinion that during the vast majority of all in-person IRS audits of individual taxpayers, the IRS auditor will decide within the first five minutes of the meeting whether or not there will be an additional assessment of tax related to that taxpayer. After only a few questions, they will know if there is anything to be found on that tax return. They will ask to see your business bank statements, and then maybe the employee forms to support your wages, some or all of the forms you learned about in this book, or maybe your home office deduction support. If you produce neat and exact answers to these questions, the interview will most likely be over. Period! Those neat and exact answers are almost always in the form of paperwork.

I spent several hundred words depressing you about the chances of being audited and how much more likely those chances are just because we are self-employed business owners. I saved some of the good news for now. Of all those IRS audits of small business taxpayers like us, about one in eight actually result in a refund. Yes, a refund, meaning the IRS initiated the audit process, the small business owner provided the necessary documentation and support, and ultimately made a deposit rather than writing a check. The only way to ensure that you are one of the eight, the one who receives the refund instead of the bill, is to complete the paperwork.

I know you have seen the often-reproduced scene in the movies of the bad guys exchanging secrets, or drugs, or guns for money at some remote airstrip or warehouse. You can see that big black Mercedes, driven by big, beefy bodyguards with unnecessarily dark sunglasses. The good guys produce the Gucci briefcase with stacks and stacks of one-hundred-dollar bills all lined up inside.

But wait.....upon further inspection, only the top one-hundred-dollar bill of each stack is real, while all other bills are just blank pieces of money colored paper. However, the perception of having a lot of money has already been established. By just looking at the Gucci case and the stacks of money, the bad guys have already concluded that everything is in order. The deal is going through! The image was successful, and the connection was complete.

Please take this example in the intended vein, but I am convinced that the same process of perception applies to the IRS audit. Visualize stacks and stacks of paper and folders, IRS forms and publications and other records available to support each number on your tax return. The IRS agent looks across the table at folders and stacks of paper, presumably supporting your tax return numbers, all neat and orderly, ready for review. The IRS agent looks at their watch and then glances at the large note on their calendar, indicating that the soccer game is imminent. The perception of order and compliance will push the agent to conclusions. Conclusions that indicate that they are not likely to find any error or understatement of tax based on that sack of paper in front of you. But in actuality, only the top piece of paper in each stack, in each folder, has anything written on it. The remaining pages are all empty pieces of copy paper. The perception of order and compliance would still generate the correct perception in the eyes of the IRS agent, and the con would be complete. It would still work!

The IRS would make that first five-minute judgment that you indeed had homerun answers to any potential question that they might ask. End of meeting. Not because everything was perfect, but because of perception and because of the soccer game.

This is obviously tongue-in-cheek, and I would certainly NOT recommend such a strategy, but the point is still valid. The perception of accuracy and of compliance is a very important one. That perception begins with the paperwork, its organization, and its completeness. The perception ends in the same place.

The bottom line is that it's all about the paperwork. Don't just say you did the stuff and then take a deduction. Do the stuff. Follow the steps outlined in this book from getting your new EIN to paying your new employee and reporting wages to the Internal Revenue Service and the Social Security Administration. You won't have to guess what to do or when to do it; all the details are here in one spot.

It's all about the paper!!!

9

A Call to Action!

I hope at this point I have convinced you that hiring your child to provide services to your sole proprietorship is a no-brainer. There is literally a basket full of money waiting for you to claim in lower taxes simply by taking action. But you must take action. This won't happen by itself, but it depends on you taking the first step. The money is yours, and it is up to you to claim the savings. I have conducted literally hundreds of seminars and webinars before thousands of small business owners, yet many of those owners have yet to hire their kids. I don't like saying it out loud, but I just don't get it.

The Department of Labor makes special provisions for children whose parents hire them. Every state workforce commission expressly addresses and exempts from state unemployment insurance the wages paid by a parent to their child in providing services to their parent's business. The IRS provides a specific exemption from federal payroll taxes for wages paid to children working for their parents' sole proprietorship. My point here is that I didn't come up with this all by myself. This is not a new thing.

You own the business. You are the boss. You decide who works for your business, what they do, and how much you pay them. You have all the knowledge and tools necessary to hire your child and save thousands of dollars in taxes, but you must take action. It won't happen by itself. As always, you have several options, but your call to action is to select one of them. It doesn't matter which one works best for you, but you must choose to act. The sooner you make that choice the sooner you can start saving tax dollars.

Option Number 1: Do It Yourself

This is the reason I wrote this book. The fact is that you don't need anyone to help you with this process. You don't need a consulting service, a CPA, a payroll expert, or anyone else. It is my opinion that you will have absolutely no problem accomplishing everything that I have outlined in this book in less than a few minutes every other week in paying your child, about thirty minutes in setting up numbers and time cards and job descriptions and then maybe another thirty minutes at the end of the year for tax forms and filings. Less than two hours per year — let me say that again — less than two hours per year can lead to over $5,000 in tax savings. Two thousand five hundred dollars an hour is a very good hourly rate.

The primary benefit of accomplishing all tasks yourself is the cost savings. As we noted in Chapter 7, you will need to purchase the forms for the machine-readable W-2 and W-3, so the process isn't entirely free. But the total cost will be something less than $25. Total!!! All other forms and publications can be obtained for free online. Following the step-by-step instructions provided in this Hire Your Kid guide will meet every single requirement necessary to achieve your maximum tax savings. There is no real need to give anyone the money you can save, since you can do all of this entirely on your own.

It may feel daunting and a bit overwhelming before you actually sit down to fill out the forms, but you will soon see that your personal capabilities are well-suited for saving $5,000. And even if you choose to do this yourself, you will not be by yourself.

As I mentioned earlier, I have conducted hundreds of seminars and webinars with thousands of small business owners. I start and end each of those seminars and webinars with the same message:

You Are Not Alone!

As a small business owner, it's easy to feel like you are in this alone. It's late Saturday night, and you finally get the kids off to bed. You're sitting at the kitchen table with hundreds of things to do in your business, and it's totally normal to feel like there is no one to help. But it just isn't true. If you have an internet connection, you have resources. And when it comes to hiring your kid, you will never be alone, because we are here to help. Even if you are handling all the paperwork yourself, you can still ask us for help. Open your email account and simply type your question, any question, about hiring your child, and we will get back to you right away. Keep a note of the following email address:

Info@HireYourKid.com

That's all you need to know. If you have a question, I am prepared to bet an hour of my time that I have the answer. And if I don't, I will be able to find out. Test me! I am ready!

There are numerous other resources available, including the IRS, the Small Business Administration, and thousands of other accountants and payroll experts ready to help or answer questions. But you CAN do this yourself. It may be hard to get started, and it may seem more of a mountain than a mole hill at this point, but you CAN do this.

Option Number 2:

HireYourKid.com

Info@HireYourKid.com

The only downside to option number 1 is my concern that you may not do it. I apologize if that sounds critical, but that worry stems from the hundreds of seminars I've attended with thousands of small business owners just like you, and my instinct tells me that you won't do it. And then, when you get to next April 15th, you will be sorry that you didn't, and you will have lost one full year of savings. If that sounds like you, then let me give you a few more options.

The best advice I can offer is to let us help you achieve your goals. We will do the work for you! We have developed a streamlined process for hiring your child that essentially handles all the paperwork for you, and the only thing you need to do is pay the child each pay period.

In this Hire Your Kid guide, we have identified seven key steps to hiring your child and saving over $5,000 in taxes:

1. Obtaining an EIN
2. Developing a detailed job description
3. Hiring the new employee, including Forms I-9 and W-4
4. Reporting to your state's new hire reporting system
5. Preparing a work schedule with detailed timecards.

6. Actually paying your new employee.
7. Preparing all of the year-end paperwork:

    a. Form W-2, Wage Statement
    b. Form W-3, Wage Transmittal Statement
    c. Form 944, Annual Payroll Tax Return
    d. Form 940, Unemployment Tax Return

As I mentioned under option number 1, you can certainly accomplish ALL of these tasks yourself. However, if you don't think you will follow the plan, then let us help you realize the savings available by handling all the paperwork for you.

Check out our website at www.HireYourKid.com for more information. We charge $499 for everything you have seen in this guide. You pay the kid, and we do the rest. If you would like to discuss if this is right for you, just send us a note and let's get started.

Info@HireYourKid.com

Also, keep in mind that we are not the only people out there with a service like this. There are over 33,000,000 small businesses just like you, so the market for this concept is bigger than either of us can imagine. Take a few minutes to search for similar options in your area. I would love to say this is an idea that we own, but this is not proprietary. Anyone can do this for you. And don't forget, YOU can do this for yourself!

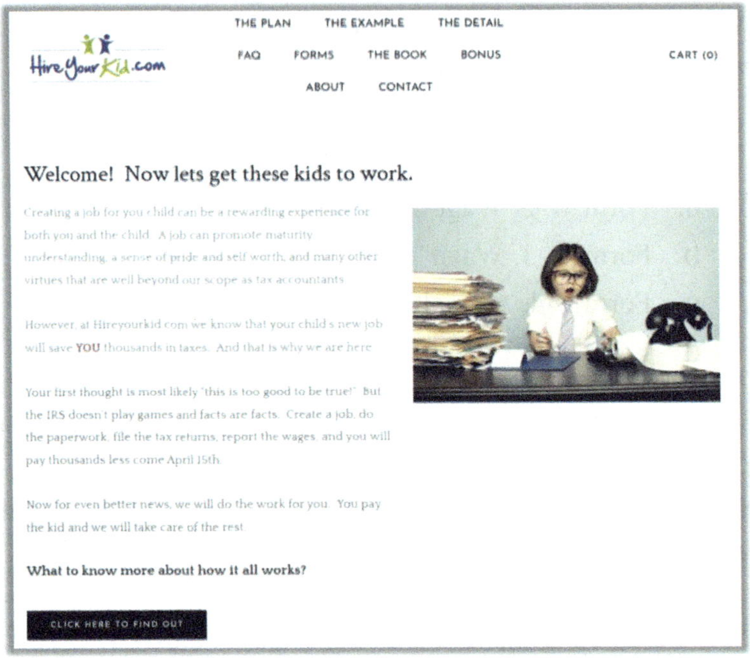

THE PLAN THE EXAMPLE THE DETAIL
FAQ FORMS THE BOOK BONUS CART (0)
ABOUT CONTACT

Welcome! Now lets get these kids to work.

Creating a job for you child can be a rewarding experience for both you and the child. A job can promote maturity understanding, a sense of pride and self worth, and many other virtues that are well beyond our scope as tax accountants.

However, at Hireyourkid.com we know that your child's new job will save **YOU** thousands in taxes. And that is why we are here.

Your first thought is most likely "this is too good to be true!" But the IRS doesn't play games and facts are facts. Create a job, do the paperwork, file the tax returns, report the wages, and you will pay thousands less come April 15th.

Now for even better news, we will do the work for you. You pay the kid and we will take care of the rest.

What to know more about how it all works?

CLICK HERE TO FIND OUT

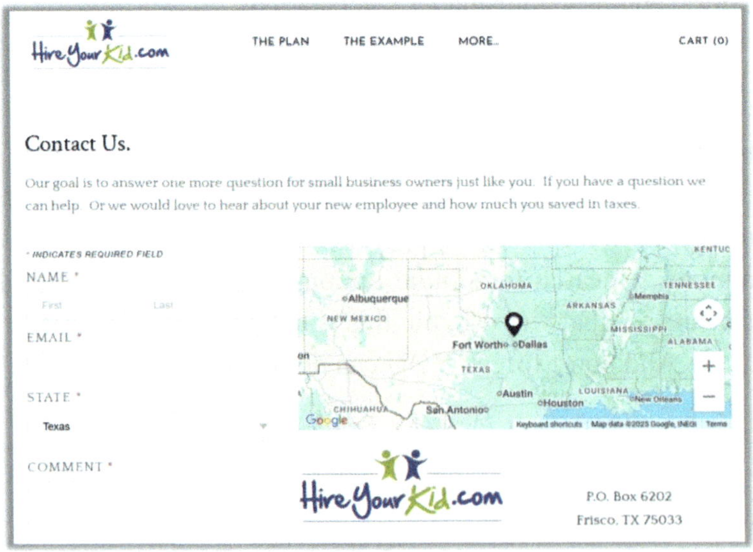

THE PLAN THE EXAMPLE MORE... CART (0)

Contact Us.

Our goal is to answer one more question for small business owners just like you. If you have a question we can help. Or we would love to hear about your new employee and how much you saved in taxes.

* INDICATES REQUIRED FIELD

NAME *

First Last

EMAIL *

STATE *

Texas

COMMENT *

P.O. Box 6202
Frisco, TX 75033

Option Number 3: Use a Payroll Service

There are many options for payroll services that can help you with some of the paperwork for hiring your kid. They handle payment, reporting, compliance, and all the tedious paperwork for millions of employees and employers every day. They know what they are doing and will alleviate most of the headaches.

They will most likely NOT obtain your EIN for you, nor will they help you with the job description or the time cards, but you can accomplish those tasks with the help of this Hire Your Kid guide. The scariest part for most small business owners in hiring any employee is the annual reporting requirements. The annual payroll tax returns and the W-2s for each employee are not brain surgery, but can be cumbersome and a bit scary, especially if you have never completed the process from beginning to end. The payroll services are excellent at meeting all of those obligations and very rarely make mistakes.

There are many companies to choose from, but perhaps the three most well-known are:

www.Gusto.com

www.ADP.com

PAYCHEX®

www.PAYCHEX.com

It is often difficult to obtain a specific quote online or over the phone, as companies tend to focus on selling their services. However, in most cases, the processing companies will ultimately compete with each other. Each of these companies will charge somewhere between $35 and $50 per month for a basic payroll service that includes year-end paperwork for one employee. That's around $400 to $600 for the whole year.

Using a payroll processing company is a great option, as it not only saves you tax dollars by helping you hire your child but also saves you a significant amount of money by alleviating many of the payroll headaches. Again, they do a great job, but are relatively expensive when compared to options 1 and 2.

If this option is the best for you, be sure to consult with several different companies. They are all very competitive and will occasionally offer discounts to new business owners. Take a few minutes to ask for a quote from each of these and from others that may provide local service in your area. Ensure you are comparing apples to apples and ask for all their current discounts and specials.

Option Number 4: Have your CPA do it for you

Of all the options available, this is certainly the easiest. But it will also be a relatively expensive option. The only time I would recommend this option is when you are already my client and I am your CPA.

Just kidding about that part, of course, but your CPA will still most likely end up being the most expensive, but can also be the easiest and most secure, since they already have all of your specific information. The process will likely also be the best and most comfortable for you, as you already have a good relationship with your CPA and trust that they will do a good job for you. There is no real substitute for personal one-on-one service. Having said that, let me give you a question to ask your CPA to make sure you are on the same page:

1. Why didn't you tell me about hiring my kid before now?

If you are working with a business manager, financial planner, CPA, or advisor, I strongly recommend discussing this idea with them before taking any further action. There is a good chance that they already know a great deal about your business and the goals you have set for it. Their input is extremely valuable, and you should most assuredly discuss this concept with them.

As I am sure you already know, CPAs and financial advisors charge for their time. Most charge somewhere between $100 and $150 an hour, and up from there. My best guess is that your CPA or financial advisor would likely charge you for four to five hours per year to accomplish all of the goals we have set forth in hiring your child. That translates to approximately $750 in fees to initiate the process and then an additional $600 annually to prepare the payroll tax returns, including the W-2, W-3, etc. There may very well be an opportunity to renegotiate your overall annual relationship with your accountant. This is a great opportunity to review all the services provided and, by adding this new facet of work, you may be able to save a few dollars on the other tasks currently fulfilled by this particular consultant.

If this option is a potential fit for your situation, take some time to visit with your advisor. Ask a variety of questions about the process, fees, and deliverables. Ensure that both of you have a clear understanding of the expectations and exactly who will be responsible for each key component of hiring your child. The bottom line in this scenario is that you are splitting the savings with your CPA in exchange for their helping you with the paperwork.

Summary of Options

Regardless of which of these four options makes the most sense for your specific situation, make sure that you choose one of them. The bottom line is that you must take action. You may be tired of me saying this by now, but $5,000 is waiting for you to take that action. Decide which option is best for you and then get started. The quicker you take action, the more money you will save.

Option	Cost
Do it yourself	$25
HireYourKid.com	$499
Use a Payroll Service	$600
Use your CPA	$750
Do Nothing	$5,000

I assume you noticed that I added a fifth option to the bottom of the chart. Obviously, I am making the point here that doing nothing indeed incurs a cost. That cost will vary based on your specific circumstances, but the cost of doing nothing can be as much as $5,000, or more.

Don't start out with the idea of meeting all of these goals by yourself if you know that you won't follow through with them. There is $5,000 waiting for you at the end of the process, but no one knows you as well as you know yourself. Choose the option that gives you the best chance for success and the best chance to reduce the amount of tax that you have to pay.

My call to action is to DO SOMETHING. Any of the options noted in this chapter are far better than doing nothing. It is my sincere hope that these pages have shown you the opportunity to save thousands of dollars in taxes, to help accomplish additional tasks in your small business, and even to find a way to make an additional difference in the growth of your child. Everything you need to know has been included in this Hire Your Kid guide. The rest is up to you!

One last push for YOUR CALL TO ACTION

The following list of articles and posts was obtained directly from a Google search for 'Hire Your Kid'. The list includes the Texas Workforce Commission, the IRS, TurboTax, software companies, CPAs, and even the Small Business Administration. All of the links lead to the benefits of hiring your kid.

I would love to convince you that I am singularly responsible for creating this amazing tax strategy, but the wealth of information available should convince you that thousands of small business owners have already hired their kids and are saving thousands of tax dollars.

CNBC MARKETS BUSINESS INVESTING TECH POLITICS VIDEO INVESTING CLUB PRO LIVESTREAM

PERSONAL FINANCE

You could score a tax break for hiring your own kids this summer — if you follow the rules

PUBLISHED MON, MAY 27 2024-9:00 AM EDT

Kate Dore, CFP®, EA
@IN/KATEDORE/

SHARE

KEY POINTS
- If you're self-employed, hiring your kids could provide tax benefits.

"You could score a tax break…"

https://www.cnbc.com/2024/05/27/hiring-yourkids-tax-breaks.html

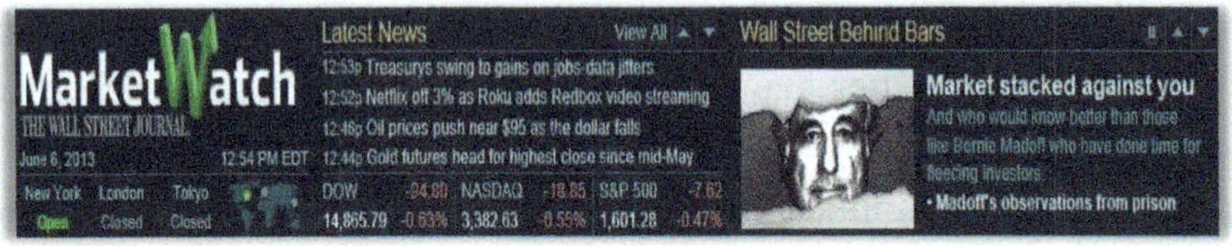

“Hire your kid, get a tax break” http://tinyurl.com/WallStreetJounral-HireYourKids

“This Summer, Hire Your Kids”http://tinyurl.com/Forbes-HireYourKids

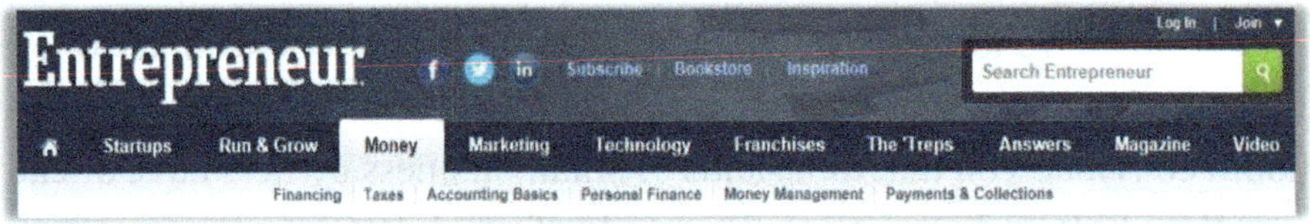

“Why You Should Hire Your Kids This Summer” http://tinyurl.com/Entrepreneur-HireYourKids

Take a few minutes to do your own search. Start with the above articles or start a new search for “Hire Your Kid” and let your own eyes be your guide. As I mentioned earlier in this chapter, always remember that you are not alone. You have resources to call upon, and after reading this guide, you should know that you now have yet another one. As you read and evaluate how much you can save, please let me know if I can assist with any questions. Send me your questions at:

Info@HireYourKid.com

I am here to help. My goal is always to answer one more question, and I hope that the next question will come from you. However, regardless of the questions, it is time to take action. It's time to hire your kid. Don't forget that over 70% of all new jobs in the United States come from small business owners just like you. Congratulations on creating one more job, and from one small business owner to another:

Keep Up the Good Work!!!

Bonus Chapter

Hire Your Kid – Retire Your Kid

This Chapter may be the first Chapter. This Chapter may include the most shocking numbers of all. Now that you have created a job for your child and paid them a reasonable wage, there is an additional benefit that you may not be aware of. Now that your child has a job, they will also have earned income. The earned income makes them eligible to contribute to a qualified retirement plan such as a traditional IRA or a Roth IRA. For 2025, an individual can contribute up to 100% of their earned income, with a maximum amount of $7,000, to a qualified retirement plan. Retirement plan options would include traditional IRAs, 401(k) plans, SIMPLE Plans, and Roth IRA plans. The most commonly known benefit of qualified retirement plans is that a taxpayer can defer, or delay, tax on qualified contributions until after retirement. Contributing to such a plan for most taxpayers is a great tax savings idea for the current year and should always be considered before hitting 'SEND' on your current year tax return.

Our new employee, your child, is not worried about paying tax since the whole idea here is that the child will have no federal income tax to pay and therefore will not have to defer or delay any such tax. Our new employee doesn't need a deduction on their latest tax return. Instead, our new employee can choose to make contributions to a Roth IRA.

Roth IRA contributions do not generate a current deduction for federal income tax. However, the earnings on those accounts are excluded from tax. EXCLUDED from tax as opposed to deferred from paying tax. That means that the earnings on qualified Roth IRA accounts are NEVER subject to federal income tax. EVER!!!

Please allow me to remind you what we have accomplished so far in creating a new job for your child:

1. We have paid your child $15,000 in wages for services provided to your small business.
2. The $15,000 is money that you were already spending on the child anyway—clothes, trips, camps, travel, allowances, etc.
3. You saved about $5,000 in federal and state income tax.

So, you are $5,000 ahead of the game. The wages you paid to the kid will be used for the same things you were spending before creating the job, so that hiring your kid, including $15,000 in wages, actually costs you absolutely nothing. The federal income tax savings of $5,000 are new money to spend on anything you see fit. But what if....

What if you took that $5,000 savings and opened a Roth IRA account for your child? Then each year from the time they were eight years old until they turned eighteen, you did exactly the same thing. Each year, a brand new $5,000 contribution to their Roth IRA account. That would be ten years of Hire Your Kid. Ten years of Roth IRA contributions that cost you exactly zero.

The long-term growth within the Roth IRA account will obviously depend on market performance over the years. The average stock market return over the past 100 years is about 10% per year. There are certainly some good years and some that are bad, but 10% is the overall average based on the S&P 500 index. In an article for NerdWallet dated April 10, 2025, Dr. James Royal, Ph.D., indicates the following average rates of return:

5-year, 10-year, 20-year and 30-year S&P 500 returns

Below is a table showing the S&P 500's price returns over different timeframes, as of the end of 2024.

The table shows that while the market has a long-term average annual return of 10%, year-to-year returns can vary significantly. The five-year return factors in the post-pandemic surge and the 2023 recovery. The 20-year return includes the Great Recession, and the 30-year return includes the dot-com crash of the early 2000s.

Period (start-of-year to end-of-2024)	Average annual S&P 500 return
5 years (2020-2024)	14.25%
10 years (2015-2024)	12.21%
15 years (2010-2024)	12.62%
20 years (2005-2024)	9.72%
25 years (2000-2024)	7.33%
30 years (1995-2024)	10.49%

Source: macrotrends.net

A simple average of those six calculations would yield an annual return of 11.1%. Indeed, things change, and the future is unknown. But let's not be greedy and assume a conservative rate of return for your child's investment opportunity of 8%, or about three-fourths of the actual historical rate. Again, who knows what returns will actually be during your child's lifetime, but history would indicate that an 8% return would be a conservative and reasonable guess.

Here's the best part. If you Hire Your Kid for those ten years from age 8 to 18, and use the tax savings you get from the IRS to fund a Roth IRA for your child, you will have invested $5,000 per year for ten years using the IRS money. This account balance will literally have been funded for free by the IRS. ZERO dollars of your out-of-pocket investment. If stock market history continues and the account experiences an average rate of return of 8%, the balance in your child's tax-free Roth IRA on their normal full retirement age of 67 will be....

$3,434,718.31

Imagine the conversation at your child's retirement party. "I am so proud of you! And, I have a surprise for you!"

Hire Your Kid!

Retire Your Kid!

And let the IRS pay for it!!!

Appendix A:
The Case Study – Meet Kelsey

Meet Kelsey Busby from Plano, Texas. Kelsey and her husband, Grady, are truly Middle America and are living the American Dream. At least living the American Dream until tax time. For most of us, April doesn't just mean April showers, looking forward to May flowers, but also means filing the dreaded tax return. In this appendix, I will prepare a complete federal income tax return with actual numbers and actual forms to explore how hiring your kid can help save thousands of dollars in taxes. As we discussed in Chapter 3, the actual savings will depend on your personal marginal income tax bracket, so your specific savings can be a bit lower or a bit higher.

Kelsey and Grady have been married for eighteen years and have two kids, Samantha, who is sixteen, and Jeremy, who is fourteen. Samantha has had her driver's license for two months, and both Kelsey and Grady agree that the hardest thing they have ever done is to give her the keys and watch her drive away. Jeremy loves soccer and baseball but hates his new braces and refuses to admit that he has a ‘thing’ for Emily, a brown-haired girl on his soccer team.

Grady just turned forty-three, is an assistant principal, and teaches algebra to tenth graders in Plano, Texas. His favorite pastime is golf, followed closely by the quadratic equation, but he tries to keep that last part quiet. His annual salary from the school district is $127,232. The following is a copy of his W-2 from last year, used to complete their joint income tax return:

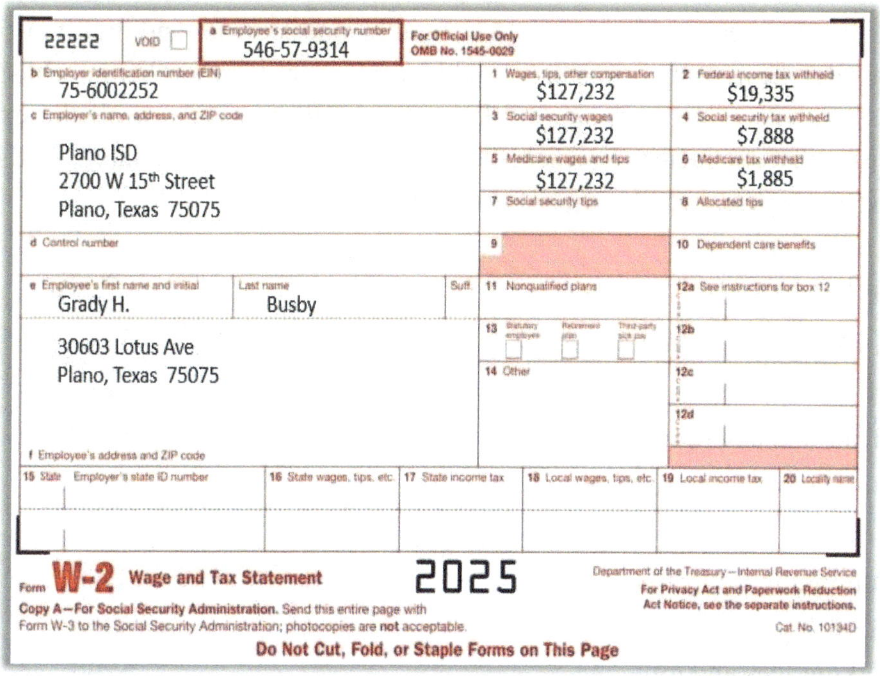
22222 VOID
a Employee's social security number 546-57-9314
For Official Use Only OMB No. 1545-0029
b Employer identification number (EIN) 75-6002252
1 Wages, tips, other compensation $127,232
2 Federal income tax withheld $19,335
c Employer's name, address, and ZIP code
Plano ISD
2700 W 15th Street
Plano, Texas 75075
3 Social security wages $127,232
4 Social security tax withheld $7,888
5 Medicare wages and tips $127,232
6 Medicare tax withheld $1,885
7 Social security tips
8 Allocated tips
d Control number
9
10 Dependent care benefits
e Employee's first name and initial Grady H.
Last name Busby
Suff.
11 Nonqualified plans
12a See instructions for box 12
13 Statutory employee Retirement plan Third-party sick pay
12b
30603 Lotus Ave
Plano, Texas 75075
14 Other
12c
12d
f Employee's address and ZIP code
15 State Employer's state ID number
16 State wages, tips, etc.
17 State income tax
18 Local wages, tips, etc.
19 Local income tax
20 Locality name
Form W-2 Wage and Tax Statement 2025
Department of the Treasury—Internal Revenue Service
For Privacy Act and Paperwork Reduction Act Notice, see the separate instructions.
Copy A—For Social Security Administration. Send this entire page with Form W-3 to the Social Security Administration; photocopies are not acceptable.
Cat. No. 10134D
Do Not Cut, Fold, or Staple Forms on This Page

Grady Busby, Form W-2

Kelsey is a licensed real estate professional and has worked for a local bank and mortgage lender specializing in residential lending for over fifteen years. Issues with the economy and the Texas real estate market led to her position being eliminated at the beginning of 2020. After several months of job hunting, she decided to start her own small business providing retail real estate services in the North Texas area. Her skill and reputation, built over many years, provided her with a number of referrals to jump-start her business. It was very scary at first, but she soon realized the need that she was fulfilling and settled into developing a new and growing small business. She won't say for sure how old she is, but says it is less than 40 and that she expects it to stay that way.

She collected $191,506 last year in real estate sales commissions and referral fees, for which she is very proud. When she first started, it never occurred to her that she was now a small business owner and didn't even consider the new tax forms that would be necessary to report her new business activity. However, she did keep outstanding records of all the expenses that she incurred, which she believed were business-related. At the end of the year, her files included the following items:

Broker dues and fees	$7,550
Marketing signs and mailers	$3,612
Office supplies	$1,662
Meals and entertainment	$1,016
Mobile telephone service	$626
Umbrella liability policy	$460
Continuing Education	$450
Licensing fees	$300
Parking fees and tolls	$240

Kelsey maintained receipts for each of the above items and also kept a detailed mileage log for the business use of her car. That log indicates that she drove 13,127 miles in connection with her business, including showing properties to clients, trips to the office supply store and post office, weekend trade shows, etc.

Kelsey is very happy with the way her business is growing, but doesn't really understand all that self-employment entails. She works hard and provides top-level service to her clients, but from a tax standpoint, she simply gives her receipts to her CPA in March and then hopes for the best by April 15th. The income and expenses related to Kelsey's real estate business are not included on a separate income tax return. Instead, they are included on a Schedule C, Profit or Loss from Business, which is then attached to her personal income tax return. Based on Kelsey's detailed records, her Schedule C would look as follows:

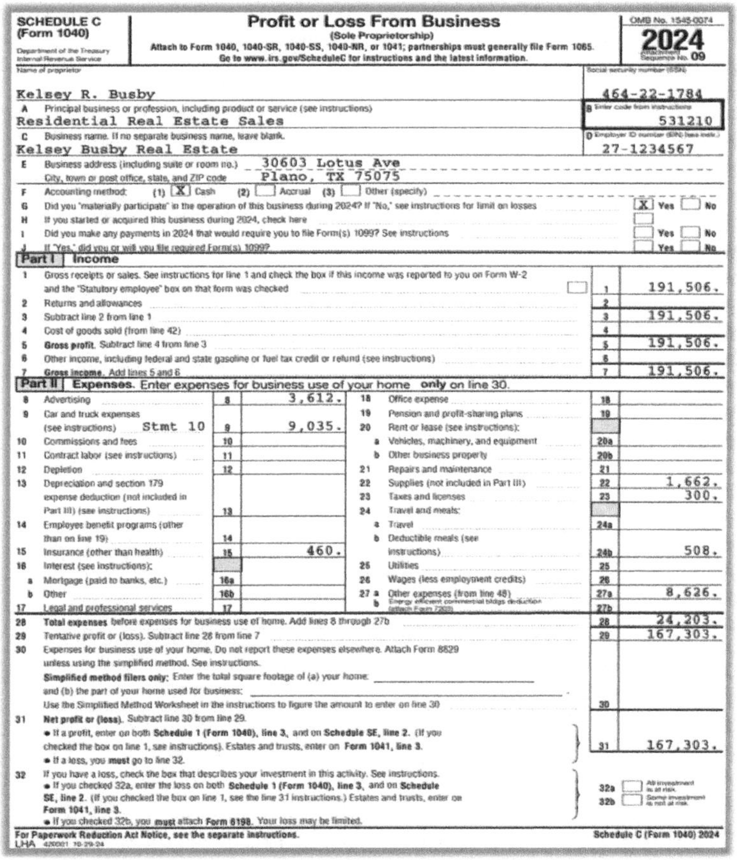

SCHEDULE C (Form 1040)
Department of the Treasury Internal Revenue Service

Profit or Loss From Business
(Sole Proprietorship)
Attach to Form 1040, 1040-SR, 1040-SS, 1040-NR, or 1041; partnerships must generally file Form 1065.
Go to www.irs.gov/ScheduleC for instructions and the latest information.

OMB No. 1545-0074
2024
Attachment Sequence No. 09

Name of proprietor: Kelsey R. Busby
Social security number (SSN): 464-22-1784

A Principal business or profession, including product or service (see instructions): Residential Real Estate Sales
B Enter code from instructions: 531210
C Business name. If no separate business name, leave blank.: Kelsey Busby Real Estate
D Employer ID number (EIN) (see instr.): 27-1234567
E Business address (including suite or room no.): 30603 Lotus Ave
City, town or post office, state, and ZIP code: Plano, TX 75075
F Accounting method: (1) [X] Cash (2) [ ] Accrual (3) [ ] Other (specify)
G Did you "materially participate" in the operation of this business during 2024? If "No," see instructions for limit on losses [X] Yes [ ] No
H If you started or acquired this business during 2024, check here [ ]
I Did you make any payments in 2024 that would require you to file Form(s) 1099? See instructions [ ] Yes [ ] No
J If "Yes," did you or will you file required Form(s) 1099? [ ] Yes [ ] No

Part I Income

1	Gross receipts or sales. See instructions for line 1 and check the box if this income was reported to you on Form W-2 and the "Statutory employee" box on that form was checked [ ]	1	191,506.
2	Returns and allowances	2	
3	Subtract line 2 from line 1	3	191,506.
4	Cost of goods sold (from line 42)	4	
5	**Gross profit.** Subtract line 4 from line 3	5	191,506.
6	Other income, including federal and state gasoline or fuel tax credit or refund (see instructions)	6	
7	**Gross income.** Add lines 5 and 6	7	191,506.

Part II Expenses. Enter expenses for business use of your home **only** on line 30.

8	Advertising	8	3,612.	18	Office expense	18	
9	Car and truck expenses (see instructions) Stmt 10	9	9,035.	19	Pension and profit-sharing plans	19	
10	Commissions and fees	10		20	Rent or lease (see instructions):		
11	Contract labor (see instructions)	11		a	Vehicles, machinery, and equipment	20a	
12	Depletion	12		b	Other business property	20b	
13	Depreciation and section 179 expense deduction (not included in Part III) (see instructions)	13		21	Repairs and maintenance	21	
14	Employee benefit programs (other than on line 19)	14		22	Supplies (not included in Part III)	22	1,662.
15	Insurance (other than health)	15	460.	23	Taxes and licenses	23	300.
16	Interest (see instructions):			24	Travel and meals:		
a	Mortgage (paid to banks, etc.)	16a		a	Travel	24a	
b	Other	16b		b	Deductible meals (see instructions)	24b	508.
17	Legal and professional services	17		25	Utilities	25	
				26	Wages (less employment credits)	26	
				27 a	Other expenses (from line 48)	27a	8,626.
				b	Energy efficient commercial bldgs deduction (attach Form 7205)	27b	

28	**Total expenses** before expenses for business use of home. Add lines 8 through 27b	28	24,203.
29	Tentative profit or (loss). Subtract line 28 from line 7	29	167,303.
30	Expenses for business use of your home. Do not report these expenses elsewhere. Attach Form 8829 unless using the simplified method. See instructions. **Simplified method filers only:** Enter the total square footage of (a) your home: ____ and (b) the part of your home used for business: ____. Use the Simplified Method Worksheet in the instructions to figure the amount to enter on line 30	30	
31	**Net profit or (loss).** Subtract line 30 from line 29. • If a profit, enter on both **Schedule 1 (Form 1040), line 3,** and on **Schedule SE, line 2.** (If you checked the box on line 1, see instructions). Estates and trusts, enter on **Form 1041, line 3.** • If a loss, you **must** go to line 32.	31	167,303.
32	If you have a loss, check the box that describes your investment in this activity. See instructions. • If you checked 32a, enter the loss on both **Schedule 1 (Form 1040), line 3,** and on **Schedule SE, line 2.** (If you checked the box on line 1, see the line 31 instructions.) Estates and trusts, enter on **Form 1041, line 3.** • If you checked 32b, you **must** attach **Form 6198.** Your loss may be limited.	32a [ ] All investment is at risk. 32b [ ] Some investment is not at risk.	

For Paperwork Reduction Act Notice, see the separate instructions. Schedule C (Form 1040) 2024
LHA 420001 10-29-24

Kelsey Busby Real Estate Schedule C, Page One

Schedule C (Form 1040) 2024 Kelsey R. Busby 464-22-1784 Page 2

Part III **Cost of Goods Sold** (see instructions)

33 Method(s) used to value closing inventory: a ☐ Cost b ☐ Lower of cost or market c ☐ Other (attach explanation)

34 Was there any change in determining quantities, costs, or valuations between opening and closing inventory? If "Yes," attach explanation ☐ Yes ☐ No

35 Inventory at beginning of year. If different from last year's closing inventory, attach explanation	35	
36 Purchases less cost of items withdrawn for personal use	36	
37 Cost of labor. Do not include any amounts paid to yourself	37	
38 Materials and supplies	38	
39 Other costs	39	
40 Add lines 35 through 39	40	
41 Inventory at end of year	41	
42 **Cost of goods sold.** Subtract line 41 from line 40. Enter the result here and on line 4	42	

Part IV **Information on Your Vehicle.** Complete this part **only** if you are claiming car or truck expenses on line 9 and are not required to file Form 4562 for this business. See the instructions for line 13 to find out if you must file Form 4562.

43 When did you place your vehicle in service for business purposes? (month/day/year) 01/01/23

44 Of the total number of miles you drove your vehicle during 2024, enter the number of miles you used your vehicle for:

a Business 13,127 b Commuting 1,020 c Other 5,453

45 Was your vehicle available for personal use during off-duty hours? ☒ Yes ☐ No

46 Do you (or your spouse) have another vehicle available for personal use? ☒ Yes ☐ No

47a Do you have evidence to support your deduction? ☒ Yes ☐ No

b If "Yes," is the evidence written? ☒ Yes ☐ No

Part V **Other Expenses.** List below business expenses not included on lines 8-26, line 27b, or line 30.

Broker Dues and Fees		7,550.
Telephone		626.
Continuing Education		450.
48 **Total other expenses.** Enter here and on line 27a	48	8,626.

420002 10-28-24 **Schedule C (Form 1040) 2024**

Kelsey Busby Real Estate Schedule C, Page Two

Notice that the bottom line, Line 31, on page one of Kelsey's Schedule C, shows a net profit of $167,303. Total collected real estate commissions and referral fees of $191,506 less deductible business expenses of $24,203, including the business use of her car, generate a net profit from her business of $167,303. Unfortunately, this is not the amount of money that she gets to keep.

Before any other deductions or credits, exemptions, or calculations, the small business owner must pay self-employment tax (SE tax) on their net earnings from the business. Many new small business owners are unaware of the SE tax and fail to plan for this part of self-employment. In addition to new small business owners, many experienced small business owners still don't quite understand the need for this 'additional' tax on their business income, and many view the tax as quite unfair.

Self-employment tax is basically just another name for Social Security tax. The SE tax paid by the self-employed business owner is exactly the same as the FICA and Medicare tax paid by employees. The typical employee must pay 6.2% of their wages in FICA tax and another 1.45% of their wages in Medicare tax. Combined, these two represent 7.65% of wages that are withheld from their paychecks and sent directly to the Social Security Administration to fund benefits under the Social Security system. Many employees are not aware that their employer, the company they work for, also must send a matching 7.65% of wages paid to the Social Security system. Therefore, a total of 15.3% of wages paid to each employee is sent to the Social Security Administration, half paid by the employee and half paid by the employer.

The real issue for the self-employed business owner is that they are, in essence, both the employee and the employer in terms of who must pay the Social Security tax. So instead of having the responsibility for half of the tax, the self-employed business owner has the distinct honor of paying BOTH halves of the tax. That's 7.65% for the employee AND 7.65% for the employer, resulting in a combined self-employment tax of 15.3%. Without any judgment of fair, Kelsey must pay $23,639 in self-employment tax. Her Schedule SE, Self-Employment Tax would be as follows:

SCHEDULE SE (Form 1040)

Department of the Treasury Internal Revenue Service

Self-Employment Tax

Attach to Form 1040, 1040-SR, 1040-SS, or 1040-NR.

Go to www.irs.gov/ScheduleSE for instructions and the latest information.

OMB No. 1545-0074

2024

Attachment Sequence No. **17**

Name of person with self-employment income (as shown on Form 1040, 1040-SR, 1040-SS, or 1040-NR): Kelsey R. Busby

Social security number of person with **self-employment** income: 464 22 1784

Part I Self-Employment Tax

Note: If your only income subject to self-employment tax is **church employee income,** see instructions for how to report your income and the definition of church employee income.

A If you are a minister, member of a religious order, or Christian Science practitioner **and** you filed Form 4361, but you had $400 or more of **other** net earnings from self-employment, check here and continue with Part I ☐

Skip lines 1a and 1b if you use the farm optional method in Part II. See instructions.

1a	Net farm profit or (loss) from Sch. F, line 34, and farm partnerships, Sch. K-1 (Form 1065), box 14, code A	1a	
b	If you received social security retirement or disability benefits, enter the amount of Conservation Reserve Program payments included on Schedule F, line 4b, or listed on Schedule K-1 (Form 1065), box 20, code AQ	1b	
	Skip line 2 if you use the nonfarm optional method in Part II. See instructions.		
2	Net profit or (loss) from Schedule C, line 31; and Schedule K-1 (Form 1065), box 14, code A (other than farming). See instructions for other income to report or if you are a minister or member of a religious order — See Statement 11	2	167,303.
3	Combine lines 1a, 1b, and 2	3	167,303.
4a	If line 3 is more than zero, multiply line 3 by 92.35% (0.9235). Otherwise, enter amount from line 3	4a	154,504.
	Note: If line 4a is less than $400 due to Conservation Reserve Program payments on line 1b, see instructions		
b	If you elect one or both of the optional methods, enter the total of lines 15 and 17 here	4b	
c	Combine lines 4a and 4b. If less than $400, **stop;** you don't owe self-employment tax. **Exception:** If less than $400 and you had **church employee income,** enter -0- and continue	4c	154,504.
5a	Enter your **church employee income** from Form W-2. See instructions for definition of church employee income	5a	
b	Multiply line 5a by 92.35% (0.9235). If less than $100, enter -0-	5b	
6	Add lines 4c and 5b	6	154,504.
7	Maximum amount of combined wages and self-employment earnings subject to social security tax or the 6.2% portion of the 7.65% railroad retirement (tier 1) tax for 2024	7	168,600
8a	Total social security wages and tips (total of boxes 3 and 7 on Form(s) W-2) and railroad retirement (tier 1) compensation. If $168,600 or more, skip lines 8b through 10, and go to line 11	8a	
b	Unreported tips subject to social security tax from Form 4137, line 10	8b	
c	Wages subject to social security tax from Form 8919, line 10	8c	
d	Add lines 8a, 8b, and 8c	8d	
9	Subtract line 8d from line 7. If zero or less, enter -0- here and on line 10 and go to line 11	9	168,600.
10	Multiply the **smaller** of line 6 or line 9 by 12.4% (0.124)	10	19,158.
11	Multiply line 6 by 2.9% (0.029)	11	4,481.
12	**Self-employment tax.** Add lines 10 and 11. Enter here and on **Schedule 2 (Form 1040), line 4, or Form 1040-SS, Part I, line 3**	12	23,639.
13	**Deduction for one-half of self-employment tax.** Multiply line 12 by 50% (0.50). Enter here and on **Schedule 1 (Form 1040), line 15**	13	11,820.

For Paperwork Reduction Act Notice, see your tax return instructions. **Schedule SE (Form 1040) 2024**

Kelsey Busby Real Estate
Schedule SE, Self-Employment Tax

If there is good news associated with the self-employment tax, it is that half of that tax paid is also a deduction. The deduction is not nearly as good as if the tax had not been paid, but the deduction for one-half of the self-employment tax does offset some of the impact of having to pay both halves of the Social Security tax. The logic here is that the employer's portion paid by companies on behalf of their employees is a valid business deduction for large corporations. Therefore, half of our self-employment tax is considered the employer-equivalent portion of that tax, and we get a deduction for that amount as detailed on Line 13 of Kelsey's Schedule SE.

As you might guess, there is still a bit more detail necessary to complete the annual tax return for Kelsey and Grady, beyond just their income and the real estate business expenses. They purchased their current home six years ago and paid $555,000, on which they currently owe $381,500 on a first mortgage with CitiMortgage. According to the IRS Form 1098 that they received from CitiMortgage, they paid $16,122.25 in mortgage interest during the year and paid $7,556.01 in property taxes, plus an allocated general sales tax amount for Plano, Texas, of $2,282.

The family health plan is with Blue Cross Blue Shield, and their monthly premiums are $787 per month, but do not include Jeremy's braces or annual physicals for the family. In addition to the health insurance premiums, the family paid $1,712 in non-covered prescription medicines and $1,797 in doctor bills and co-payments in connection with the Blue Cross medical plan. They also paid $2,709 in dental bills for the family and orthodontics bills for Jeremy's braces. They paid $540 for new glasses for Grady and a $500 deductible related to an emergency room visit for Jeremy due to an unfortunate altercation between his skateboard and the empty end of a swimming pool.

They also contributed $4,650 to various charities, including their church, the United Way, and the Boy Scouts of America. Kelsey also contributed old clothes, some furniture, and sundry items to the Salvation Army, valued at approximately $450. Based on all of these details, the Busbys' Schedule A, Itemized Deductions, will look like this:

SCHEDULE A (Form 1040)
Department of the Treasury Internal Revenue Service

Itemized Deductions

Attach to Form 1040 or 1040-SR.
Go to www.irs.gov/ScheduleA for instructions and the latest information.
Caution: If you are claiming a net qualified disaster loss on Form 4684, see the instructions for line 16.

OMB No. 1545-0074
2024
Attachment Sequence No. **07**

Name(s) shown on Form 1040 or 1040-SR	Your social security number
Grady H. & Kelsey R. Busby	546 57 9314

Section	Line	Description	Box	Amount	Box	Total
Medical and Dental Expenses		**Caution:** Do not include expenses reimbursed or paid by others.				
	1	Medical and dental expenses (see instructions)	1			
	2	Enter amount from Form 1040 or 1040-SR, line 11 [2]				
	3	Multiply line 2 by 7.5% (0.075)	3			
	4	Subtract line 3 from line 1. If line 3 is more than line 1, enter -0-			4	
Taxes You Paid	5	State and local taxes.				
	a	State and local income taxes or general sales taxes. You may include either income taxes or general sales taxes on line 5a, but not both. If you elect to include general sales taxes instead of income taxes, check this box See Statement 8 [X]	5a	2,282.		
	b	State and local real estate taxes (see instructions)	5b	7,556.		
	c	State and local personal property taxes	5c			
	d	Add lines 5a through 5c	5d	9,838.		
	e	Enter the smaller of line 5d or $10,000 ($5,000 if married filing separately)	5e	9,838.		
	6	Other taxes. List type and amount:	6			
	7	Add lines 5e and 6			7	9,838.
Interest You Paid Caution: Your mortgage interest deduction may be limited. See instructions.	8	Home mortgage interest and points. If you didn't use all of your home mortgage loan(s) to buy, build, or improve your home, see instructions and check this box [ ]				
	a	Home mortgage interest and points reported to you on Form 1098. See instructions if limited	8a	16,122.		
	b	Home mortgage interest not reported to you on Form 1098. See instructions if limited. If paid to the person from whom you bought the home, see instructions and show that person's name, identifying no., and address	8b			
	c	Points not reported to you on Form 1098. See instructions for special rules	8c			
	d	Reserved for future use	8d			
	e	Add lines 8a through 8c	8e	16,122.		
	9	Investment interest. Attach Form 4952 if required. See instructions	9			
	10	Add lines 8e and 9			10	16,122.
Gifts to Charity Caution: If you made a gift and got a benefit for it, see instructions.	11	Gifts by cash or check. If you made any gift of $250 or more, see instructions	11	5,100.		Stmt 7
	12	Other than by cash or check. If you made any gift of $250 or more, see instructions. You **must** attach Form 8283 if over $500	12			
	13	Carryover from prior year	13			
	14	Add lines 11 through 13			14	5,100.
Casualty and Theft Losses	15	Casualty and theft loss(es) from a federally declared disaster (other than net qualified disaster losses). Attach Form 4684 and enter the amount from line 18 of that form. See instructions			15	
Other Itemized Deductions	16	Other - from list in instructions. List type and amount:			16	
Total Itemized Deductions	17	Add the amounts in the far right column for lines 4 through 16. Also, enter this amount on Form 1040 or 1040-SR, line 12			17	31,060.
	18	If you elect to itemize deductions even though they are less than your standard deduction, check this box [ ]				

LHA **For Paperwork Reduction Act Notice, see the Instructions for Form 1040.** 419501 12-08-24 **Schedule A (Form 1040) 2024**

Grady and Kelsey Busby
Schedule A, Itemized Deductions

Almost there! Just a few more numbers, and we will have the details we need to complete the full tax return. Grady has a small IRA account that he has contributed to for several years, which has a balance of about $46,000 as of the end of the year. Kelsey had contributed to a 401(k) plan while she was at the mortgage company and has about the same amount in her subsequent rollover IRA account. Both of them recognize that they are way behind on retirement planning, and it has become a source of concern lately.

They have a small amount of cash saved, mainly from an inheritance received when Kelsey's grandmother passed away several years ago. It is currently invested in government securities and mutual funds at Charles Schwab. They received $122 in interest income for the year from Chase Bank and received $312 in dividends from the Charles Schwab account, of which $156 were qualified dividends. The Charles Schwab year-end tax statement also showed $81 in capital gain distributions. Their total interest and dividend income would be reported on IRS Schedule B, Interest and Ordinary Dividends.

In addition to all of this information, Kelsey met with her CPA early during the year for tax planning. The CPA convinced her that, in addition to federal income tax, self-employment tax, and all of the business expenses that she will be expected to cover, she should also make quarterly estimated tax payments based on her planned business income. Based on her planned closings and her goals for the business, the CPA helped her calculate quarterly payments to avoid any potential IRS penalties and interest for underpayment of tax. Therefore, each quarter, Kelsey sent an estimated tax payment to the IRS for $9,500, totaling $38,000 for the year.

Okay! Finally! After all of that, we finally have enough detail to finish their return. Along with names, addresses, and Social Security numbers, dependents, child tax credits, making work pay credits, and so much more, we finally have enough to make the IRS happy. Despite rumors of a paperless society, we still have to provide the IRS with a stack of paper each year. The completed Form 1040, pages one and two, are now ready to review.

Form 1040 Department of the Treasury - Internal Revenue Service
U.S. Individual Income Tax Return **2024** OMB No. 1545-0074 IRS Use Only - Do not write or staple in this space.

For the year Jan. 1 - Dec. 31, 2024, or other tax year beginning ______ ending ______ See separate instructions.

Your first name and middle initial	Last name	Your social security number
Grady H.	Busby	546 57 9314
If joint return, spouse's first name and middle initial	Last name	Spouse's social security number
Kelsey R.	Busby	464 22 1784

Home address (number and street). If you have a P.O. box, see instructions. Apt. no.
30603 Lotus Ave

City, town, or post office. If you have a foreign address, also complete spaces below. State ZIP code
Plano TX 75075

Foreign country name | Foreign province/state/county | Foreign postal code

Presidential Election Campaign Check here if you, or your spouse if filing jointly, want $3 to go to this fund. Checking a box below will not change your tax or refund. ☐ You ☐ Spouse

Filing Status Check only one box.
☐ Single
☒ Married filing jointly (even if only one had income)
☐ Married filing separately (MFS)
☐ Head of household (HOH)
☐ Qualifying surviving spouse (QSS)
If you checked the MFS box, enter the name of your spouse. If you checked the HOH or QSS box, enter the child's name if the qualifying person is a child but not your dependent:
☐ If treating a nonresident alien or dual-status alien spouse as a U.S. resident for the entire tax year, check the box and enter their name (see instructions and attach statement if required):

Digital Assets At any time during 2024, did you: (a) receive (as a reward, award, or payment for property or services); or (b) sell, exchange, or otherwise dispose of a digital asset (or a financial interest in a digital asset)? (See instructions.) ☐ Yes ☒ No

Standard Deduction Someone can claim: ☐ You as a dependent ☐ Your spouse as a dependent
☐ Spouse itemizes on a separate return or you were a dual-status alien

Age/Blindness You: ☐ Were born before January 2, 1960 ☐ Are blind **Spouse:** ☐ Was born before January 2, 1960 ☐ Is blind

Dependents (see instructions): If more than four dependents, see instr. and check here ☐

(1) First name Last name	(2) Social security number	(3) Relationship to you	(4) Child tax credit	(4) Credit for other dependents
Samantha Busby	457-27-3901	Daughter	☒	☐
Jeremy Busby	457-27-9827	Son	☒	☐
			☐	☐
			☐	☐

Income
Attach Form(s) W-2 here. Also attach Forms W-2G and 1099-R if tax was withheld.
If you did not get a Form W-2, see instructions.

1a	Total amount from Form(s) W-2, box 1 (see instructions) Stmt 2	1a	127,232.
b	Household employee wages not reported on Form(s) W-2	1b	
c	Tip income not reported on line 1a (see instructions)	1c	
d	Medicaid waiver payments not reported on Form(s) W-2 (see instructions)	1d	
e	Taxable dependent care benefits from Form 2441, line 26	1e	
f	Employer-provided adoption benefits from Form 8839, line 29	1f	
g	Wages from Form 8919, line 6	1g	
h	Other earned income (see instructions)	1h	
i	Nontaxable combat pay election (see instructions) 1i		
z	Add lines 1a through 1h	1z	127,232.
2a	Tax-exempt interest 2a ___ b Taxable interest	2b	122.
3a	Qualified dividends 3a 156. b Ordinary dividends	3b	312.
4a	IRA distributions 4a ___ b Taxable amount	4b	
5a	Pensions and annuities 5a ___ b Taxable amount	5b	
6a	Social security benefits 6a ___ b Taxable amount	6b	
c	If you elect to use the lump-sum election method, check here (see instructions) ☐		
7	Capital gain or (loss). Attach Schedule D if required. If not required, check here ☒	7	81.
8	Additional income from Schedule 1, line 10	8	167,303.
9	Add lines 1z, 2b, 3b, 4b, 5b, 6b, 7, and 8. This is your **total income**	9	295,050.
10	Adjustments to income from Schedule 1, line 26	10	21,264.
11	Subtract line 10 from line 9. This is your **adjusted gross income**	11	273,786.
12	**Standard deduction or itemized deductions** (from Schedule A)	12	31,060.
13	Qualified business income deduction from Form 8995 or Form 8995-A	13	29,208.
14	Add lines 12 and 13	14	60,268.
15	Subtract line 14 from line 11. If zero or less, enter -0-. This is your **taxable income**	15	213,518.

Attach Sch. B if required.

Standard Deduction for -
- Single or Married filing separately, $14,600
- Married filing jointly or Qualifying surviving spouse, $29,200
- Head of household, $21,900
- If you checked any box under Standard Deduction, see instructions

For Disclosure, Privacy Act, and Paperwork Reduction Act Notice, see separate instructions. Form **1040** (2024)
LHA 413921 12-30-24

Grady and Kelsey Busby.
Form 1040, U.S. Individual Income Tax Return, Page One

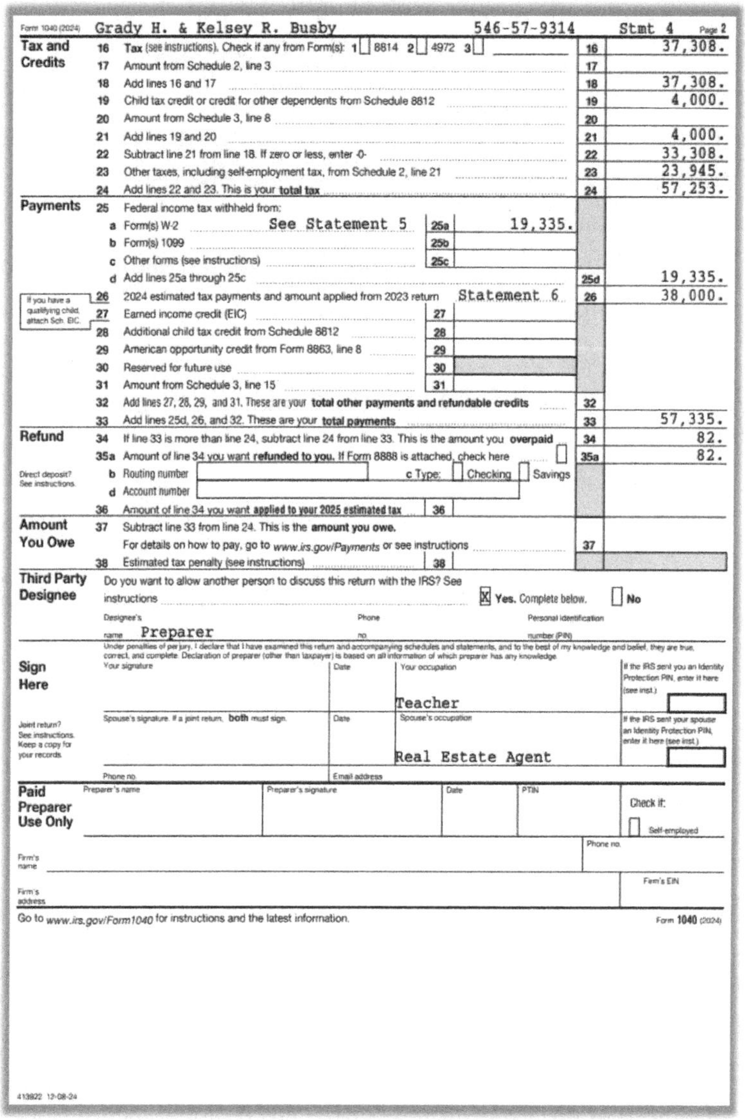

Form 1040 (2024) Grady H. & Kelsey R. Busby 546-57-9314 Stmt 4 Page 2

Section	Line	Description	Box	Amount	Line	Amount
Tax and Credits	16	Tax (see instructions). Check if any from Form(s): 1 ☐ 8814 2 ☐ 4972 3 ☐			16	37,308.
	17	Amount from Schedule 2, line 3			17	
	18	Add lines 16 and 17			18	37,308.
	19	Child tax credit or credit for other dependents from Schedule 8812			19	4,000.
	20	Amount from Schedule 3, line 8			20	
	21	Add lines 19 and 20			21	4,000.
	22	Subtract line 21 from line 18. If zero or less, enter -0-			22	33,308.
	23	Other taxes, including self-employment tax, from Schedule 2, line 21			23	23,945.
	24	Add lines 22 and 23. This is your **total tax**			24	57,253.
Payments	25	Federal income tax withheld from:				
	a	Form(s) W-2 See Statement 5	25a	19,335.		
	b	Form(s) 1099	25b			
	c	Other forms (see instructions)	25c			
	d	Add lines 25a through 25c			25d	19,335.
If you have a qualifying child, attach Sch. EIC.	26	2024 estimated tax payments and amount applied from 2023 return Statement 6			26	38,000.
	27	Earned income credit (EIC)	27			
	28	Additional child tax credit from Schedule 8812	28			
	29	American opportunity credit from Form 8863, line 8	29			
	30	Reserved for future use	30			
	31	Amount from Schedule 3, line 15	31			
	32	Add lines 27, 28, 29, and 31. These are your **total other payments and refundable credits**			32	
	33	Add lines 25d, 26, and 32. These are your **total payments**			33	57,335.
Refund	34	If line 33 is more than line 24, subtract line 24 from line 33. This is the amount you **overpaid**			34	82.
	35a	Amount of line 34 you want **refunded to you.** If Form 8888 is attached, check here ☐			35a	82.
Direct deposit? See instructions.	b	Routing number c Type: ☐ Checking ☐ Savings				
	d	Account number				
	36	Amount of line 34 you want **applied to your 2025 estimated tax**	36			
Amount You Owe	37	Subtract line 33 from line 24. This is the **amount you owe.** For details on how to pay, go to *www.irs.gov/Payments* or see instructions			37	
	38	Estimated tax penalty (see instructions)	38			

Third Party Designee Do you want to allow another person to discuss this return with the IRS? See instructions ☒ **Yes.** Complete below. ☐ **No**

Designee's name Preparer Phone no. Personal identification number (PIN)

Sign Here Under penalties of perjury, I declare that I have examined this return and accompanying schedules and statements, and to the best of my knowledge and belief, they are true, correct, and complete. Declaration of preparer (other than taxpayer) is based on all information of which preparer has any knowledge.

Your signature | Date | Your occupation: Teacher | If the IRS sent you an Identity Protection PIN, enter it here (see inst.)

Joint return? See instructions. Keep a copy for your records.

Spouse's signature. If a joint return, **both** must sign. | Date | Spouse's occupation: Real Estate Agent | If the IRS sent your spouse an Identity Protection PIN, enter it here (see inst.)

Phone no. | Email address

Paid Preparer Use Only Preparer's name | Preparer's signature | Date | PTIN | Check if: ☐ Self-employed

Firm's name | Phone no.

Firm's address | Firm's EIN

Go to *www.irs.gov/Form1040* for instructions and the latest information. Form **1040** (2024)

413922 12-08-24

Grady and Kelsey Busby

Form 1040, U.S. Individual Income Tax Return, Page Two

Whew! That is a lot of detail, but then again, this is a full federal income tax return. Nobody ever said that it was going to be easy, but let me point out a few key numbers. The Busbys' tax return worked out very well for them, which, for most of us, isn't usually the way that it works out each April 15th. After lots of number crunching, they ended up with a small refund totaling $82, as you can see below. This wasn't an accident but was based on good tax planning and Kelsey's commitment to making her quarterly estimated tax payments when they were due. Even though the tax return worked out about even, making Grady and Kelsey very happy, the family still paid over $57,000 in taxes to Uncle Sam, including over $23,500 in self-employment tax.

Form 1040 (2024)	Grady H. & Kelsey R. Busby	546-57-9314	Stmt 4		Page 2
Tax and Credits	16 Tax (see instructions). Check if any from Form(s): 1 ☐ 8814 2 ☐ 4972 3 ☐			16	37,308.
	17 Amount from Schedule 2, line 3			17	
	18 Add lines 16 and 17			18	37,308.
	19 Child tax credit or credit for other dependents from Schedule 8812			19	4,000.
	20 Amount from Schedule 3, line 8			20	
	21 Add lines 19 and 20			21	4,000.
	22 Subtract line 21 from line 18. If zero or less, enter -0-			22	33,308.
	23 Other taxes, including self-employment tax, from Schedule 2, line 21			23	23,945.
	24 Add lines 22 and 23. This is your **total tax**			24	57,253.
Payments	25 Federal income tax withheld from:				
	a Form(s) W-2	See Statement 5	25a 19,335.		
	b Form(s) 1099		25b		
	c Other forms (see instructions)		25c		
	d Add lines 25a through 25c			25d	19,335.
If you have a qualifying child, attach Sch. EIC.	26 2024 estimated tax payments and amount applied from 2023 return	Statement 6		26	38,000.
	27 Earned income credit (EIC)		27		
	28 Additional child tax credit from Schedule 8812		28		
	29 American opportunity credit from Form 8863, line 8		29		
	30 Reserved for future use		30		
	31 Amount from Schedule 3, line 15		31		
	32 Add lines 27, 28, 29, and 31. These are your **total other payments and refundable credits**			32	
	33 Add lines 25d, 26, and 32. These are your **total payments**			33	57,335.
Refund	34 If line 33 is more than line 24, subtract line 24 from line 33. This is the amount you **overpaid**			34	82.
	35a Amount of line 34 you want **refunded to you.** If Form 8888 is attached, check here ☐			35a	82.

The goal of this book is to reduce that amount. Pure and simple, I want to help you pay less in tax. So now, let's create a job. In fact, that is exactly what Kelsey did at the first of the year for her daughter Samantha. She did everything that she was supposed to do, including obtaining an Employer Identification Number and developing a job description. She formalized the work that Samantha was already doing to help in the business. Samantha completed time cards for the hours she worked, about twelve hours per week, and Kelsey paid her $25.00 per hour. At the end of the year, the total of the payments was $15,000, of which a majority was transferred to Samantha's college savings account. Don't forget, this was money that Kelsey and Grady were transferring to that college account anyway. They were already spending this money out of their overall family budget. Now the amounts they pay are more formal and considered wages instead of simply an allowance or a college savings deposit. Let's go back to the actual tax return to see exactly what that means.

Remember the Schedule C, Profit or Loss from Business for Kelsey's real estate business from page 141? Note Line 26, Wages, was blank since Kelsey had no employees and therefore no wages.

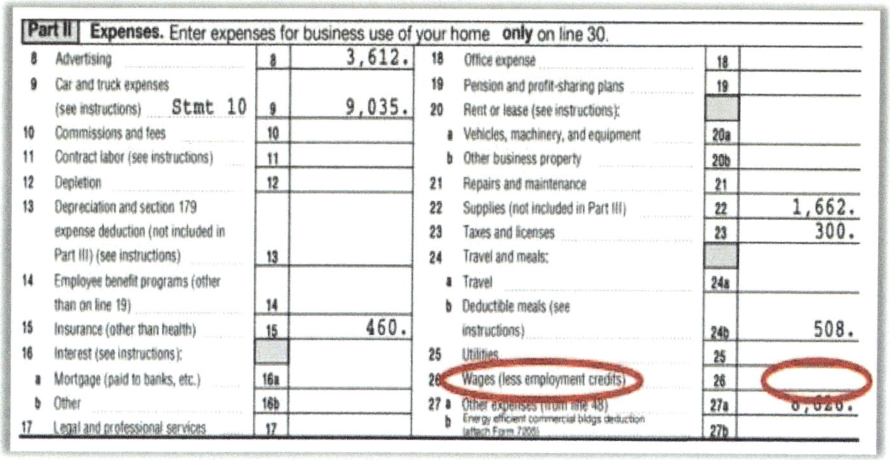

Part II Expenses. Enter expenses for business use of your home **only** on line 30.

8 Advertising	8	3,612.	18 Office expense	18	
9 Car and truck expenses (see instructions) Stmt 10	9	9,035.	19 Pension and profit-sharing plans	19	
			20 Rent or lease (see instructions):		
10 Commissions and fees	10		a Vehicles, machinery, and equipment	20a	
11 Contract labor (see instructions)	11		b Other business property	20b	
12 Depletion	12		21 Repairs and maintenance	21	
13 Depreciation and section 179 expense deduction (not included in Part III) (see instructions)	13		22 Supplies (not included in Part III)	22	1,662.
			23 Taxes and licenses	23	300.
			24 Travel and meals:		
14 Employee benefit programs (other than on line 19)	14		a Travel	24a	
15 Insurance (other than health)	15	460.	b Deductible meals (see instructions)	24b	508.
16 Interest (see instructions):			25 Utilities	25	
a Mortgage (paid to banks, etc.)	16a		26 Wages (less employment credits)	26	
b Other	16b		27 a Other expenses (from line 48)	27a	[illegible]
17 Legal and professional services	17		b Energy efficient commercial bldgs deduction (attach Form 7205)	27b	

By following the steps in this book and creating a job for Samantha, Kelsey's business now has a full tax deduction for the $15,000 she paid in wages for amounts that formerly were personal expenses and completely non-deductible. Note below the same section of Schedule C but with the new amount on line 26 for wages.

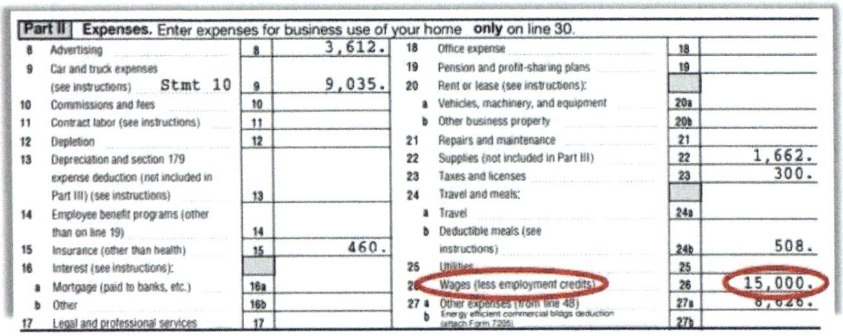

Part II **Expenses.** Enter expenses for business use of your home **only** on line 30.

Line	Description	Box	Amount	Line	Description	Box	Amount
8	Advertising	8	3,612.	18	Office expense	18	
9	Car and truck expenses (see instructions) Stmt 10	9	9,035.	19	Pension and profit-sharing plans	19	
10	Commissions and fees	10		20	Rent or lease (see instructions):		
11	Contract labor (see instructions)	11		a	Vehicles, machinery, and equipment	20a	
12	Depletion	12		b	Other business property	20b	
13	Depreciation and section 179 expense deduction (not included in Part III) (see instructions)	13		21	Repairs and maintenance	21	
14	Employee benefit programs (other than on line 19)	14		22	Supplies (not included in Part III)	22	1,662.
15	Insurance (other than health)	15	460.	23	Taxes and licenses	23	300.
16	Interest (see instructions):			24	Travel and meals:		
a	Mortgage (paid to banks, etc.)	16a		a	Travel	24a	
b	Other	16b		b	Deductible meals (see instructions)	24b	508.
17	Legal and professional services	17		25	Utilities	25	
				26	Wages (less employment credits)	26	15,000.
				27 a	Other expenses (from line 48)	27a	[illegible]
				b	Energy efficient commercial bldgs deduction (attach Form 7205)	27b	

The $15,000 deduction for wages generates a new Schedule C for Kelsey Busby Real Estate as follows:

SCHEDULE C (Form 1040)
Department of the Treasury Internal Revenue Service

Profit or Loss From Business

(Sole Proprietorship)

Attach to Form 1040, 1040-SR, 1040-SS, 1040-NR, or 1041; partnerships must generally file Form 1065.
Go to www.irs.gov/ScheduleC for instructions and the latest information.

OMB No. 1545-0074
2024
Attachment Sequence No. 09

Name of proprietor: Kelsey R. Busby
Social security number (SSN): 464-22-1784

A Principal business or profession, including product or service (see instructions): Residential Real Estate Sales
B Enter code from instructions: 531210

C Business name. If no separate business name, leave blank.: Kelsey Busby Real Estate
D Employer ID number (EIN) (see instr.): 27-1234567

E Business address (including suite or room no.): 30603 Lotus Ave
City, town or post office, state, and ZIP code: Plano, TX 75075

F Accounting method: (1) [X] Cash (2) [ ] Accrual (3) [ ] Other (specify)

G Did you "materially participate" in the operation of this business during 2024? If "No," see instructions for limit on losses [X] Yes [ ] No

H If you started or acquired this business during 2024, check here [ ]

I Did you make any payments in 2024 that would require you to file Form(s) 1099? See instructions [ ] Yes [ ] No

J If "Yes," did you or will you file required Form(s) 1099? [ ] Yes [ ] No

Part I Income

		Line	Amount
1	Gross receipts or sales. See instructions for line 1 and check the box if this income was reported to you on Form W-2 and the "Statutory employee" box on that form was checked [ ]	1	191,506.
2	Returns and allowances	2	
3	Subtract line 2 from line 1	3	191,506.
4	Cost of goods sold (from line 42)	4	
5	**Gross profit.** Subtract line 4 from line 3	5	191,506.
6	Other income, including federal and state gasoline or fuel tax credit or refund (see instructions)	6	
7	**Gross income.** Add lines 5 and 6	7	191,506.

Part II Expenses. Enter expenses for business use of your home **only** on line 30.

		Line	Amount			Line	Amount
8	Advertising	8	3,612.	18	Office expense	18	
9	Car and truck expenses (see instructions) Stmt 10	9	9,035.	19	Pension and profit-sharing plans	19	
10	Commissions and fees	10		20	Rent or lease (see instructions):		
11	Contract labor (see instructions)	11		a	Vehicles, machinery, and equipment	20a	
12	Depletion	12		b	Other business property	20b	
13	Depreciation and section 179 expense deduction (not included in Part III) (see instructions)	13		21	Repairs and maintenance	21	
14	Employee benefit programs (other than on line 19)	14		22	Supplies (not included in Part III)	22	1,662.
15	Insurance (other than health)	15	460.	23	Taxes and licenses	23	300.
16	Interest (see instructions):			24	Travel and meals:		
a	Mortgage (paid to banks, etc.)	16a		a	Travel	24a	
b	Other	16b		b	Deductible meals (see instructions)	24b	508.
17	Legal and professional services	17		25	Utilities	25	
				26	Wages (less employment credits)	26	15,000.
				27 a	Other expenses (from line 48)	27a	8,626.
				b	Energy efficient commercial bldgs deduction (attach Form 7205)	27b	

		Line	Amount
28	**Total expenses** before expenses for business use of home. Add lines 8 through 27b	28	39,203.
29	Tentative profit or (loss). Subtract line 28 from line 7	29	152,303.
30	Expenses for business use of your home. Do not report these expenses elsewhere. Attach Form 8829 unless using the simplified method. See instructions. **Simplified method filers only:** Enter the total square footage of (a) your home: ____ and (b) the part of your home used for business: ____ . Use the Simplified Method Worksheet in the instructions to figure the amount to enter on line 30	30	
31	**Net profit or (loss).** Subtract line 30 from line 29. • If a profit, enter on both **Schedule 1 (Form 1040), line 3,** and on **Schedule SE, line 2.** (If you checked the box on line 1, see instructions). Estates and trusts, enter on **Form 1041, line 3.** • If a loss, you **must** go to line 32.	31	152,303.
32	If you have a loss, check the box that describes your investment in this activity. See instructions. • If you checked 32a, enter the loss on both **Schedule 1 (Form 1040), line 3,** and on **Schedule SE, line 2.** (If you checked the box on line 1, see the line 31 instructions.) Estates and trusts, enter on **Form 1041, line 3.** • If you checked 32b, you **must** attach **Form 6198.** Your loss may be limited.	32a [ ] All investment is at risk. 32b [ ] Some investment is not at risk.	

For Paperwork Reduction Act Notice, see the separate instructions. **Schedule C (Form 1040) 2024**
LHA 420001 10-29-24

The only difference between the original income tax return and the new tax return is the entry on Line 26. The new tax return:

Form **1040** Department of the Treasury - Internal Revenue Service
U.S. Individual Income Tax Return **2024** OMB No. 1545-0074 IRS Use Only - Do not write or staple in this space.

For the year Jan. 1 - Dec. 31, 2024, or other tax year beginning , ending See separate instructions.

Your first name and middle initial: Grady H.	Last name: Busby	Your social security number: 546 57 9314
If joint return, spouse's first name and middle initial: Kelsey R.	Last name: Busby	Spouse's social security number: 464 22 1784
Home address (number and street). If you have a P.O. box, see instructions.: 30603 Lotus Ave	Apt. no.	**Presidential Election Campaign** Check here if you, or your spouse if filing jointly, want $3 to go to this fund. Checking a box below will not change your tax or refund. ☐ You ☐ Spouse
City, town, or post office. If you have a foreign address, also complete spaces below.: Plano	State: TX ZIP code: 75075	
Foreign country name	Foreign province/state/county	Foreign postal code

Filing Status Check only one box.
☐ Single
☒ Married filing jointly (even if only one had income)
☐ Married filing separately (MFS)
☐ Head of household (HOH)
☐ Qualifying surviving spouse (QSS)
If you checked the MFS box, enter the name of your spouse. If you checked the HOH or QSS box, enter the child's name if the qualifying person is a child but not your dependent:
☐ If treating a nonresident alien or dual-status alien spouse as a U.S. resident for the entire tax year, check the box and enter their name (see instructions and attach statement if required):

Digital Assets At any time during 2024, did you: (a) receive (as a reward, award, or payment for property or services); or (b) sell, exchange, or otherwise dispose of a digital asset (or a financial interest in a digital asset)? (See instructions.) ☐ Yes ☒ No

Standard Deduction Someone can claim: ☐ You as a dependent ☐ Your spouse as a dependent
☐ Spouse itemizes on a separate return or you were a dual-status alien

Age/Blindness You: ☐ Were born before January 2, 1960 ☐ Are blind **Spouse:** ☐ Was born before January 2, 1960 ☐ Is blind

Dependents (see instructions): If more than four dependents, see instr. and check here ☐

(1) First name Last name	(2) Social security number	(3) Relationship to you	(4) Child tax credit	Credit for other dependents
Samantha Busby	457-27-3901	Daughter	☒	☐
Jeremy Busby	457-27-9827	Son	☒	☐
			☐	☐
			☐	☐

Income Attach Form(s) W-2 here. Also attach Forms W-2G and 1099-R if tax was withheld. If you did not get a Form W-2, see instructions.

1a	Total amount from Form(s) W-2, box 1 (see instructions)	Stmt 2	1a	127,232.
b	Household employee wages not reported on Form(s) W-2		1b	
c	Tip income not reported on line 1a (see instructions)		1c	
d	Medicaid waiver payments not reported on Form(s) W-2 (see instructions)		1d	
e	Taxable dependent care benefits from Form 2441, line 26		1e	
f	Employer-provided adoption benefits from Form 8839, line 29		1f	
g	Wages from Form 8919, line 6		1g	
h	Other earned income (see instructions)		1h	
i	Nontaxable combat pay election (see instructions)	1i		
z	Add lines 1a through 1h		1z	127,232.
2a	Tax-exempt interest	2a	2b Taxable interest	122.
3a	Qualified dividends	3a 156.	3b Ordinary dividends	312.
4a	IRA distributions	4a	4b Taxable amount	
5a	Pensions and annuities	5a	5b Taxable amount	
6a	Social security benefits	6a	6b Taxable amount	
c	If you elect to use the lump-sum election method, check here (see instructions) ☐			
7	Capital gain or (loss). Attach Schedule D if required. If not required, check here ☒		7	81.
8	Additional income from Schedule 1, line 10		8	152,303.
9	Add lines 1z, 2b, 3b, 4b, 5b, 6b, 7, and 8. This is your **total income**		9	280,050.
10	Adjustments to income from Schedule 1, line 26		10	20,204.
11	Subtract line 10 from line 9. This is your **adjusted gross income**		11	259,846.
12	**Standard deduction or itemized deductions** (from Schedule A)		12	31,060.
13	Qualified business income deduction from Form 8995 or Form 8995-A		13	26,420.
14	Add lines 12 and 13		14	57,480.
15	Subtract line 14 from line 11. If zero or less, enter -0-. This is your **taxable income**		15	202,366.

Attach Sch. B if required.

Standard Deduction for -
- Single or Married filing separately, $14,600
- Married filing jointly or Qualifying surviving spouse, $29,200
- Head of household, $21,900
- If you checked any box under Standard Deduction, see instructions.

For Disclosure, Privacy Act, and Paperwork Reduction Act Notice, see separate instructions. Form **1040** (2024)
LHA 413921 12-30-24

Grady and Kelsey Busby
Form 1040, U.S. Individual Income Tax Return, Page One with Samantha's Wages Included

Form 1040 (2024) Grady H. & Kelsey R. Busby 546-57-9314 Stmt 4 Page 2

Tax and Credits	16	**Tax** (see instructions). Check if any from Form(s): 1 ☐ 8814 2 ☐ 4972 3 ☐		16	34,632.
	17	Amount from Schedule 2, line 3		17	
	18	Add lines 16 and 17		18	34,632.
	19	Child tax credit or credit for other dependents from Schedule 8812		19	4,000.
	20	Amount from Schedule 3, line 8		20	
	21	Add lines 19 and 20		21	4,000.
	22	Subtract line 21 from line 18. If zero or less, enter -0-		22	30,632.
	23	Other taxes, including self-employment tax, from Schedule 2, line 21		23	21,701.
	24	Add lines 22 and 23. This is your **total tax**		24	52,333.
Payments	25	Federal income tax withheld from:			
	a	Form(s) W-2 See Statement 5	25a 19,335.		
	b	Form(s) 1099	25b		
	c	Other forms (see instructions)	25c		
	d	Add lines 25a through 25c		25d	19,335.
If you have a qualifying child, attach Sch. EIC.	26	2024 estimated tax payments and amount applied from 2023 return Statement 6		26	38,000.
	27	Earned income credit (EIC)	27		
	28	Additional child tax credit from Schedule 8812	28		
	29	American opportunity credit from Form 8863, line 8	29		
	30	Reserved for future use	30		
	31	Amount from Schedule 3, line 15	31		
	32	Add lines 27, 28, 29, and 31. These are your **total other payments and refundable credits**		32	
	33	Add lines 25d, 26, and 32. These are your **total payments**		33	57,335.
Refund	34	If line 33 is more than line 24, subtract line 24 from line 33. This is the amount you **overpaid**		34	5,002.
	35a	Amount of line 34 you want **refunded to you.** If Form 8888 is attached, check here ☐		35a	5,002.
Direct deposit? See instructions.	b	Routing number c Type: ☐ Checking ☐ Savings			
	d	Account number			
	36	Amount of line 34 you want **applied to your 2025 estimated tax**	36		
Amount You Owe	37	Subtract line 33 from line 24. This is the **amount you owe.** For details on how to pay, go to *www.irs.gov/Payments* or see instructions		37	
	38	Estimated tax penalty (see instructions)	38		

Third Party Designee Do you want to allow another person to discuss this return with the IRS? See instructions ☒ **Yes.** Complete below. ☐ **No**

Designee's name Preparer Phone no. Personal identification number (PIN)

Sign Here Under penalties of perjury, I declare that I have examined this return and accompanying schedules and statements, and to the best of my knowledge and belief, they are true, correct, and complete. Declaration of preparer (other than taxpayer) is based on all information of which preparer has any knowledge.

Your signature | Date | Your occupation: Teacher | If the IRS sent you an Identity Protection PIN, enter it here (see inst.)

Joint return? See instructions. Keep a copy for your records.

Spouse's signature. If a joint return, **both** must sign. | Date | Spouse's occupation: Real Estate Agent | If the IRS sent your spouse an Identity Protection PIN, enter it here (see inst.)

Phone no. | Email address

Paid Preparer Use Only Preparer's name | Preparer's signature | Date | PTIN | Check if: ☐ Self-employed

Firm's name | Phone no.

Firm's address | Firm's EIN

Go to *www.irs.gov/Form1040* for instructions and the latest information. Form **1040** (2024)

413922 12-08-24

Grady and Kelsey Busby

Form 1040, U.S. Individual Income Tax Return, Page Two with Samantha's Wages Included

Let's take a look at the new pages one and two of the Busbys' federal income tax return, Form 1040. Notice line 8 shows net business income of $152,303 compared to the original amount of $167,303 (see page 148). The reduction in total Adjusted Gross Income is not the full $15,000, since the deduction for one-half of the SE Tax is also lower. In addition, the qualified Business Income deduction on Line 13 is lower. Each number that is changed can affect many others, and we know nothing is ever easy with the IRS.

The bottom line: The new tax return, including Samantha's wages, shows a net tax refund for Kelsey and Grady of $5,002. Let me say that again…A net tax refund of $5,002 instead of the original $82.

This tax return is real. The numbers are real. And the savings are real. The only difference between the first return and the second return is the wages paid to Samantha for the work she was already doing. Kelsey created a job by doing everything that was asked of her in this book. She adopted a job description and paid Samantha twice a month. She did the paperwork, and she was rewarded with a significantly higher refund from the IRS.

I know there is a lot of detail in this chapter, and most of it is pure tax boredom, but the savings are real. If you file a Schedule C and have a child at home who can help in your business, there is over $5,000 waiting for you. All you have to do is ACT. Create a job just like Kelsey did, do the paperwork, pay attention to the detail, and the savings will be yours. And don't forget that you are not alone.

Appendix B
Hire Your Kid Checklist

We have been through a lot of detail and forms, and calculations, but the process is really quite easy. There are a number of hoops to jump through, but all of them are close to the ground and easy to clear. Do your best to avoid the shortcuts. The process is easy, but it is important that you fulfill each step. As we discussed in great detail in Chapter 8, it's all about the paperwork. Take things one step at a time, and you will be rewarded with significant tax savings when it is time to file your next tax return.

To summarize the process and the steps you need to accomplish, we have developed a comprehensive step-by-step to-do list. Each step includes point-by-point detail, and you can always go back to specific chapters for more information or examples. As you go through the process, check the box to make sure you have completed each step along the way.

It's a great idea to make a copy of the checklist and use it to build a file or binder to maintain a comprehensive file of all your paperwork in one place. Take your time; check the boxes, and you will be happy you did.

And don't forget that you are NOT ALONE. We are here to help in any way we can. If you have questions or if we can help in any way, just email your question to:

Info@HireYourKid.com

Congratulations on creating your new job and congratulations on keeping more of your hard-earned money.

Hire Your Kid Checklist

1. Obtain an Employer Identification Number □ Complete Form SS-4

    - Call, mail or go online at www.irs.gov
    - Make sure you indicate Form 944 on line 14
    - Record your new EIN

2. Develop a Detailed Job Description

    - Detail duties to be assigned
    - Make the duties match your child's skill set
    - Determine a reasonable wage per hour
    - Review the job description with your new employee
    - Have your new employee sign the job description
    - Include the signed copy in a new "Personnel File"

3. Hire Your New Employee

    - Verify eligibility by Completing Form I-9
    - Keep the complete I-9 in the "Personnel File"
    - Complete IRS Form W-4, and have the employee sign the form
    - Keep the signed W-4 in the "Personnel File"

4. Complete New Hire Reporting for Your State

    - Find the URL for your State's New Hire Reporting

    (See Appendix D)

    - Complete the form for each new hire within 10 days
    - Mail, fax, or file the new hire report online
    - Keep a copy of the new hire report in the "Personnel File"

Hire Your Kid Checklist

5. Prepare a Work Schedule for the New Employee □ Prepare time cards

   - Make sure total hours meet your expectations
   - Document hours worked each pay period
   - Have the new employee sign each time card
   - Keep completed and signed cards in the "Personnel File"

6. Pay your new employee

   - Calculate gross pay based on time cards
   - Determine method of payment: physical check, automatic transfer, direct deposit, cash
   - Pay the employee at the end of each pay period
   - Keep a record of payments made in the "Personnel File"

7. Prepare and file year-end paperwork
   - Complete a W-2 for each employee
   - Complete a W-3 Transmittal form for all W-2's
   - Mail W-3 and W-2 to the Social Security Administration by the last day of February, keeping copies for your files.
   - Complete Forms 944 and 940 payroll tax returns.
   - Mail Forms 944 and 940 to the IRS by January 31st, keeping copies for your files

8. Save $5,000 or more when filing your tax return
   - Include total wages on Line 26, Wages, of your Schedule C, Profit or Loss from Business
   - Reduce taxable income by $15,000 or more
   - Increase your refund by over $5,000

Appendix C
Completed Sample Forms

The Hire Your Kid Checklist included in Appendix B outlines 8 specific steps to saving over $5,000 by hiring your child, from obtaining a new Employer Identification Number to developing a formal job description to filing annual payroll tax returns. Each of these forms plays its own role in supporting your new tax deduction. The following pages include completed forms for each of these steps for Kelsey Busby and her new employee, Samantha. If you pay your child as we have outlined in this guide, your forms will be the same as those included in this Appendix. The following forms are included as a sample of completed forms for Kelsey Busby Real Estate:

Form SS-4, Application for Employer Identification Number

Formal Job Description

Form I-9, Employee Eligibility Verification

Texas New Hire Reporting Form

Sample Employee Time Cards

Completed Form W-4

Completed Form W-2 Completed Form W-3

Form 944, Employer's Annual Tax Return

Form 940, Employer's Federal Unemployment Tax Return.

Form 1040, Grady and Kelsey's Completed

Federal Income Tax Return

Form **SS-4** (Rev. December 2023) Department of the Treasury Internal Revenue Service

Application for Employer Identification Number

(For use by employers, corporations, partnerships, trusts, estates, churches, government agencies, Indian tribal entities, certain individuals, and others.)

See separate instructions for each line. Keep a copy for your records.

Go to *www.irs.gov/FormSS4* for instructions and the latest information.

OMB No. 1545-0003

EIN

Type or print clearly.

1 Legal name of entity (or individual) for whom the EIN is being requested: Kelsey Busby

2 Trade name of business (if different from name on line 1)

3 Executor, administrator, trustee, "care of" name

4a Mailing address (room, apt., suite no. and street, or P.O. box): 30603 Lotus Ave

5a Street address (if different) (Don't enter a P.O. box.)

4b City, state, and ZIP code (if foreign, see instructions): Plano, Texas 75075

5b City, state, and ZIP code (if foreign, see instructions)

6 County and state where principal business is located: Collin, Texas

7a Name of responsible party: Kelsey Busby

7b SSN, ITIN, or EIN: 464-22-1784

8a Is this application for a limited liability company (LLC) (or a foreign equivalent)? ☐ Yes ☑ No

8b If 8a is "Yes," enter the number of LLC members

8c If 8a is "Yes," was the LLC organized in the United States? ☐ Yes ☐ No

9a **Type of entity** (check only one box). **Caution:** If 8a is "Yes," see the instructions for the correct box to check.

- ☑ Sole proprietor (SSN) 464-22-1784
- ☐ Partnership
- ☐ Corporation (enter form number to be filed)
- ☐ Personal service corporation
- ☐ Church or church-controlled organization
- ☐ Other nonprofit organization (specify)
- ☐ Other (specify)
- ☐ Estate (SSN of decedent)
- ☐ Plan administrator (TIN)
- ☐ Trust (TIN of grantor)
- ☐ Military/National Guard
- ☐ State/local government
- ☐ Farmers' cooperative
- ☐ Federal government
- ☐ REMIC
- ☐ Indian tribal governments/enterprises

Group Exemption Number (GEN) if any

9b If a corporation, name the state or foreign country (if applicable) where incorporated — State — Foreign country

10 **Reason for applying** (check only one box)

- ☐ Started new business (specify type)
- ☑ Hired employees (Check the box and see line 13.)
- ☐ Compliance with IRS withholding regulations
- ☐ Other (specify)
- ☐ Banking purpose (specify purpose)
- ☐ Changed type of organization (specify new type)
- ☐ Purchased going business
- ☐ Created a trust (specify type)
- ☐ Created a pension plan (specify type)

11 Date business started or acquired (month, day, year). See instructions. June 1, 2020

12 Closing month of accounting year: December

13 Highest number of employees expected in the next 12 months (enter -0- if none). If no employees expected, skip line 14.

Agricultural	Household	Other
		1

14 If you expect your employment tax liability to be $1,000 or less in a full calendar year **and** want to file Form 944 annually instead of Forms 941 quarterly, check here. (Your employment tax liability will generally be $1,000 or less if you expect to pay $5,000 or less, $6,536 or less if you're in a U.S. territory, in total wages.) If you don't check this box, you must file Form 941 for every quarter. ☑

15 First date wages or annuities were paid (month, day, year). **Note:** If applicant is a withholding agent, enter date income will first be paid to nonresident alien (month, day, year): January 1, 2025

16 Check **one** box that best describes the principal activity of your business.

- ☐ Health care & social assistance
- ☐ Wholesale—agent/broker
- ☐ Construction
- ☐ Rental & leasing
- ☐ Transportation & warehousing
- ☐ Accommodation & food service
- ☐ Wholesale—other
- ☐ Retail
- ☑ Real estate
- ☐ Manufacturing
- ☐ Finance & insurance
- ☐ Other (specify)

17 Indicate principal line of merchandise sold, specific construction work done, products produced, or services provided. Residential Real Estate Sales

18 Has the applicant entity shown on line 1 ever applied for and received an EIN? ☐ Yes ☑ No

If "Yes," write previous EIN here

Third Party Designee

Complete this section **only** if you want to authorize the named individual to receive the entity's EIN and answer questions about the completion of this form.

Designee's name — Designee's telephone number (include area code)

Address and ZIP code — Designee's fax number (include area code)

Under penalties of perjury, I declare that I have examined this application, and to the best of my knowledge and belief, it is true, correct, and complete.

Name and title (type or print clearly) Kelsey Busby, Owner

Applicant's telephone number (include area code): 214-620-2437

Applicant's fax number (include area code)

Signature *Kelsey Busby* Date 1-1-25

For Privacy Act and Paperwork Reduction Act Notice, see separate instructions. Cat. No. 16055N Form **SS-4** (Rev. 12-2023)

Kelsey Busby Real Estate

Completed Form SS-4, Application for EIN

Kelsey Busby Real Estate Sales

Job Description

Job Title: Administrative Assistant   Reports to: Owner

Wages, Hourly: $25.00   Last Revision: January 1, 2025

SUMMARY

Provide administrative support to the company Owner and Manager. Duties include general clerical, receptionist, and project-based work. Project a professional company image through in-person and phone interaction.

PRIMARY RESPONSIBILITIES

1. Answer the telephone and transfer to the appropriate staff member.
2. Meet and greet clients and visitors as needed.
3. Create and modify documents using Microsoft Office software.
4. Perform general clerical duties to include: photocopying, faxing, mailing, and filing.
5. Maintain a hard copy and electronic filing system.
6. Sign for and distribute UPS/FedEx/Airborne packages.
7. Coordinate and maintain records for staff office space, phones, parking, etc.
8. Set up and coordinate meetings and conferences.
9. Support staff in assigned project-based work.
10. Other duties as assigned.

ADDITIONAL DUTIES

1. Maintain overall safety and cleanliness of the office.
2. Accomplish travel and delivery-related duties outside the office as necessary.

KNOWLEDGE AND SKILL REQUIREMENTS

1. Basic reading, writing, and arithmetic skills required.
2. Knowledge of Microsoft Office and telephone protocol.

WORKING CONDITIONS

1. Working conditions are normal for an office environment.
2. No hazardous duties will be assigned.

__________________________   ____________________

Employee Signature   Date

Employment Eligibility Verification
Department of Homeland Security
U.S. Citizenship and Immigration Services

USCIS
Form I-9
OMB No.1615-0047
Expires 05/31/2027

START HERE: Employers must ensure the form instructions are available to employees when completing this form. Employers are liable for failing to comply with the requirements for completing this form. See below and the Instructions.

ANTI-DISCRIMINATION NOTICE: All employees can choose which acceptable documentation to present for Form I-9. Employers cannot ask employees for documentation to verify information in **Section 1**, or specify which acceptable documentation employees must present for **Section 2** or Supplement B, Reverification and Rehire. Treating employees differently based on their citizenship, immigration status, or national origin may be illegal.

Section 1. Employee Information and Attestation: Employees must complete and sign Section 1 of Form I-9 no later than the **first day of employment**, but not before accepting a job offer.

Last Name (Family Name)	First Name (Given Name)	Middle Initial (if any)	Other Last Names Used (if any)
Busby	Samantha	R	

Address (Street Number and Name)	Apt. Number (if any)	City or Town	State	ZIP Code
30603 Lotus Ave		Plano	TX	75075

Date of Birth (mm/dd/yyyy)	U.S. Social Security Number	Employee's Email Address	Employee's Telephone Number
07/26/2008	4 5 7 2 7 3 9 0 1	Sammy.Busby@gmail.com	(214) 620-2437

I am aware that federal law provides for imprisonment and/or fines for false statements, or the use of false documents, in connection with the completion of this form. I attest, under penalty of perjury, that this information, including my selection of the box attesting to my citizenship or immigration status, is true and correct.

Check one of the following boxes to attest to your citizenship or immigration status (See page 2 and 3 of the instructions.):

- [X] 1. A citizen of the United States
- [ ] 2. A noncitizen national of the United States (See Instructions.)
- [ ] 3. A lawful permanent resident (Enter USCIS or A-Number.)
- [ ] 4. An alien authorized to work until (exp. date, if any)

If you check **Item Number 4.**, enter one of these:

USCIS A-Number	OR	Form I-94 Admission Number	OR	Foreign Passport Number and Country of Issuance

Signature of Employee	Today's Date (mm/dd/yyyy)
Samantha Busby	01/01/2025

If a preparer and/or translator assisted you in completing Section 1, that person MUST complete the Preparer and/or Translator Certification on Page 3.

Section 2. Employer Review and Verification: Employers or their authorized representative must complete and sign **Section 2** within three business days after the employee's first day of employment, and must physically examine, or examine consistent with an alternative procedure authorized by the Secretary of DHS, documentation from List A OR a combination of documentation from List B and List C. Enter any additional documentation in the Additional Information box; see Instructions.

	List A	OR	List B	AND	List C
Document Title 1			Minor Under Age 18		Social Security Card
Issuing Authority			Hospital Records		
Document Number (if any)					
Expiration Date (if any)					
Document Title 2 (if any)			**Additional Information**		
Issuing Authority					
Document Number (if any)					
Expiration Date (if any)					
Document Title 3 (if any)					
Issuing Authority					
Document Number (if any)					
Expiration Date (if any)			[ ] Check here if you used an alternative procedure authorized by DHS to examine documents.		

Certification: I attest, under penalty of perjury, that (1) I have examined the documentation presented by the above-named employee, (2) the above-listed documentation appears to be genuine and to relate to the employee named, and (3) to the best of my knowledge, the employee is authorized to work in the United States.

First Day of Employment (mm/dd/yyyy):

Last Name, First Name and Title of Employer or Authorized Representative	Signature of Employer or Authorized Representative	Today's Date (mm/dd/yyyy)
Busby, Kelsey - Owner	*Kelsey Busby*	01/01/2025

Employer's Business or Organization Name	Employer's Business or Organization Address, City or Town, State, ZIP Code
Kelsey Busby Real Estate	30603 Lotus Ave, Plano, Texas 75075

For reverification or rehire, complete Supplement B, Reverification and Rehire on Page 4.

Form I-9 Edition 01/20/25

Page 1 of 4

Kelsey Busby Real Estate – Samantha Busby
Completed Form I-9

Texas Employer New Hire Reporting Form

Submit within 20 calendar days of new employee's first day of work to:
Central File Maintenance
P.O. Box 12048
Austin, TX 78711-2048
Phone: 1-800-850-6442 FAX: 1-800-732-5015
Online: www.employer.oag.texas.gov

To ensure the highest level of accuracy, please print neatly in capital letters and avoid contact with the edges of the boxes. The following will serve as an example:

A B C   1 2 3

Employer Information

1. Federal Employer ID Number (FEIN): *Please use the same FEIN that appears on quarterly wage reports*
   2 7 1 2 3 4 5 6 7
2. State Employer ID Number (Optional):
3. Employer Name: KELSEY BUSBY REAL ESTATE
4. Employer Address (Please indicate the address where the Income Withholding Orders should be sent): 30603 LOTUS AVE
5. Employer City (if US): PLANO
6. State (if US): TX
7. ZIP Code (if US): 75075 -
8. Province/Region (if foreign):
9. Country (if foreign):
10. Postal Code (if foreign):
11. Employer Telephone (Optional): 2 1 4 6 2 0 2 4 3 7
12. Employer FAX (Optional):
13. New Hire Contact Person (Optional): KELSEY BUSBY

Employee Information

14. Social Security Number (SSN): 4 5 7 2 7 3 9 0 1
15. Date of Hire (MM/DD/YYYY): 01 01 2025
16. Employee First Name: SAMANTHA
17. Employee Middle Name: RENEE
18. Employee Last Name: BUSBY
19. Employee Home Address: 30603 LOTUS AVE
20. Employee City (if US): PLANO
21. State (if US): TX
22. ZIP Code (if US): 75075 -
23. Province/Region (if foreign):
24. Country (if foreign):
25. Postal Code (if foreign):
26. State Where Employee Was Hired (Optional): TX
27. Employee DOB (MM/DD/YYYY) (Optional): 07 26 2008
28. Employee's Salary (Dollars and Cents) (Optional): 25.00
29. Salary Frequency (Check One ONLY) (Optional):
   [X] Hourly [ ] Weekly [ ] Biweekly [ ] Semi-Monthly [ ] Monthly [ ] Annually

REV 05/23   ENHR RPT FORM

Kelsey Busby Real Estate
Completed Texas New Hire Form

Kelsey Busby Real Estate **Pay Period # 1 January 1 - January 15, 2025**

Time Card

Position: **Administrative Assistant** Employee: **Samantha Busby**

	Wed 1-Jan	Thu 2-Jan	Fri 3-Jan	Sat 4-Jan	Sun 5-Jan	Mon 6-Jan	Tue 7-Jan	Wed 8-Jan	Thu 9-Jan	Fri 10-Jan	Sat 11-Jan	Sun 12-Jan	Mon 13-Jan	Tue 14-Jan	Wed 15-Jan
Hours Worked		3	1	3	3		3		4		3	2		3	
Overtime Hours															
Total Hours	0	3	1	3	3	0	3	0	4	0	3	2	0	3	0

Total Hours - Pay Period #15 25.00

Samantha Busby 1/15/25

Employee Signature Date

Kelsey Busby Real Estate **Pay Period # 2 January 16 - January 31, 2025**

Time Card

Position: **Administrative Assistant** Employee: **Samantha Busby**

	Thu 16-Jan	Fri 17-Jan	Sat 18-Jan	Sun 19-Jan	Mon 20-Jan	Tue 21-Jan	Wed 22-Jan	Thu 23-Jan	Fri 24-Jan	Sat 25-Jan	Sun 26-Jan	Mon 27-Jan	Tue 28-Jan	Wed 29-Jan	Thu 30-Jan	Fri 31-Jan
Hours Worked	2	1	3	2		2		3	2	3	2	0	2		2	1
Overtime Hours																
Total Hours	2	1	3	2	0	2	0	3	2	3	2	0	2	0	2	1

Total Hours - Pay Period #15 25.00

Samantha Busby 1/31/25

Employee Signature Date

Kelsey Busby Real Estate **Pay Period # 3 February - February 15, 2025**

Time Card

Position: **Administrative Assistant** Employee: **Samantha Busby**

	Sat 1-Feb	Sun 2-Feb	Mon 3-Feb	Tue 4-Feb	Wed 5-Feb	Thu 6-Feb	Fri 7-Feb	Sat 8-Feb	Sun 9-Feb	Mon 10-Feb	Tue 11-Feb	Wed 12-Feb	Thu 13-Feb	Fri 14-Feb	Sat 15-Feb
Hours Worked	1	4		2		3		3	4		2		2		4
Overtime Hours															
Total Hours	1	4	0	2	0	3	0	3	4	0	2	0	2	0	4

Total Hours - Pay Period #15 25.00

Samantha Busby 2/15/25

Employee Signature Date

Kelsey Busby Real Estate **Pay Period # 4 February 16 - February 28, 2025**

Time Card

Position: **Administrative Assistant** Employee: **Samantha Busby**

	Sun 16-Feb	Mon 17-Feb	Tue 18-Feb	Wed 19-Feb	Thu 20-Feb	Fri 21-Feb	Sat 22-Feb	Sun 23-Feb	Mon 24-Feb	Tue 25-Feb	Wed 26-Feb	Thu 27-Feb	Fri 28-Feb
Hours Worked	4		3		3	1	4	3		2		3	2
Overtime Hours													
Total Hours	4	0	3	0	3	1	4	3	0	2	0	3	2

Total Hours - Pay Period #15 25.00

Samantha Busby 2/28/25

Employee Signature Date

Kelsey Busby Real Estate
Sample Employee Time Cards

Form **W-4**

Department of the Treasury
Internal Revenue Service

Employee's Withholding Certificate

Complete Form W-4 so that your employer can withhold the correct federal income tax from your pay.
Give Form W-4 to your employer.
Your withholding is subject to review by the IRS.

OMB No. 1545-0074

2025

Step 1: Enter Personal Information

(a) First name and middle initial	Last name	(b) Social security number
Samantha R	Busby	457-27-3901

Address: 30603 Lotus Ave

City or town, state, and ZIP code: Plano, Texas 75075

Does your name match the name on your social security card? If not, to ensure you get credit for your earnings, contact SSA at 800-772-1213 or go to *www.ssa.gov.*

(c)
- [x] **Single** or **Married filing separately**
- [ ] **Married filing jointly** or **Qualifying surviving spouse**
- [ ] **Head of household** (Check only if you're unmarried and pay more than half the costs of keeping up a home for yourself and a qualifying individual.)

TIP: Consider using the estimator at *www.irs.gov/W4App* to determine the most accurate withholding for the rest of the year if: you are completing this form after the beginning of the year; expect to work only part of the year; or have changes during the year in your marital status, number of jobs for you (and/or your spouse if married filing jointly), dependents, other income (not from jobs), deductions, or credits. Have your most recent pay stub(s) from this year available when using the estimator. At the beginning of next year, use the estimator again to recheck your withholding.

Complete Steps 2–4 ONLY if they apply to you; otherwise, skip to Step 5. See page 2 for more information on each step, who can claim exemption from withholding, and when to use the estimator at *www.irs.gov/W4App.*

Step 2: Multiple Jobs or Spouse Works

Complete this step if you (1) hold more than one job at a time, or (2) are married filing jointly and your spouse also works. The correct amount of withholding depends on income earned from all of these jobs.

Do **only one** of the following.

(a) Use the estimator at *www.irs.gov/W4App* for the most accurate withholding for this step (and Steps 3–4). If you or your spouse have self-employment income, use this option; **or**

(b) Use the Multiple Jobs Worksheet on page 3 and enter the result in Step 4(c) below; **or**

(c) If there are only two jobs total, you may check this box. Do the same on Form W-4 for the other job. This option is generally more accurate than (b) if pay at the lower paying job is more than half of the pay at the higher paying job. Otherwise, (b) is more accurate . . . . ☐

Complete Steps 3–4(b) on Form W-4 for only ONE of these jobs. Leave those steps blank for the other jobs. (Your withholding will be most accurate if you complete Steps 3–4(b) on the Form W-4 for the highest paying job.)

Step 3: Claim Dependent and Other Credits

If your total income will be $200,000 or less ($400,000 or less if married filing jointly):

Multiply the number of qualifying children under age 17 by $2,000 $ ______

Multiply the number of other dependents by $500 . . . . . $ ______

Add the amounts above for qualifying children and other dependents. You may add to this the amount of any other credits. Enter the total here . . . . **3** $

Step 4 (optional): Other Adjustments

(a) Other income (not from jobs). If you want tax withheld for other income you expect this year that won't have withholding, enter the amount of other income here. This may include interest, dividends, and retirement income . . . . **4(a)** $

(b) Deductions. If you expect to claim deductions other than the standard deduction and want to reduce your withholding, use the Deductions Worksheet on page 3 and enter the result here . . . . **4(b)** $

(c) Extra withholding. Enter any additional tax you want withheld each **pay period** . . **4(c)** $

Step 5: Sign Here

Under penalties of perjury, I declare that this certificate, to the best of my knowledge and belief, is true, correct, and complete.

Employee's signature (This form is not valid unless you sign it.) **Date**

Employers Only

Employer's name and address	First date of employment	Employer identification number (EIN)
Kelsey Busby Real Estate 30603 Lotus Ave Plano, Texas 75075	01-01-2025	27-1234567

For Privacy Act and Paperwork Reduction Act Notice, see page 3. Cat. No. 10220Q Form **W-4** (2025)

Kelsey Busby Real Estate
Samantha Busby Completed
IRS Form W-4

22222 VOID ☐ | a Employee's social security number: 457-27-9314 | For Official Use Only OMB No. 1545-0029

b Employer identification number (EIN) 27-1234567	1 Wages, tips, other compensation $15,000	2 Federal income tax withheld $0
c Employer's name, address, and ZIP code Kelsey Busby Real Estate 30603 Lotus Ave Plano, Texas 75075	3 Social security wages $0	4 Social security tax withheld $0
	5 Medicare wages and tips $0	6 Medicare tax withheld $0
	7 Social security tips	8 Allocated tips
d Control number	9	10 Dependent care benefits
e Employee's first name and initial: Samantha — Last name: Busby — Suff.	11 Nonqualified plans	12a See instructions for box 12
30603 Lotus Ave Plano, Texas 75075	13 Statutory employee ☐ Retirement plan ☐ Third-party sick pay ☐	12b
	14 Other	12c
f Employee's address and ZIP code		12d

15 State Employer's state ID number	16 State wages, tips, etc.	17 State income tax	18 Local wages, tips, etc.	19 Local income tax	20 Locality name

Form **W-2** **Wage and Tax Statement** 2025

Department of the Treasury—Internal Revenue Service

Copy A—For Social Security Administration. Send this entire page with Form W-3 to the Social Security Administration; photocopies are **not** acceptable.

For Privacy Act and Paperwork Reduction Act Notice, see the separate instructions.

Cat. No. 10134D

Do Not Cut, Fold, or Staple Forms on This Page

Kelsey Busby Real Estate
Samantha Busby Completed Form W-2

DO NOT STAPLE

33333	a Control number	For Official Use Only: OMB No. 1545-0029

b **Kind of Payer** (Check one): 941 ☐ Military ☐ 943 ☐ 944 [X] CT-1 ☐ Hshld. emp. ☐ Medicare govt. emp. ☐

Kind of Employer (Check one): None apply [X] 501c non-govt. ☐ State/local non-501c ☐ State/local 501c ☐ Federal govt. ☐

Third-party sick pay (Check if applicable) ☐

c Total number of Forms W-2: 1	d Establishment number	1 Wages, tips, other compensation: $15,000	2 Federal income tax withheld: $0
e Employer identification number (EIN): 27-1234567		3 Social security wages: $0	4 Social security tax withheld: $0
f Employer's name: Kelsey Busby Real Estate		5 Medicare wages and tips: $0	6 Medicare tax withheld: $0
30603 Lotus Ave Plano, Texas 75075		7 Social security tips	8 Allocated tips
		9	10 Dependent care benefits
g Employer's address and ZIP code		11 Nonqualified plans	12a Deferred compensation
h Other EIN used this year		13 For third-party sick pay use only	12b
15 State / Employer's state ID number		14 Income tax withheld by payer of third-party sick pay	
16 State wages, tips, etc.	17 State income tax	18 Local wages, tips, etc.	19 Local income tax
Employer's contact person: Kelsey Busby		Employer's telephone number: 214-620-2437	For Official Use Only
Employer's fax number		Employer's email address: K.Busby@BusbyRE.com	

Under penalties of perjury, I declare that I have examined this return and accompanying documents, and, to the best of my knowledge and belief, they are true, correct, and complete.

Signature: *Kelsey Busby* Title: Owner Date: Jan 31, 2025

Form **W-3** **Transmittal of Wage and Tax Statements** 2025 Department of the Treasury Internal Revenue Service

Send this entire page with the entire Copy A page of Form(s) W-2 to the Social Security Administration (SSA). Photocopies are not acceptable. Do not send Form W-3 if you filed electronically with the SSA.
Do not send any payment (cash, checks, money orders, etc.) with Forms W-2 and W-3.

Reminder

Separate instructions. See the 2025 General Instructions for Forms W-2 and W-3 for information on completing this form. Do not file Form W-3 for Form(s) W-2 that were submitted electronically to the SSA.

Purpose of Form

Complete a Form W-3 transmittal only when filing paper Copy A of Form(s) W-2, Wage and Tax Statement. Don't file Form W-3 alone. All paper forms **must** comply with IRS standards and be machine readable. Photocopies are **not** acceptable. Use a Form W-3 even if only one paper Form W-2 is being filed. Make sure both the Form W-3 and Form(s) W-2 show the correct tax year and employer identification number (EIN). Make a copy of this form and keep it with Copy D (For Employer) of Form(s) W-2 for your records. The IRS recommends retaining copies of these forms for at least 4 years.

E-Filing

The SSA strongly suggests employers report Form W-3 and Forms W-2 Copy A electronically instead of on paper. The SSA provides two free e-filing options on its Business Services Online (BSO) website.

- **W-2 Online.** Use fill-in forms to create, save, print, and submit up to 50 Forms W-2 at a time to the SSA.
- **File Upload.** Upload wage files to the SSA you have created using payroll or tax software that formats the files according to the SSA's *Specifications for Filing Forms W-2 Electronically (EFW2).*

W-2 Online fill-in forms or file uploads will be on time if submitted by **February 02, 2026**. For more information, go to *www.SSA.gov/bso*.

When To File Paper Forms

Mail Form W-3 with Copy A of Form(s) W-2 by **February 02, 2026**.

Where To File Paper Forms

Send this entire page with the entire Copy A page of Form(s) W-2 to:

Social Security Administration
Direct Operations Center
Wilkes-Barre, PA 18769-0001

Note: If you use "Certified Mail" to file, change the ZIP code to "18769-0002." If you use an IRS-approved private delivery service, add "ATTN: W-2 Process, 1150 E. Mountain Dr." to the address and change the ZIP code to "18702-7997." Go to *www.irs.gov/PDS* for a list of IRS-approved private delivery services.

For Privacy Act and Paperwork Reduction Act Notice, see the separate instructions.

Cat. No. 10159Y

Kelsey Busby Real Estate Completed Form W-3

Form **944 for 2024: Employer's ANNUAL Federal Tax Return**

Department of the Treasury — Internal Revenue Service

OMB No. 1545-0029

Employer identification number (EIN)	2 7 – 1 2 3 4 5 6 7
Name *(not your trade name)*	Kelsey Busby
Trade name *(if any)*	Kesley Busby Real Estate
Address	30603 Lotus Ave
	Number / Street / Suite or room number
	Plano / TX / 75075
	City / State / ZIP code
	Foreign country name / Foreign province/county / Foreign postal code

Who Must File Form 944

You must file annual Form 944 instead of filing quarterly Forms 941 **only if the IRS notified you in writing**.

Go to *www.irs.gov/Form944* for instructions and the latest information.

Read the separate instructions before you complete Form 944. Type or print within the boxes.

Part 1: Answer these questions for this year. Employers in American Samoa, Guam, the Commonwealth of the Northern Mariana Islands, the U.S. Virgin Islands, and Puerto Rico can skip lines 1 and 2, unless you have employees who are subject to U.S. income tax withholding.

1	**Wages, tips, and other compensation**	1	15,000 . 00
2	**Federal income tax withheld from wages, tips, and other compensation**	2	0 . 00
3	**If no wages, tips, and other compensation are subject to social security or Medicare tax**	3	[X] **Check here and go to line 5.**
4	**Taxable social security and Medicare wages and tips:**		

	Column 1		Column 2
4a **Taxable social security wages**	.	× 0.124 =	.
4b **Taxable social security tips**	.	× 0.124 =	.
4c **Taxable Medicare wages & tips**	.	× 0.029 =	.
4d **Taxable wages & tips subject to Additional Medicare Tax withholding**	.	× 0.009 =	.

4e	**Total social security and Medicare taxes.** Add Column 2 from lines 4a, 4b, 4c, and 4d	4e	.
5	**Total taxes before adjustments.** Add lines 2 and 4e	5	0 . 00
6	**Current year's adjustments** (see instructions)	6	.
7	**Total taxes after adjustments.** Combine lines 5 and 6	7	0 . 00
8	**Qualified small business payroll tax credit for increasing research activities.** Attach Form 8974	8	.
9	**Total taxes after adjustments and nonrefundable credits.** Subtract line 8 from line 7	9	0 . 00
10	**Total deposits for this year, including overpayment applied from a prior year and overpayments applied from Form 944-X, 941-X, or 941-X (PR)**	10	0 . 00
11	**Balance due.** If line 9 is more than line 10, enter the difference and see instructions	11	. 00
12	**Overpayment.** If line 10 is more than line 9, enter the difference: 0 . 00 — Check one: [ ] Apply to next return. [ ] Send a refund.		

You MUST complete both pages of Form 944 and SIGN it.

For Privacy Act and Paperwork Reduction Act Notice, see separate instructions. Cat. No. 39316N Form **944** (2024)

Kelsey Busby Real Estate Completed Form 944, Page 1

Name (not your trade name): Kelsey Busby

Employer identification number (EIN): 27 – 1234567

Part 2: Tell us about your deposit schedule and tax liability for this year.

13 Check one: [X] **Line 9 is less than $2,500. Go to Part 3.**

[ ] **Line 9 is $2,500 or more. Enter your tax liability for each month. If you're a semiweekly schedule depositor or you became one because you accumulated $100,000 or more of liability on any day during a deposit period, you must complete Form 945-A instead of the boxes below.**

13a	Jan.	13d	Apr.	13g	July	13j	Oct.
13b	Feb.	13e	May	13h	Aug.	13k	Nov.
13c	Mar.	13f	June	13i	Sept.	13l	Dec.

Total liability for year. Add lines 13a through 13l. Total must equal line 9. **13m**

Part 3: Tell us about your business. If question 14 does NOT apply to your business, leave it blank.

14 If your business has closed or you stopped paying wages . . . . [ ] Check here, and

enter the final date you paid wages / / ; also attach a statement to your return. See instructions.

Part 4: May we speak with your third-party designee?

Do you want to allow an employee, a paid tax preparer, or another person to discuss this return with the IRS? See the instructions for details.

[ ] Yes. Designee's name and phone number

Select a 5-digit personal identification number (PIN) to use when talking to the IRS.

[X] No.

Part 5: Sign here. You MUST complete both pages of Form 944 and SIGN it.

Under penalties of perjury, I declare that I have examined this return, including accompanying schedules and statements, and to the best of my knowledge and belief, it is true, correct, and complete. Declaration of preparer (other than taxpayer) is based on all information of which preparer has any knowledge.

Sign your name here *Kelsey Busby*

Print your name here: Kelsey Busby

Print your title here: Owner

Date: 1-31-25

Best daytime phone: 214-620-2437

Paid Preparer Use Only

Check if you're self-employed [ ]

Preparer's name

PTIN

Preparer's signature

Date

Firm's name (or yours if self-employed)

EIN

Address

Phone

City

State

ZIP code

Page **2** Form **944** (2024)

Kelsey Busby Real Estate

Completed Form 944, Page 2

Form **940 for 2024: Employer's Annual Federal Unemployment (FUTA) Tax Return** 850113

Department of the Treasury — Internal Revenue Service

OMB No. 1545-0029

Employer identification number (EIN) 27 - 1234567

Name *(not your trade name)* Kelsey Busby

Trade name *(if any)* Kelsey Busby Real Estate

Address 30603 Lotus Ave

Number Street Suite or room number

Plano TX 75075

City State ZIP code

Foreign country name Foreign province/county Foreign postal code

Type of Return (Check all that apply.)

- ☐ **a.** Amended
- ☐ **b.** Successor employer
- ☐ **c.** No payments to employees in 2024
- ☐ **d.** Final: Business closed or stopped paying wages

Go to *www.irs.gov/Form940* for instructions and the latest information.

Read the separate instructions before you complete this form. Please type or print within the boxes.

Part 1: Tell us about your return. If any line does NOT apply, leave it blank. See instructions before completing Part 1.

1a	**If you had to pay state unemployment tax in one state only, enter the state abbreviation**	1a	T X
1b	**If you had to pay state unemployment tax in more than one state, you are a multi-state employer**	1b	☐ Check here. Complete Schedule A (Form 940).
2	**If you paid wages in a state that is subject to CREDIT REDUCTION**	2	☐ Check here. Complete Schedule A (Form 940).

Part 2: Determine your FUTA tax before adjustments. If any line does NOT apply, leave it blank.

Line	Description		Amount
3	**Total payments to all employees**	3	15,000.00
4	**Payments exempt from FUTA tax**	4	15,000.00
	Check all that apply: 4a ☐ Fringe benefits; 4b ☐ Group-term life insurance; 4c ☐ Retirement/Pension; 4d ☐ Dependent care; 4e ☒ Other		
5	**Total of payments made to each employee in excess of $7,000**	5	.
6	**Subtotal** (line 4 + line 5 = line 6)	6	15,000.00
7	**Total taxable FUTA wages** (line 3 – line 6 = line 7). See instructions.	7	0.00
8	**FUTA tax before adjustments** (line 7 x 0.006 = line 8)	8	0.00

Part 3: Determine your adjustments. If any line does NOT apply, leave it blank.

Line	Description		Amount
9	**If ALL of the taxable FUTA wages you paid were excluded from state unemployment tax, multiply line 7 by 0.054** (line 7 × 0.054 = line 9). Go to line 12	9	.
10	**If SOME of the taxable FUTA wages you paid were excluded from state unemployment tax, OR you paid ANY state unemployment tax late** (after the due date for filing Form 940), complete the worksheet in the instructions. Enter the amount from line 7 of the worksheet	10	.
11	**If credit reduction applies**, enter the total from Schedule A (Form 940)	11	.

Part 4: Determine your FUTA tax and balance due or overpayment. If any line does NOT apply, leave it blank.

Line	Description		Amount
12	**Total FUTA tax after adjustments** (lines 8 + 9 + 10 + 11 = line 12)	12	.
13	**FUTA tax deposited for the year, including any overpayment applied from a prior year**	13	.
14	**Balance due.** If line 12 is more than line 13, enter the excess on line 14. • If line 14 is more than $500, you must deposit your tax. • If line 14 is $500 or less, you may pay with this return. See instructions	14	0.00
15	**Overpayment.** If line 13 is more than line 12, enter the excess on line 15 and check a box below	15	0.00

You **MUST** complete both pages of this form and **SIGN** it. Check one: ☐ Apply to next return. ☐ Send a refund.

For Privacy Act and Paperwork Reduction Act Notice, see separate instructions. Cat. No. 11234O Form **940** (2024)

Kelsey Busby Real Estate

Completed Form 940, Page 1

850212

Name (not your trade name)	Employer identification number (EIN)
Kelsey Busby	27 – 1234567

Part 5: Report your FUTA tax liability by quarter only if line 12 is more than $500. If not, go to Part 6.

16 **Report the amount of your FUTA tax liability for each quarter; do NOT enter the amount you deposited. If you had no liability for a quarter, leave the line blank.**

16a **1st quarter** (January 1 – March 31)	16a	.
16b **2nd quarter** (April 1 – June 30)	16b	.
16c **3rd quarter** (July 1 – September 30)	16c	.
16d **4th quarter** (October 1 – December 31)	16d	.
17 **Total tax liability for the year** (lines 16a + 16b + 16c + 16d = line 17)	17	0 . 00 **Total must equal line 12.**

Part 6: May we speak with your third-party designee?

Do you want to allow an employee, a paid tax preparer, or another person to discuss this return with the IRS? See the instructions for details.

☐ **Yes.** Designee's name and phone number

Select a 5-digit personal identification number (PIN) to use when talking to the IRS.

☒ **No.**

Part 7: Sign here. You MUST complete both pages of this form and SIGN it.

Under penalties of perjury, I declare that I have examined this return, including accompanying schedules and statements, and to the best of my knowledge and belief, it is true, correct, and complete, and that no part of any payment made to a state unemployment fund claimed as a credit was, or is to be, deducted from the payments made to employees. Declaration of preparer (other than taxpayer) is based on all information of which preparer has any knowledge.

Sign your name here Kelsey Busby	Print your name here: Kelsey Busby
	Print your title here: Owner
Date 1/31/25	Best daytime phone: 214-620-2437

Paid Preparer Use Only Check if you are self-employed ☐

Preparer's name		PTIN	
Preparer's signature		Date	/ /
Firm's name (or yours if self-employed)		EIN	
Address		Phone	
City	State	ZIP code	

Page **2** Form **940** (2024)

Kelsey Busby Real Estate
Completed Form 940, Page 2

Form **1040** Department of the Treasury - Internal Revenue Service
U.S. Individual Income Tax Return **2024** OMB No. 1545-0074 IRS Use Only - Do not write or staple in this space.

For the year Jan. 1 - Dec. 31, 2024, or other tax year beginning , ending See separate instructions.

Your first name and middle initial	Last name	Your social security number
Grady H.	Busby	546 57 9314
If joint return, spouse's first name and middle initial	Last name	Spouse's social security number
Kelsey R.	Busby	464 22 1784

Home address (number and street). If you have a P.O. box, see instructions.			Apt. no.
30603 Lotus Ave			
City, town, or post office. If you have a foreign address, also complete spaces below.		State	ZIP code
Plano		TX	75075
Foreign country name	Foreign province/state/county	Foreign postal code	

Presidential Election Campaign Check here if you, or your spouse if filing jointly, want $3 to go to this fund. Checking a box below will not change your tax or refund. ☐ You ☐ Spouse

Filing Status Check only one box.
☐ Single
☒ Married filing jointly (even if only one had income)
☐ Married filing separately (MFS)
☐ Head of household (HOH)
☐ Qualifying surviving spouse (QSS)
If you checked the MFS box, enter the name of your spouse. If you checked the HOH or QSS box, enter the child's name if the qualifying person is a child but not your dependent:
☐ If treating a nonresident alien or dual-status alien spouse as a U.S. resident for the entire tax year, check the box and enter their name (see instructions and attach statement if required):

Digital Assets At any time during 2024, did you: (a) receive (as a reward, award, or payment for property or services); or (b) sell, exchange, or otherwise dispose of a digital asset (or a financial interest in a digital asset)? (See instructions.) ☐ Yes ☒ No

Standard Deduction Someone can claim: ☐ You as a dependent ☐ Your spouse as a dependent
☐ Spouse itemizes on a separate return or you were a dual-status alien

Age/Blindness You: ☐ Were born before January 2, 1960 ☐ Are blind **Spouse:** ☐ Was born before January 2, 1960 ☐ Is blind

Dependents (see instructions): If more than four dependents, see instr. and check here ☐

(1) First name Last name	(2) Social security number	(3) Relationship to you	(4) Child tax credit	Credit for other dependents
Samantha Busby	457-27-3901	Daughter	X	
Jeremy Busby	457-27-9827	Son	X	

Income

Attach Form(s) W-2 here. Also attach Forms W-2G and 1099-R if tax was withheld.

If you did not get a Form W-2, see instructions.

1a	Total amount from Form(s) W-2, box 1 (see instructions)	Stmt 2	1a	127,232.
b	Household employee wages not reported on Form(s) W-2		1b	
c	Tip income not reported on line 1a (see instructions)		1c	
d	Medicaid waiver payments not reported on Form(s) W-2 (see instructions)		1d	
e	Taxable dependent care benefits from Form 2441, line 26		1e	
f	Employer-provided adoption benefits from Form 8839, line 29		1f	
g	Wages from Form 8919, line 6		1g	
h	Other earned income (see instructions)		1h	
i	Nontaxable combat pay election (see instructions)	1i		
z	Add lines 1a through 1h		1z	127,232.
2a	Tax-exempt interest	2a	b Taxable interest 2b	122.
3a	Qualified dividends	3a 156.	b Ordinary dividends 3b	312.
4a	IRA distributions	4a	b Taxable amount 4b	
5a	Pensions and annuities	5a	b Taxable amount 5b	
6a	Social security benefits	6a	b Taxable amount 6b	
c	If you elect to use the lump-sum election method, check here (see instructions) ☐			
7	Capital gain or (loss). Attach Schedule D if required. If not required, check here ☒		7	81.
8	Additional income from Schedule 1, line 10		8	152,303.
9	Add lines 1z, 2b, 3b, 4b, 5b, 6b, 7, and 8. This is your **total income**		9	280,050.
10	Adjustments to income from Schedule 1, line 26		10	20,204.
11	Subtract line 10 from line 9. This is your **adjusted gross income**		11	259,846.
12	**Standard deduction or itemized deductions** (from Schedule A)		12	31,060.
13	Qualified business income deduction from Form 8995 or Form 8995-A		13	26,420.
14	Add lines 12 and 13		14	57,480.
15	Subtract line 14 from line 11. If zero or less, enter -0-. This is your **taxable income**		15	202,366.

Attach Sch. B if required.

Standard Deduction for -
- Single or Married filing separately, $14,600
- Married filing jointly or Qualifying surviving spouse, $29,200
- Head of household, $21,900
- If you checked any box under Standard Deduction, see instructions.

For Disclosure, Privacy Act, and Paperwork Reduction Act Notice, see separate instructions. Form **1040** (2024)
LHA 413921 12-30-24

Form 1040 (2024) Grady H. & Kelsey R. Busby 546-57-9314 Stmt 4 Page 2

Tax and Credits	16	**Tax** (see instructions). Check if any from Form(s): 1 ☐ 8814 2 ☐ 4972 3 ☐		16	34,632.
	17	Amount from Schedule 2, line 3		17	
	18	Add lines 16 and 17		18	34,632.
	19	Child tax credit or credit for other dependents from Schedule 8812		19	4,000.
	20	Amount from Schedule 3, line 8		20	
	21	Add lines 19 and 20		21	4,000.
	22	Subtract line 21 from line 18. If zero or less, enter -0-		22	30,632.
	23	Other taxes, including self-employment tax, from Schedule 2, line 21		23	21,701.
	24	Add lines 22 and 23. This is your **total tax**		24	52,333.
Payments	25	Federal income tax withheld from:			
	a	Form(s) W-2 See Statement 5	25a 19,335.		
	b	Form(s) 1099	25b		
	c	Other forms (see instructions)	25c		
	d	Add lines 25a through 25c		25d	19,335.
If you have a qualifying child, attach Sch. EIC	26	2024 estimated tax payments and amount applied from 2023 return Statement 6		26	38,000.
	27	Earned income credit (EIC)	27		
	28	Additional child tax credit from Schedule 8812	28		
	29	American opportunity credit from Form 8863, line 8	29		
	30	Reserved for future use	30		
	31	Amount from Schedule 3, line 15	31		
	32	Add lines 27, 28, 29, and 31. These are your **total other payments and refundable credits**		32	
	33	Add lines 25d, 26, and 32. These are your **total payments**		33	57,335.
Refund	34	If line 33 is more than line 24, subtract line 24 from line 33. This is the amount you **overpaid**		34	5,002.
	35a	Amount of line 34 you want **refunded to you.** If Form 8888 is attached, check here ☐		35a	5,002.
Direct deposit? See instructions.	b	Routing number	c Type: ☐ Checking ☐ Savings		
	d	Account number			
	36	Amount of line 34 you want **applied to your 2025 estimated tax**	36		
Amount You Owe	37	Subtract line 33 from line 24. This is the **amount you owe.** For details on how to pay, go to *www.irs.gov/Payments* or see instructions		37	
	38	Estimated tax penalty (see instructions)	38		

Third Party Designee Do you want to allow another person to discuss this return with the IRS? See instructions ☒ **Yes.** Complete below. ☐ **No**

Designee's name Preparer | Phone no. | Personal identification number (PIN)

Sign Here

Under penalties of perjury, I declare that I have examined this return and accompanying schedules and statements, and to the best of my knowledge and belief, they are true, correct, and complete. Declaration of preparer (other than taxpayer) is based on all information of which preparer has any knowledge.

Your signature	Date	Your occupation Teacher	If the IRS sent you an Identity Protection PIN, enter it here (see inst.)
Spouse's signature. If a joint return, **both** must sign.	Date	Spouse's occupation Real Estate Agent	If the IRS sent your spouse an Identity Protection PIN, enter it here (see inst.)
Phone no.	Email address		

Joint return? See instructions. Keep a copy for your records.

Paid Preparer Use Only

Preparer's name	Preparer's signature	Date	PTIN	Check if: ☐ Self-employed
Firm's name				Phone no.
Firm's address				Firm's EIN

Go to *www.irs.gov/Form1040* for instructions and the latest information. Form **1040** (2024)

413922 12-08-24

161

SCHEDULE 1
(Form 1040)

Department of the Treasury
Internal Revenue Service

Additional Income and Adjustments to Income

Attach to Form 1040, 1040-SR, or 1040-NR.
Go to www.irs.gov/Form1040 for instructions and the latest information.

OMB No. 1545-0074
2024
Attachment Sequence No. **01**

Name(s) shown on Form 1040, 1040-SR, or 1040-NR	Your social security number
Grady H. & Kelsey R. Busby	546-57-9314

For 2024, enter the amount reported to you on Form(s) 1099-K that was included in error or for personal items sold at a loss

Note: The remaining amounts reported to you on Form(s) 1099-K should be reported elsewhere on your return depending on the nature of the transaction. See *www.irs.gov/1099k.*

Part I Additional Income

1	Taxable refunds, credits, or offsets of state and local income taxes			1	
2a	Alimony received			2a	
b	Date of original divorce or separation agreement (see instructions)				
3	Business income or (loss). Attach Schedule C			3	152,303.
4	Other gains or (losses). Attach Form 4797			4	
5	Rental real estate, royalties, partnerships, S corporations, trusts, etc. Attach Schedule E			5	
6	Farm income or (loss). Attach Schedule F			6	
7	Unemployment compensation			7	
8	Other income:				
a	Net operating loss	8a	( )		
b	Gambling	8b			
c	Cancellation of debt	8c			
d	Foreign earned income exclusion from Form 2555	8d	( )		
e	Income from Form 8853	8e			
f	Income from Form 8889	8f			
g	Alaska Permanent Fund dividends	8g			
h	Jury duty pay	8h			
i	Prizes and awards	8i			
j	Activity not engaged in for profit income	8j			
k	Stock options	8k			
l	Income from the rental of personal property if you engaged in the rental for profit but were not in the business of renting such property	8l			
m	Olympic and Paralympic medals and USOC prize money (see instructions)	8m			
n	Section 951(a) inclusion (see instructions)	8n			
o	Section 951A(a) inclusion (see instructions)	8o			
p	Section 461(l) excess business loss adjustment	8p			
q	Taxable distributions from an ABLE account (see instructions)	8q			
r	Scholarship and fellowship grants not reported on Form W-2	8r			
s	Nontaxable amount of Medicaid waiver payments included on Form 1040, line 1a or 1d	8s	( )		
t	Pension or annuity from a nonqualifed deferred compensation plan or a nongovernmental section 457 plan	8t			
u	Wages earned while incarcerated	8u			
v	Digital assets received as ordinary income not reported elsewhere. See instructions	8v			
z	Other income. List type and amount:	8z			
9	Total other income. Add lines 8a through 8z			9	
10	Combine lines 1 through 7 and 9. This is your **additional income.** Enter here and on Form 1040, 1040-SR, or 1040-NR, line 8			10	152,303.

For Paperwork Reduction Act Notice, see your tax return instructions. Schedule 1 (Form 1040) 2024

LHA 414141 12-08-24

Schedule 1 (Form 1040) 2024 Page 2

Part II Adjustments to Income

11	Educator expenses	11	
12	Certain business expenses of reservists, performing artists, and fee-basis government officials. Attach Form 2106	12	
13	Health savings account deduction. Attach Form 8889	13	
14	Moving expenses for members of the Armed Forces. Attach Form 3903	14	
15	Deductible part of self-employment tax. Attach Schedule SE	15	10,760.
16	Self-employed SEP, SIMPLE, and qualified plans	16	
17	Self-employed health insurance deduction	17	9,444.
18	Penalty on early withdrawal of savings	18	
19a	Alimony paid	19a	
b	Recipient's SSN		
c	Date of original divorce or separation agreement (see instructions):		
20	IRA deduction	20	
21	Student loan interest deduction	21	
22	Reserved for future use	22	
23	Archer MSA deduction	23	
24	Other adjustments:		
a	Jury duty pay (see instructions)	24a	
b	Deductible expenses related to income reported on line 8l from the rental of personal property engaged in for profit	24b	
c	Nontaxable amount of the value of Olympic and Paralympic medals and USOC prize money reported on line 8m	24c	
d	Reforestation amortization and expenses	24d	
e	Repayment of supplemental unemployment benefits under the Trade Act of 1974	24e	
f	Contributions to section 501(c)(18)(D) pension plans	24f	
g	Contributions by certain chaplains to section 403(b) plans	24g	
h	Attorney fees and court costs for actions involving certain unlawful discrimination claims (see instructions)	24h	
i	Attorney fees and court costs you paid in connection with an award from the IRS for information you provided that helped the IRS detect tax law violations	24i	
j	Housing deduction from Form 2555	24j	
k	Excess deductions of section 67(e) expenses from Schedule K-1 (Form 1041)	24k	
z	Other adjustments. List type and amount:	24z	
25	Total other adjustments. Add lines 24a through 24z	25	
26	Add lines 11 through 23 and 25. These are your **adjustments to income.** Enter here and on Form 1040, 1040-SR, or 1040-NR, line 10	26	20,204.

Schedule 1 (Form 1040) 2024

411012 12-08-24

SCHEDULE 2 (Form 1040)

Department of the Treasury Internal Revenue Service

Additional Taxes

Attach to Form 1040, 1040-SR, or 1040-NR.

Go to www.irs.gov/Form1040 for instructions and the latest information.

OMB No. 1545-0074

2024

Attachment Sequence No. **02**

Name(s) shown on Form 1040, 1040-SR, or 1040-NR: Grady H. & Kelsey R. Busby

Your social security number: 546-57-9314

Part I Tax

1	Additions to tax:				
a	Excess advance premium tax credit repayment. Attach Form 8962	1a			
b	Repayment of new clean vehicle credit(s) transferred to a registered dealer from Schedule A (Form 8936), Part II. Attach Form 8936 and Schedule A (Form 8936)	1b			
c	Repayment of previously owned clean vehicle credit(s) transferred to a registered dealer from Schedule A (Form 8936), Part IV. Attach Form 8936 and Schedule A (Form 8936)	1c			
d	Recapture of net EPE from Form 4255, line 2a, column (l)	1d			
e	Excessive payments (EP) from Form 4255. Check applicable box and enter amount. (i) ☐ Line 1a, column (n) (ii) ☐ Line 1c, column (n) (iii) ☐ Line 1d, column (n) (iv) ☐ Line 2a, column (n)	1e			
f	20% EP from Form 4255. Check applicable box and enter amount. See instructions (i) ☐ Line 1a, column (o) (ii) ☐ Line 1c, column (o) (iii) ☐ Line 1d, column (o) (iv) ☐ Line 2a, column (o)	1f			
y	Other additions to tax (see instructions):	1y			
z	Add lines 1a through 1y			1z	
2	Alternative minimum tax. Attach Form 6251			2	
3	Add lines 1z and 2. Enter here and on Form 1040, 1040-SR, or 1040-NR, line 17			3	0.

Part II Other Taxes

4	Self-employment tax. Attach Schedule SE			4	21,520.
5	Social security and Medicare tax on unreported tip income. Attach Form 4137	5			
6	Uncollected social security and Medicare tax on wages. Attach Form 8919	6			
7	Total additional social security and Medicare tax. Add lines 5 and 6			7	
8	Additional tax on IRAs or other tax-favored accounts. Attach Form 5329 if required. If not required, check here ☐			8	
9	Household employment taxes. Attach Schedule H			9	
10	Repayment of first-time homebuyer credit. Attach Form 5405 if required			10	
11	Additional Medicare Tax. Attach Form 8959			11	161.
12	Net investment income tax. Attach Form 8960			12	20.
13	Uncollected social security and Medicare or RRTA tax on tips or group-term life insurance from Form W-2, box 12			13	
14	Interest on tax due on installment income from the sale of certain residential lots and timeshares			14	
15	Interest on the deferred tax on gain from certain installment sales with a sales price over $150,000			15	
16	Recapture of low-income housing credit. Attach Form 8611			16	

(continued on page 2)

For Paperwork Reduction Act Notice, see your tax return instructions. **Schedule 2 (Form 1040) 2024**

LHA 414151 01-02-25

Schedule 2 (Form 1040) 2024 Page **2**

Part II **Other Taxes** *(continued)*

17	Other additional taxes:				
a	Recapture of other credits. List type, form number, and amount	17a			
b	Recapture of federal mortgage subsidy, if you sold your home see instructions	17b			
c	Additional tax on HSA distributions. Attach Form 8889	17c			
d	Additional tax on an HSA because you didn't remain an eligible individual. Attach Form 8889	17d			
e	Additional tax on Archer MSA distributions. Attach Form 8853	17e			
f	Additional tax on Medicare Advantage MSA distributions. Attach Form 8853	17f			
g	Recapture of a charitable contribution deduction related to a fractional interest in tangible personal property	17g			
h	Income you received from a nonqualified deferred compensation plan that fails to meet the requirements of section 409A	17h			
i	Compensation you received from a nonqualified deferred compensation plan described in section 457A	17i			
j	Section 72(m)(5) excess benefits tax	17j			
k	Golden parachute payments	17k			
l	Tax on accumulation distribution of trusts	17l			
m	Excise tax on insider stock compensation from an expatriated corporation	17m			
n	Look-back interest under section 167(g) or 460(b) from Form 8697 or 8866	17n			
o	Tax on non-effectively connected income for any part of the year you were a nonresident alien from Form 1040-NR	17o			
p	Any interest from Form 8621, line 16f, relating to distributions from, and dispositions of, stock of a section 1291 fund	17p			
q	Any interest from Form 8621, line 24	17q			
z	Any other taxes. List type and amount:	17z			
18	Total additional taxes. Add lines 17a through 17z			18	
19	Recapture of net EPE from Form 4255, line 1d, column (l)			19	
20	Section 965 net tax liability installment from Form 965-A	20			
21	Add lines 4, 7 through 16, 18, and 19. These are your **total other taxes.** Enter here and on Form 1040 or 1040-SR, line 23, or Form 1040-NR, line 23b			21	21,701.

Schedule 2 (Form 1040) 2024

414152 01-02-25

SCHEDULE A (Form 1040)

Department of the Treasury Internal Revenue Service

Itemized Deductions

Attach to Form 1040 or 1040-SR.

Go to www.irs.gov/ScheduleA for instructions and the latest information.

Caution: If you are claiming a net qualified disaster loss on Form 4684, see the instructions for line 16.

OMB No. 1545-0074

2024

Attachment Sequence No. 07

Name(s) shown on Form 1040 or 1040-SR	Your social security number
Grady H. & Kelsey R. Busby	546 57 9314

Section	Line	Description	Line no.	Amount	Line no.	Total
Medical and Dental Expenses		**Caution:** Do not include expenses reimbursed or paid by others.				
	1	Medical and dental expenses (see instructions)	1			
	2	Enter amount from Form 1040 or 1040-SR, line 11 [2]				
	3	Multiply line 2 by 7.5% (0.075)	3			
	4	Subtract line 3 from line 1. If line 3 is more than line 1, enter -0-			4	
Taxes You Paid	5	State and local taxes.				
	a	State and local income taxes or general sales taxes. You may include either income taxes or general sales taxes on line 5a, but not both. If you elect to include general sales taxes instead of income taxes, check this box See Statement 8 [X]	5a	2,282.		
	b	State and local real estate taxes (see instructions)	5b	7,556.		
	c	State and local personal property taxes	5c			
	d	Add lines 5a through 5c	5d	9,838.		
	e	Enter the smaller of line 5d or $10,000 ($5,000 if married filing separately)	5e	9,838.		
	6	Other taxes. List type and amount:	6			
	7	Add lines 5e and 6			7	9,838.
Interest You Paid Caution: Your mortgage interest deduction may be limited. See instructions.	8	Home mortgage interest and points. If you didn't use all of your home mortgage loan(s) to buy, build, or improve your home, see instructions and check this box [ ]				
	a	Home mortgage interest and points reported to you on Form 1098. See instructions if limited	8a	16,122.		
	b	Home mortgage interest not reported to you on Form 1098. See instructions if limited. If paid to the person from whom you bought the home, see instructions and show that person's name, identifying no., and address	8b			
	c	Points not reported to you on Form 1098. See instructions for special rules	8c			
	d	Reserved for future use	8d			
	e	Add lines 8a through 8c	8e	16,122.		
	9	Investment interest. Attach Form 4952 if required. See instructions	9			
	10	Add lines 8e and 9			10	16,122.
Gifts to Charity Caution: If you made a gift and got a benefit for it, see instructions.	11	Gifts by cash or check. If you made any gift of $250 or more, see instructions	11	5,100.		Stmt 7
	12	Other than by cash or check. If you made any gift of $250 or more, see instructions. You **must** attach Form 8283 if over $500	12			
	13	Carryover from prior year	13			
	14	Add lines 11 through 13			14	5,100.
Casualty and Theft Losses	15	Casualty and theft loss(es) from a federally declared disaster (other than net qualified disaster losses). Attach Form 4684 and enter the amount from line 18 of that form. See instructions			15	
Other Itemized Deductions	16	Other - from list in instructions. List type and amount:			16	
Total Itemized Deductions	17	Add the amounts in the far right column for lines 4 through 16. Also, enter this amount on Form 1040 or 1040-SR, line 12			17	31,060.
	18	If you elect to itemize deductions even though they are less than your standard deduction, check this box [ ]				

LHA **For Paperwork Reduction Act Notice, see the Instructions for Form 1040.** 419501 12-08-24 **Schedule A (Form 1040) 2024**

SCHEDULE B (Form 1040)

Department of the Treasury Internal Revenue Service

Interest and Ordinary Dividends

Attach to Form 1040 or 1040-SR.

Go to www.irs.gov/ScheduleB for instructions and the latest information.

OMB No. 1545-0074

2024

Attachment Sequence No. **08**

Name(s) shown on return	Your social security number
Grady H. & Kelsey R. Busby	546 57 9314

Part I Interest

		Line	Amount
1	List name of payer. If any interest is from a seller-financed mortgage and the buyer used the property as a personal residence, see the instructions and list this interest first. Also, show that buyer's social security number and address:		
	JPMorgan Chase	1	122.
2	Add the amounts on line 1	2	122.
3	Excludable interest on series EE and I U.S. savings bonds issued after 1989. Attach Form 8815	3	
4	Subtract line 3 from line 2. Enter the result here and on Form 1040 or 1040-SR, line 2b	4	122.

Note: If you received a Form 1099-INT, Form 1099-OID, or substitute statement from a brokerage firm, list the firm's name as the payer and enter the total interest shown on that form.

Note: If line 4 is over $1,500, you must complete Part III.

Part II Ordinary Dividends

		Line	Amount
5	List name of payer:		
	Charles Schwab	5	312.
6	Add the amounts on line 5. Enter the total here and on Form 1040 or 1040-SR, line 3b	6	312.

Note: If you received a Form 1099-DIV or substitute statement from a brokerage firm, list the firm's name as the payer and enter the ordinary dividends shown on that form.

Note: If line 6 is over $1,500, you must complete Part III.

Part III Foreign Accounts and Trusts

Caution: If required, failure to file FinCEN Form 114 may result in substantial penalties. Additionally, you may be required to file Form 8938, Statement of Specified Foreign Financial Assets. See instr.

You must complete this part if you **(a)** had over $1,500 of taxable interest or ordinary dividends; **(b)** had a foreign account; or **(c)** received a distribution from, or were a grantor of, or a transferor to, a foreign trust.

		Yes	No
7a	At any time during 2024, did you have a financial interest in or signature authority over a financial account (such as a bank account, securities account, or brokerage account) located in a foreign country? See instructions		X
	If "Yes," are you required to file FinCEN Form 114, Report of Foreign Bank and Financial Accounts (FBAR), to report that financial interest or signature authority? See FinCEN Form 114 and its instructions for filing requirements and exceptions to those requirements		
b	If you are required to file FinCEN Form 114, list the name(s) of the foreign country(-ies) where the financial account(s) is (are) located		
8	During 2024, did you receive a distribution from, or were you the grantor of, or transferor to, a foreign trust? If "Yes," you may have to file Form 3520. See instructions		X

427501 10-25-24

LHA **For Paperwork Reduction Act Notice, see your tax return instructions.** **Schedule B (Form 1040) 2024**

SCHEDULE SE (Form 1040)

Department of the Treasury Internal Revenue Service

Self-Employment Tax

Attach to Form 1040, 1040-SR, 1040-SS, or 1040-NR.

Go to www.irs.gov/ScheduleSE for instructions and the latest information.

OMB No. 1545-0074

2024

Attachment Sequence No. **17**

Name of person with self-employment income (as shown on Form 1040, 1040-SR, 1040-SS, or 1040-NR): Kelsey R. Busby

Social security number of person with **self-employment** income: 464 22 1784

Part I Self-Employment Tax

Note: If your only income subject to self-employment tax is **church employee income,** see instructions for how to report your income and the definition of church employee income.

A If you are a minister, member of a religious order, or Christian Science practitioner **and** you filed Form 4361, but you had $400 or more of **other** net earnings from self-employment, check here and continue with Part I ☐

Skip lines 1a and 1b if you use the farm optional method in Part II. See instructions.

1a	Net farm profit or (loss) from Sch. F, line 34, and farm partnerships, Sch. K-1 (Form 1065), box 14, code A			1a	
b	If you received social security retirement or disability benefits, enter the amount of Conservation Reserve Program payments included on Schedule F, line 4b, or listed on Schedule K-1 (Form 1065), box 20, code AQ			1b	
	Skip line 2 if you use the nonfarm optional method in Part II. See instructions.				
2	Net profit or (loss) from Schedule C, line 31; and Schedule K-1 (Form 1065), box 14, code A (other than farming). See instructions for other income to report or if you are a minister or member of a religious order — See Statement 11			2	152,303.
3	Combine lines 1a, 1b, and 2			3	152,303.
4a	If line 3 is more than zero, multiply line 3 by 92.35% (0.9235). Otherwise, enter amount from line 3			4a	140,652.
	Note: If line 4a is less than $400 due to Conservation Reserve Program payments on line 1b, see instructions				
b	If you elect one or both of the optional methods, enter the total of lines 15 and 17 here			4b	
c	Combine lines 4a and 4b. If less than $400, **stop;** you don't owe self-employment tax. **Exception:** If less than $400 and you had **church employee income,** enter -0- and continue			4c	140,652.
5a	Enter your **church employee income** from Form W-2. See instructions for definition of church employee income	5a			
b	Multiply line 5a by 92.35% (0.9235). If less than $100, enter -0-			5b	
6	Add lines 4c and 5b			6	140,652.
7	Maximum amount of combined wages and self-employment earnings subject to social security tax or the 6.2% portion of the 7.65% railroad retirement (tier 1) tax for 2024			7	168,600
8a	Total social security wages and tips (total of boxes 3 and 7 on Form(s) W-2) and railroad retirement (tier 1) compensation. If $168,600 or more, skip lines 8b through 10, and go to line 11	8a			
b	Unreported tips subject to social security tax from Form 4137, line 10	8b			
c	Wages subject to social security tax from Form 8919, line 10	8c			
d	Add lines 8a, 8b, and 8c			8d	
9	Subtract line 8d from line 7. If zero or less, enter -0- here and on line 10 and go to line 11			9	168,600.
10	Multiply the **smaller** of line 6 or line 9 by 12.4% (0.124)			10	17,441.
11	Multiply line 6 by 2.9% (0.029)			11	4,079.
12	**Self-employment tax.** Add lines 10 and 11. Enter here and on **Schedule 2 (Form 1040), line 4, or Form 1040-SS, Part I, line 3**			12	21,520.
13	**Deduction for one-half of self-employment tax.** Multiply line 12 by 50% (0.50). Enter here and on **Schedule 1 (Form 1040), line 15**	13	10,760.		

For Paperwork Reduction Act Notice, see your tax return instructions. **Schedule SE (Form 1040) 2024**

LHA 424501 10-23-24

SCHEDULE C (Form 1040)

Department of the Treasury Internal Revenue Service

Profit or Loss From Business

(Sole Proprietorship)

Attach to Form 1040, 1040-SR, 1040-SS, 1040-NR, or 1041; partnerships must generally file Form 1065.

Go to www.irs.gov/ScheduleC for instructions and the latest information.

OMB No. 1545-0074

2024

Attachment Sequence No. 09

Name of proprietor: Kelsey R. Busby

Social security number (SSN): 464-22-1784

A Principal business or profession, including product or service (see instructions): Residential Real Estate Sales

B Enter code from instructions: 531210

C Business name. If no separate business name, leave blank.: Kelsey Busby Real Estate

D Employer ID number (EIN) (see instr.): 27-1234567

E Business address (including suite or room no.): 30603 Lotus Ave

City, town or post office, state, and ZIP code: Plano, TX 75075

F Accounting method: (1) [X] Cash (2) [ ] Accrual (3) [ ] Other (specify)

G Did you "materially participate" in the operation of this business during 2024? If "No," see instructions for limit on losses [X] Yes [ ] No

H If you started or acquired this business during 2024, check here [ ]

I Did you make any payments in 2024 that would require you to file Form(s) 1099? See instructions [ ] Yes [ ] No

J If "Yes," did you or will you file required Form(s) 1099? [ ] Yes [ ] No

Part I Income

1	Gross receipts or sales. See instructions for line 1 and check the box if this income was reported to you on Form W-2 and the "Statutory employee" box on that form was checked [ ]	1	191,506.
2	Returns and allowances	2	
3	Subtract line 2 from line 1	3	191,506.
4	Cost of goods sold (from line 42)	4	
5	**Gross profit.** Subtract line 4 from line 3	5	191,506.
6	Other income, including federal and state gasoline or fuel tax credit or refund (see instructions)	6	
7	**Gross income.** Add lines 5 and 6	7	191,506.

Part II Expenses. Enter expenses for business use of your home only on line 30.

8	Advertising	8	3,612.	18	Office expense	18	
9	Car and truck expenses (see instructions) Stmt 10	9	9,035.	19	Pension and profit-sharing plans	19	
10	Commissions and fees	10		20	Rent or lease (see instructions):		
11	Contract labor (see instructions)	11		a	Vehicles, machinery, and equipment	20a	
12	Depletion	12		b	Other business property	20b	
13	Depreciation and section 179 expense deduction (not included in Part III) (see instructions)	13		21	Repairs and maintenance	21	
				22	Supplies (not included in Part III)	22	1,662.
				23	Taxes and licenses	23	300.
14	Employee benefit programs (other than on line 19)	14		24	Travel and meals:		
				a	Travel	24a	
15	Insurance (other than health)	15	460.	b	Deductible meals (see instructions)	24b	508.
16	Interest (see instructions):			25	Utilities	25	
a	Mortgage (paid to banks, etc.)	16a		26	Wages (less employment credits)	26	15,000.
b	Other	16b		27 a	Other expenses (from line 48)	27a	8,626.
17	Legal and professional services	17		b	Energy efficient commercial bldgs deduction (attach Form 7205)	27b	

28	**Total expenses** before expenses for business use of home. Add lines 8 through 27b	28	39,203.
29	Tentative profit or (loss). Subtract line 28 from line 7	29	152,303.
30	Expenses for business use of your home. Do not report these expenses elsewhere. Attach Form 8829 unless using the simplified method. See instructions. **Simplified method filers only:** Enter the total square footage of (a) your home: ______ and (b) the part of your home used for business: ______ . Use the Simplified Method Worksheet in the instructions to figure the amount to enter on line 30	30	
31	**Net profit or (loss).** Subtract line 30 from line 29. • If a profit, enter on both **Schedule 1 (Form 1040), line 3,** and on **Schedule SE, line 2.** (If you checked the box on line 1, see instructions). Estates and trusts, enter on **Form 1041, line 3.** • If a loss, you **must** go to line 32.	31	152,303.
32	If you have a loss, check the box that describes your investment in this activity. See instructions. • If you checked 32a, enter the loss on both **Schedule 1 (Form 1040), line 3,** and on **Schedule SE, line 2.** (If you checked the box on line 1, see the line 31 instructions.) Estates and trusts, enter on **Form 1041, line 3.** • If you checked 32b, you **must** attach **Form 6198.** Your loss may be limited.	32a / 32b	[ ] All investment is at risk. [ ] Some investment is not at risk.

For Paperwork Reduction Act Notice, see the separate instructions. LHA 420001 10-29-24 **Schedule C (Form 1040) 2024**

Schedule C (Form 1040) 2024 Kelsey R. Busby 464-22-1784 Page 2

Part III Cost of Goods Sold (see instructions)

33 Method(s) used to value closing inventory: a ☐ Cost b ☐ Lower of cost or market c ☐ Other (attach explanation)

34 Was there any change in determining quantities, costs, or valuations between opening and closing inventory? If "Yes," attach explanation ☐ Yes ☐ No

35 Inventory at beginning of year. If different from last year's closing inventory, attach explanation	35	
36 Purchases less cost of items withdrawn for personal use	36	
37 Cost of labor. Do not include any amounts paid to yourself	37	
38 Materials and supplies	38	
39 Other costs	39	
40 Add lines 35 through 39	40	
41 Inventory at end of year	41	
42 **Cost of goods sold.** Subtract line 41 from line 40. Enter the result here and on line 4	42	

Part IV Information on Your Vehicle. Complete this part **only** if you are claiming car or truck expenses on line 9 and are not required to file Form 4562 for this business. See the instructions for line 13 to find out if you must file Form 4562.

43 When did you place your vehicle in service for business purposes? (month/day/year) 01/01/23

44 Of the total number of miles you drove your vehicle during 2024, enter the number of miles you used your vehicle for:

a Business 13,127 b Commuting 1,020 c Other 5,453

45 Was your vehicle available for personal use during off-duty hours? ☒ Yes ☐ No

46 Do you (or your spouse) have another vehicle available for personal use? ☒ Yes ☐ No

47a Do you have evidence to support your deduction? ☒ Yes ☐ No

b If "Yes," is the evidence written? ☒ Yes ☐ No

Part V Other Expenses. List below business expenses not included on lines 8-26, line 27b, or line 30.

Broker Dues and Fees		7,550.
Telephone		626.
Continuing Education		450.
48 **Total other expenses.** Enter here and on line 27a	48	8,626.

420002 10-29-24 Schedule C (Form 1040) 2024

SCHEDULE SE (Form 1040)

Department of the Treasury Internal Revenue Service

Self-Employment Tax

Attach to Form 1040, 1040-SR, 1040-SS, or 1040-NR.

Go to www.irs.gov/ScheduleSE for instructions and the latest information.

OMB No. 1545-0074

2024

Attachment Sequence No. **17**

Name of person with self-employment income (as shown on Form 1040, 1040-SR, 1040-SS, or 1040-NR)	Social security number of person with **self-employment** income
Kelsey R. Busby	464 22 1784

Part I Self-Employment Tax

Note: If your only income subject to self-employment tax is **church employee income,** see instructions for how to report your income and the definition of church employee income.

A	If you are a minister, member of a religious order, or Christian Science practitioner **and** you filed Form 4361, but you had $400 or more of **other** net earnings from self-employment, check here and continue with Part I		☐
	Skip lines 1a and 1b if you use the farm optional method in Part II. See instructions.		
1a	Net farm profit or (loss) from Sch. F, line 34, and farm partnerships, Sch. K-1 (Form 1065), box 14, code A	1a	
b	If you received social security retirement or disability benefits, enter the amount of Conservation Reserve Program payments included on Schedule F, line 4b, or listed on Schedule K-1 (Form 1065), box 20, code AQ	1b	
	Skip line 2 if you use the nonfarm optional method in Part II. See instructions.		
2	Net profit or (loss) from Schedule C, line 31; and Schedule K-1 (Form 1065), box 14, code A (other than farming). See instructions for other income to report or if you are a minister or member of a religious order See Statement 11	2	152,303.
3	Combine lines 1a, 1b, and 2	3	152,303.
4a	If line 3 is more than zero, multiply line 3 by 92.35% (0.9235). Otherwise, enter amount from line 3	4a	140,652.
	Note: If line 4a is less than $400 due to Conservation Reserve Program payments on line 1b, see instructions		
b	If you elect one or both of the optional methods, enter the total of lines 15 and 17 here	4b	
c	Combine lines 4a and 4b. If **less** than $400, **stop;** you don't owe self-employment tax. **Exception:** If less than $400 and you had **church employee income,** enter -0- and continue	4c	140,652.
5a	Enter your **church employee income** from Form W-2. See instructions for definition of church employee income (5a)		
b	Multiply line 5a by 92.35% (0.9235). If less than $100, enter -0-	5b	
6	Add lines 4c and 5b	6	140,652.
7	Maximum amount of combined wages and self-employment earnings subject to social security tax or the 6.2% portion of the 7.65% railroad retirement (tier 1) tax for 2024	7	168,600
8a	Total social security wages and tips (total of boxes 3 and 7 on Form(s) W-2) and railroad retirement (tier 1) compensation. If $168,600 or more, skip lines 8b through 10, and go to line 11 (8a)		
b	Unreported tips subject to social security tax from Form 4137, line 10 (8b)		
c	Wages subject to social security tax from Form 8919, line 10 (8c)		
d	Add lines 8a, 8b, and 8c	8d	
9	Subtract line 8d from line 7. If zero or less, enter -0- here and on line 10 and go to line 11	9	168,600.
10	Multiply the **smaller** of line 6 or line 9 by 12.4% (0.124)	10	17,441.
11	Multiply line 6 by 2.9% (0.029)	11	4,079.
12	**Self-employment tax.** Add lines 10 and 11. Enter here and on **Schedule 2 (Form 1040), line 4, or Form 1040-SS, Part I, line 3**	12	21,520.
13	**Deduction for one-half of self-employment tax.** Multiply line 12 by 50% (0.50). Enter here and on **Schedule 1 (Form 1040), line 15** (13) 10,760.		

For Paperwork Reduction Act Notice, see your tax return instructions. **Schedule SE (Form 1040) 2024**

LHA 424501 10-23-24

SCHEDULE 8812 (Form 1040)

Department of the Treasury Internal Revenue Service

Credits for Qualifying Children and Other Dependents

Attach to Form 1040, 1040-SR, or 1040-NR.
Go to www.irs.gov/Schedule8812 for instructions and the latest information.

OMB No. 1545-0074

2024

Attachment Sequence No. **47**

Name(s) shown on return: Grady H. & Kelsey R. Busby

Your social security number: 546-57-9314

Part I Child Tax Credit and Credit for Other Dependents

Line	Description	Box	Amount
1	Enter the amount from line 11 of your Form 1040, 1040-SR, or 1040-NR	1	259,846.
2a	Enter income from Puerto Rico that you excluded — 2a		
b	Enter the amounts from lines 45 and 50 of your Form 2555 — 2b		
c	Enter the amount from line 15 of your Form 4563 — 2c		
d	Add lines 2a through 2c	2d	
3	Add lines 1 and 2d	3	259,846.
4	Number of qualifying children under age 17 with the required social security number — 4: 2		
5	Multiply line 4 by $2,000	5	4,000.
6	Number of other dependents, including any qualifying children who are not under age 17 or who do not have the required social security number — 6 **Caution:** Do not include yourself, your spouse, or anyone who is not a U.S. citizen, U.S. national, or U.S. resident alien. Also, do not include anyone you included on line 4.		
7	Multiply line 6 by $500	7	
8	Add lines 5 and 7	8	4,000.
9	Enter the amount shown below for your filing status. • Married filing jointly - $400,000 • All other filing statuses - $200,000	9	400,000.
10	Subtract line 9 from line 3. • If zero or less, enter -0-. • If more than zero and not a multiple of $1,000, enter the next multiple of $1,000. For example, if the result is $425, enter $1,000; if the result is $1,025, enter $2,000, etc.	10	0.
11	Multiply line 10 by 5% (0.05)	11	0.
12	Is the amount on line 8 more than the amount on line 11? [ ] **No. STOP.** You cannot take the child tax credit, credit for other dependents, or additional child tax credit. Skip Parts II-A and II-B. Enter -0- on lines 14 and 27. [X] **Yes.** Subtract line 11 from line 8. Enter the result.	12	4,000.
13	Enter the amount from **Credit Limit Worksheet A** — Stmt 12	13	34,632.
14	Enter the smaller of line 12 or line 13. **This is your child tax credit and credit for other dependents** Enter this amount on Form 1040, 1040-SR, or 1040-NR, line 19.	14	4,000.

If the amount on line 12 is more than the amount on line 14, you may be able to take the **additional child tax credit** on Form 1040, 1040-SR, or 1040-NR, line 28. Complete your Form 1040, 1040-SR, or 1040-NR through line 27 (also complete Schedule 3, line 11) before completing Part II-A.

For Paperwork Reduction Act Notice, see your tax return instructions. Schedule 8812 (Form 1040) 2024

LHA 403501 11-01-24

Schedule 8812 (Form 1040) 2024 Page 2

Part II-A Additional Child Tax Credit for All Filers

Caution: If you file Form 2555, you cannot claim the additional child tax credit.

15	Check this box if you **do not** want to claim the additional child tax credit. Skip Parts II-A and II-B. Enter -0- on line 27			☐
16a	Subtract line 14 from line 12. If zero, **stop here;** you cannot take the additional child tax credit. Skip Parts II-A and II-B. Enter -0- on line 27		16a	0.
b	Number of qualifying children under age 17 with the required social security number: ________ x $1,700. Enter the result. If zero, **stop here;** you cannot claim the additional child tax credit. Skip Parts II-A and II-B. Enter -0- on line 27		16b	
	TIP: The number of children you use for this line is the same as the number of children you used for line 4.			
17	Enter the **smaller** of line 16a or line 16b		17	
18a	Earned income (see instructions)	18a		
b	Nontaxable combat pay (see instructions) 18b			
19	Is the amount on line 18a more than $2,500? ☐ **No.** Leave line 19 blank and enter -0- on line 20. ☐ **Yes.** Subtract $2,500 from the amount on line 18a. Enter the result	19		
20	Multiply the amount on line 19 by 15% (0.15) and enter the result		20	
	Next. On line 16b, is the amount $5,100 or more? ☐ **No.** If you are a bona fide resident of Puerto Rico, go to line 21. Otherwise, skip Part II-B and enter the **smaller** of line 17 or line 20 on line 27. ☐ **Yes.** If line 20 is equal to or more than line 17, skip Part II-B and enter the amount from line 17 on line 27. Otherwise, go to line 21.			

Part II-B Certain Filers Who Have Three or More Qualifying Children and Bona Fide Residents of Puerto Rico

21	Withheld social security, Medicare, and Additional Medicare taxes from Form(s) W-2, boxes 4 and 6. If married filing jointly, include your spouse's amounts with yours. If your employer withheld or you paid Additional Medicare Tax or tier 1 RRTA taxes, or if you are a bona fide resident of Puerto Rico, see instructions	21		
22	Enter the total of the amounts from Schedule 1 (Form 1040), line 15; Schedule 2 (Form 1040), line 5; Schedule 2 (Form 1040), line 6; and Schedule 2 (Form 1040), line 13	22		
23	Add lines 21 and 22	23		
24	**1040 and 1040-SR filers:** Enter the total of the amounts from Form 1040 or 1040-SR, line 27, and Schedule 3 (Form 1040), line 11. **1040-NR filers:** Enter the amount from Schedule 3 (Form 1040), line 11.	24		
25	Subtract line 24 from line 23. If zero or less, enter -0-		25	
26	Enter the **larger** of line 20 or line 25		26	
	Next, enter the **smaller** of line 17 or line 26 on line 27.			

Part II-C Additional Child Tax Credit

27	**This is your additional child tax credit. Enter this amount on Form 1040, 1040-SR, or 1040-NR, line 28**	27	0.

Schedule 8812 (Form 1040) 2024

403502 11-01-24

Form **8995**

Department of the Treasury
Internal Revenue Service

Qualified Business Income Deduction Simplified Computation

Attach to your tax return.

Go to www.irs.gov/Form8995 for instructions and the latest information.

OMB No. 1545-2294

2024

Attachment Sequence No. **55**

Name(s) shown on return: Grady H. & Kelsey R. Busby

Your taxpayer identification number: 546-57-9314

Note: *You can claim the qualified business income deduction* **only** *if you have qualified business income from a qualified trade or business, real estate investment trust dividends, publicly traded partnership income, or a domestic production activities deduction passed through from an agricultural or horticultural cooperative. See instructions.*

Use this form if your taxable income, before your qualified business income deduction, is at or below $191,950 ($383,900 if married filing jointly), and you aren't a patron of an agricultural or horticultural cooperative.

1	**(a)** Trade, business, or aggregation name	**(b)** Taxpayer identification number	**(c)** Qualified business income or (loss)
i	Kelsey Busby Real Estate	27-1234567	132,099.
ii			
iii			
iv			
v			

2	Total qualified business income or (loss). Combine lines 1i through 1v, column (c)	2	132,099.		
3	Qualified business net (loss) carryforward from the prior year	3	( )		
4	Total qualified business income. Combine lines 2 and 3. If zero or less, enter -0-	4	132,099.		
5	Qualified business income component. Multiply line 4 by 20% (0.20)			5	26,420.
6	Qualified REIT dividends and publicly traded partnership (PTP) income or (loss) (see instructions)	6			
7	Qualified REIT dividends and qualified PTP (loss) carryforward from the prior year	7	( )		
8	Total qualified REIT dividends and PTP income. Combine lines 6 and 7. If zero or less, enter -0-	8			
9	REIT and PTP component. Multiply line 8 by 20% (0.20)			9	
10	Qualified business income deduction before the income limitation. Add lines 5 and 9			10	26,420.
11	Taxable income before qualified business income deduction (see instructions)	11	228,786.		
12	Enter your net capital gain, if any, increased by any qualified dividends (see instructions)	12	237.		
13	Subtract line 12 from line 11. If zero or less, enter -0-	13	228,549.		
14	Income limitation. Multiply line 13 by 20% (0.20)			14	45,710.
15	Qualified business income deduction. Enter the smaller of line 10 or line 14. Also enter this amount on the applicable line of your return (see instructions)			15	26,420.
16	Total qualified business (loss) carryforward. Combine lines 2 and 3. If greater than zero, enter -0-			16	( )
17	Total qualified REIT dividends and PTP (loss) carryforward. Combine lines 6 and 7. If greater than zero, enter -0-			17	( )

LHA **For Privacy Act and Paperwork Reduction Act Notice, see instructions.** 408421 12-19-24 Form **8995** (2024)

Form **8959** Department of the Treasury Internal Revenue Service

Additional Medicare Tax

If any line does not apply to you, leave it blank. See separate instructions.
Attach to Form 1040, 1040-SR, 1040-NR, or 1040-SS.
Go to www.irs.gov/Form8959 for instructions and the latest information.

OMB No. 1545-0074
2024
Attachment Sequence No. 71

Name(s) shown on return: Grady H. & Kelsey R. Busby
Your social security number: 546-57-9314

Part I Additional Medicare Tax on Medicare Wages

1	Medicare wages and tips from Form W-2, box 5. If you have more than one Form W-2, enter the total of the amounts from box 5	1	127,232.		
2	Unreported tips from Form 4137, line 6	2			
3	Wages from Form 8919, line 6	3			
4	Add lines 1 through 3	4	127,232.		
5	Enter the following amount for your filing status: Married filing jointly $250,000; Married filing separately $125,000; Single, Head of household, or Qualifying surviving spouse $200,000	5	250,000.		
6	Subtract line 5 from line 4. If zero or less, enter -0-			6	0.
7	Additional Medicare Tax on Medicare wages. Multiply line 6 by 0.9% (0.009). Enter here and go to Part II			7	

Part II Additional Medicare Tax on Self-Employment Income

8	Self-employment income from Schedule SE (Form 1040), Part I, line 6. If you had a loss, enter -0-	8	140,652.		
9	Enter the following amount for your filing status: Married filing jointly $250,000; Married filing separately $125,000; Single, Head of household, or Qualifying surviving spouse $200,000	9	250,000.		
10	Enter the amount from line 4	10	127,232.		
11	Subtract line 10 from line 9. If zero or less, enter -0-	11	122,768.		
12	Subtract line 11 from line 8. If zero or less, enter -0-			12	17,884.
13	Additional Medicare Tax on self-employment income. Multiply line 12 by 0.9% (0.009). Enter here and go to Part III			13	161.

Part III Additional Medicare Tax on Railroad Retirement Tax Act (RRTA) Compensation

14	Railroad retirement (RRTA) compensation and tips from Form(s) W-2, box 14 (see instructions)	14			
15	Enter the following amount for your filing status: Married filing jointly $250,000; Married filing separately $125,000; Single, Head of household, or Qualifying surviving spouse $200,000	15			
16	Subtract line 15 from line 14. If zero or less, enter -0-			16	
17	Additional Medicare Tax on railroad retirement (RRTA) compensation. Multiply line 16 by 0.9% (0.009). Enter here and go to Part IV			17	

Part IV Total Additional Medicare Tax

18	Add lines 7, 13, and 17. Also include this amount on Schedule 2 (Form 1040), line 11 (Form 1040-SS filers, see instructions), and go to Part V	18	161.

Part V Withholding Reconciliation

19	Medicare tax withheld from Form W-2, box 6. If you have more than one Form W-2, enter the total of the amounts from box 6	19	1,845.		
20	Enter the amount from line 1	20	127,232.		
21	Multiply line 20 by 1.45% (0.0145). This is your regular Medicare tax withholding on Medicare wages	21	1,845.		
22	Subtract line 21 from line 19. If zero or less, enter -0-. This is your Additional Medicare Tax withholding on Medicare wages			22	0.
23	Additional Medicare Tax withholding on railroad retirement (RRTA) compensation from Form W-2, box 14 (see instructions)			23	
24	**Total Additional Medicare Tax withholding.** Add lines 22 and 23. Also include this amount with federal income tax withholding on Form 1040, 1040-SR, or 1040-NR, line 25c (Form 1040-SS filers, see instructions)			24	

423111 12-05-24 LHA **For Paperwork Reduction Act Notice, see your tax return instructions.** Form **8959** (2024)

Form **8960** Department of the Treasury Internal Revenue Service

Net Investment Income Tax - Individuals, Estates, and Trusts

Attach to your tax return.

Go to www.irs.gov/Form8960 for instructions and the latest information.

OMB No. 1545-2227 **2024** Attachment Sequence No. **72**

Name(s) shown on your tax return: Grady H. & Kelsey R. Busby

Your social security number or EIN: 546-57-9314

Part I Investment Income

☐ Section 6013(g) election (see instructions)
☐ Section 6013(h) election (see instructions)
☐ Regulations section 1.1411-10(g) election (see instructions)

1	Taxable interest (see instructions)			1	122.
2	Ordinary dividends (see instructions)			2	312.
3	Annuities (see instructions)			3	
4a	Rental real estate, royalties, partnerships, S corporations, trusts, trades or businesses, etc. (see instructions)	4a	152,303.		
b	Adjustment for net income or loss derived in the ordinary course of a non-section 1411 trade or business (see instructions) Statement 13	4b	-152,303.		
c	Combine lines 4a and 4b			4c	0.
5a	Net gain or loss from disposition of property (see instructions)	5a	81.		
b	Net gain or loss from disposition of property that is not subject to net investment income tax (see instructions)	5b			
c	Adjustment from disposition of partnership interest or S corporation stock (see instructions)	5c			
d	Combine lines 5a through 5c			5d	81.
6	Adjustments to investment income for certain CFCs and PFICs (see instructions)			6	
7	Other modifications to investment income (see instructions)			7	
8	Total investment income. Combine lines 1, 2, 3, 4c, 5d, 6, and 7			8	515.

Part II Investment Expenses Allocable to Investment Income and Modifications

9a	Investment interest expenses (see instructions)	9a			
b	State, local, and foreign income tax (see instructions)	9b			
c	Miscellaneous investment expenses (see instructions)	9c			
d	Add lines 9a, 9b, and 9c			9d	
10	Additional modifications (see instructions)			10	
11	Total deductions and modifications. Add lines 9d and 10			11	

Part III Tax Computation

12	Net investment income. Subtract Part II, line 11, from Part I, line 8. Individuals, complete lines 13-17. Estates and trusts, complete lines 18a - 21. If zero or less, enter -0-			12	515.
	Individuals:				
13	Modified adjusted gross income (see instructions)	13	259,846.		
14	Threshold based on filing status (see instructions)	14	250,000.		
15	Subtract line 14 from line 13. If zero or less, enter -0-	15	9,846.		
16	Enter the smaller of line 12 or line 15			16	515.
17	Net investment income tax for individuals. Multiply line 16 by 3.8% (0.038). **Enter here and include on your tax return** (see instructions)			17	20.
	Estates and Trusts:				
18a	Net investment income (line 12 above)	18a			
b	Deductions for distributions of net investment income and charitable deductions (see instructions)	18b			
c	Undistributed net investment income. Subtract line 18b from line 18a (see instructions). If zero or less, enter -0-	18c			
19a	Adjusted gross income (see instructions)	19a			
b	Highest tax bracket for estates and trusts for the year (see instructions)	19b			
c	Subtract line 19b from line 19a. If zero or less, enter -0-	19c			
20	Enter the smaller of line 18c or line 19c			20	
21	Net investment income tax for estates and trusts. Multiply line 20 by 3.8% (0.038). **Enter here and include on your tax return** (see instructions)			21	

For Paperwork Reduction Act Notice, see your tax return instructions. Form **8960** (2024)

Grady H. & Kelsey R. Busby 546-57-9314

Form 1040	Capital Gain Distributions	Statement 1

Name of Payer	Total Capital Gain	28% Gain
Charles Schwab	81.	
Totals to Form 1040, line 7	81.	

Form 1040	Wages Received and Taxes Withheld	Statement 2

T S	Employer's Name	Amount Paid	Federal Tax Withheld	State Tax Withheld	City SDI Tax W/H	FICA Tax	Medicare Tax
T	Plano ISD	127,232.	19,335.			7,888.	1,845.
	Totals	127,232.	19,335.			7,888.	1,845.

Form 1040	Qualified Dividends	Statement 3

Name of Payer	Ordinary Dividends	Qualified Dividends
Charles Schwab	312.	156.
Total included in Form 1040, line 3a		156.

Form 1040	Tax	Statement 4

Description	Amount
From Qualified Dividends and Capital Gain Worksheet	34,632.
Total to Form 1040, line 16	34,632.

Grady H. & Kelsey R. Busby 546-57-9314

Form 1040	Federal Income Tax Withheld - Form(s) W-2	Statement 5

T S Description	Amount
T Plano ISD	19,335.
Total to Form 1040, line 25a	19,335.

Form 1040	Current Year Estimates and Amount Applied from Previous Year	Statement 6

Description	Amount
1st Qtr Estimate Payment - Joint	9,500.
2nd Qtr Estimate Payment - Joint	9,500.
3rd Qtr Estimate Payment - Joint	9,500.
4th Qtr Estimate Payment - Joint	9,500.
Total to Form 1040, line 26	38,000.

Schedule A	Cash Contributions	Statement 7

Description	Amount 60% Limit	Amount 30% Limit
Miscellaneous	4,650. 450.	
Subtotals	5,100.	
Total to Schedule A, line 11		5,100.

Schedule A	State and Local General Sales Taxes	Statement 8

Description	Amount
State Sales Tax	1,729.
Local Sales Tax	553.
Total to Schedule A, line 5a	2,282.

Grady H. & Kelsey R. Busby 546-57-9314

Schedule A	General Sales Tax Deduction Worksheet		Statement 9
1	Enter your state general sales taxes from the applicable table. Texas If, for all of 2024, you lived only in Connecticut, the District of Columbia, Indiana, Kentucky, Maine, Maryland, Massachusetts, Michigan, New Jersey, or Rhode Island, skip lines 2 through 5, enter -0- on line 6, and go to line 7. Otherwise, go to line 2.		1,729.
2	Did you live in Alabama, Alaska, Arizona, Arkansas, Colorado, Georgia, Illinois, Kansas, Louisiana, Mississippi, Missouri, New York, North Carolina, South Carolina, Tennessee, Utah, or Virginia in 2024? If No, enter -0-. If Yes, enter your local general sales taxes from the applicable table.	0.	
3	Did your locality impose a local general sales tax in 2024? Residents of California and Nevada see instructions. If No, skip lines 3 through 5, enter -0- on line 6 and go to line 7. If Yes, enter your local general sales tax rate, but omit the percentage sign. PLANO	2.0000	
4	Did you enter -0- on line 2 above? If No, skip lines 4 and 5 and go to line 6. If Yes, Enter your state general sales tax rate, but omit the percentage sign.	6.2500	
5	Divide line 3 by line 4. Enter the result as a decimal (rounded to at least three places).	.3200	
6	Did you enter -0- on line 2 above? If No, multiply line 2 by line 3. If Yes, multiply line 1 by line 5.		553.
6a	Add line 1 and line 6.		2,282.
6b	Part-year days rate.		1.000000
6c	Multiply line 6a by line 6b.		2,282.
7	Enter your general sales taxes paid on specified items, if any.		
8	Deduction for general sales taxes. Add lines 6c and 7. Enter the result here and on Schedule A, line 5a and check box.		2,282.

Grady H. & Kelsey R. Busby — 546-57-9314

Schedule C	Car and Truck Expenses	Statement 10

Description	Amount
Vehicle Number 1 - 13127 Business Miles @ $0.670	8,795.
Car and truck expenses	240.
Total to Schedule C, line 9	9,035.

Schedule SE	Non-Farm Income	Statement 11

Description	Amount
Residential Real Estate Sales	152,303.
Total to Schedule SE, line 2	152,303.

Grady H. & Kelsey R. Busby		546-57-9314
Schedule 8812	Credit Limit Worksheet A	Statement 12

1. Enter the amount from line 18 of Form 1040 or Form 1040-NR 34,632.

2. Add the following amounts (if applicable) from:

   Schedule 3, line 1
   Schedule 3, line 2
   Schedule 3, line 3
   Schedule 3, line 4
   Schedule 3, line 5b
   Schedule 3, line 6d
   Schedule 3, line 6f
   Schedule 3, line 6l
   Schedule 3, line 6m
   Enter the total

3. Subtract line 2 from line 1 34,632.

   Complete the Credit Limit Worksheet B only if you meet all of the following:

   1. You are claiming one or more of the following credits:
      a. Mortgage interest credit, Form 8396
      b. Adoption credit, Form 8839
      c. Residential clean energy credit, Form 5695, Part I
      d. District of Columbia first-time homebuyer credit, Form 8859
   2. You are not filing Form 2555
   3. Line 4 of Schedule 8812 is more than zero

4. If you are not completing Credit Limit Worksheet B, enter -0-; otherwise, enter the amount from the Credit Limit Worksheet B. 0.

5. Subtract line 4 from line 3. Enter this amount on Schedule 8812, line 13. 34,632.

Form 8960	Trade or Business Income	Statement 13
Kelsey Busby Real Estate		-152,303.
Amount to Form 8960, line 4B		-152,303.

Appendix D
State Websites for New Hire Reporting

U.S. Department of Health and Human Services (DHHS) State New Hire Reporting Websites

https://acf.gov/css/contact-information/state-new-hirereporting-websites

Summary link via Symmetry.com for all fifty states

https://www.symmetry.com/payroll-tax-insights/new-hire-requirements-by-state

Alabama	https://adol.alabama.gov/employers/alabama-new-hire/
Alaska	https://tinyurl.com/p8saz987
California	http://www.edd.ca.gov/payroll_taxes/New_Hire_Reporting.htm
Colorado	https://newhire.state.co.us/downloads/CO_NH_reporting.pdf
Connecticut	https://www1.ctdol.state.ct.us/newhires/index2.asp
Delaware	https://www.de-newhire.com/de-Newhire/default.aspx
Florida	https://tinyurl.com/ybfxucua
Georgia	ga-newhire.com/

Hawaii	https://ag.hawaii.gov/csea/employer-information/
Idaho	https://www.labor.idaho.gov/businesses/report-new-hires/
Illinois	https://tinyurl.com/m885hync
Indiana	https://in-newhire.com/
Iowa	https://secureapp.dhs.state.ia.us/epay/
Kansas	https://tinyurl.com/2khtsjjs
Kentucky	https://ky-newhire.com/#/public/public-landing/login
Louisiana	https://newhire-reporting.com/LA-Newhire/Default.aspx
Maine	https://tinyurl.com/yc8u3x7d
Maryland	https://tinyurl.com/2as3wvu3
Massachusetts	https://tinyurl.com/r8x49u32
Michigan	https://tinyurl.com/2d9dejf3
Minnesota	https://mn-newhire.com/login
Mississippi	https://ms-newhire.com/
Missouri	https://www.missouriemployer.dss.mo.gov/NewHireInfo.aspx
Montana	https://dphhs.mt.gov/cssd/employerinfo/nhrs

Nebraska	https://ne-newhire.com/
Nevada	https://dwss.nv.gov/Support/1_1_7_01-New-Hire-Reporting/
New Hampshire	www.nhes.nh.gov/services/employers/compliance.htm
New Jersey	https://www.njcsesp.com/
New Mexico	https://nm-newhire.com/
New York	https://www.tax.ny.gov/bus/wt/newhire.htm
North Carolina	https://ncnewhires.ncdhhs.gov/
North Dakota	https://www.hhs.nd.gov/childsupport/employers/new-hire-reporting
Ohio	https://www.oh-newhire.com/#/public/public-landing/login
Oklahoma	https://www.ok.gov/oesc/newhire/app/index.php
Oregon	https://www.doj.state.or.us/child-support/for-employers/report-new-hires/
Pennsylvania	https://tinyurl.com/3ycvdduu
Rhode Island	https://ri-newhire.com/
South Carolina	https://newhire.sc.gov/#/
Tennessee	https://tnnewhire.com/
Texas	https://www.texasattorneygeneral.gov/child-support/employers/new-hire-reporting
Utah	https://tinyurl.com/4wjtm4ah
Vermont	https://labor.vermont.gov/
Virginia	https://va-newhire.com
Washington	https://tinyurl.com/b7rxhru9
Washington DC	https://dc-newhire.com
West Virginia	https://wv-newhire.com/
Wisconsin	https://wi-newhire.com/
Wyoming	https://newhire-reporting.com/WY-Newhire/default.as

Appendix E:
Small Business Resources

HireYourKid.com

Of all the things I have mentioned in this guide, there is one single fact that I hope you remember above all else:

You Are NOT Alone!

As a small business owner, it is very easy to lose track of the support that is available. It is very easy to feel like you are out there, all alone, trying to meet the goals you have set for yourself and to try and accomplish literally thousands of tasks that stand between you and those goals. But you are not alone. There are hundreds of individuals and groups just like us who have as their primary business goal helping small business owners just like you. Keep this list of resources close and always know that if you have a question, there are people who can help.

Never forget that over 70% of all new jobs in this country come from small business owners just like you. You ARE making a difference. Well Done!!!

Naturally, this is the best place to go for questions about hiring your kid.

www.HireYourKid.com

SBA.GOV
U.S. Small Business Administration

The Small Business Administration has a great website with links to all state agencies for payroll and state income tax, as well as significant resources beyond just tax information.

www.SBA.gov

IRS

The Internal Revenue Service has committed millions of dollars to its website, much of it designed to help small businesses. They have done a great job and can answer many of your questions.

www.IRS.gov

nase

The National Association for the Self-Employed is a non-profit business organization dedicated to the needs of micro-business owners with the sole goal of helping the smallest of small businesses be more successful.

www.NASE.org

The National Small Business Association is the nation's oldest small business advocacy group, helping entrepreneurs navigate legislation, connect with peers, and advance a nonpartisan agenda.

www.NSBAadvocate.org

America's SBDC is a national association representing over 1,000 local Small Business Development Centers. They provide face-to-face counseling for millions of small business owners each year.

www.americassbdc.org

Intuit provides a wide range of products and services that are geared toward meeting the needs of small business, including payroll solutions, QuickBooks, TurboTax, merchant services and more.

www.Intuit.com

SCORE, a resource partner with the U.S. Small Business Administration provides free business mentoring and low cost workshops for small business owners through over 350 local offices.

www.SCORE.org

The U.S. Department of Labor has a very good website to help with all facets of federal employment law and requirements.

www.dol.gov

Reuters supplies access to news and education and has an in-depth Small Business Resources Center to help with starting and maintaining a new small business.

www.reuters.com

The American Independent Business Coalition provides business consultants and online support for thousands of small business owners

www.AIBCoalition.com

NAWBO is the only dues-based organization representing the interests of all women entrepreneurs across all industries; with chapters across the country. With far-reaching clout and impact, NAWBO is a one-stop resource which propels women business owners into greater economic, social and political spheres of power worldwide.

www.NAWBO.org

Made in the USA
Monee, IL
03 November 2026

67386728R00115